Powerful Techniques for
Teaching Adults

Stephen D. Brookfield

Powerful
Techniques for
Teaching Adults

JOSSEY-BASS
A Wiley Imprint
www.josseybass.com

Published by Jossey-Bass
A Wiley Imprint
One Montgomery Street, Suite 1200, San Francisco, CA 94104-4594—
www.josseybass.com

Jossey-Bass books and products are available through most bookstores. To contact Jossey-Bass directly call our Customer Care Department within the U.S. at 800-956-7739, outside the U.S. at 317-572-3986, or fax 317-572-4002.

Wiley publishes in a variety of print and electronic formats and by print-on-demand. Some material included with standard print versions of this book may not be included in e-books or in print-on-demand. If this book refers to media such as a CD or DVD that is not included in the version you purchased, you may download this material at http://booksupport.wiley.com. For more information about Wiley products, visit www.wiley.com.

Library of Congress Cataloging-in-Publication Data has been applied for and is on file with the Library of Congress.

ISBN 978-1-118-0-1700-5 (cloth); ISBN 978-1-118-41570-2 (ebk),
ISBN 978-1-118-41857-4 (ebk), ISBN 978-1-118-55598-9 (ebk)

Printed in the United States of America

FIRST EDITION

HB Printing 10 9 8 7 6 5 4 3 2 1

The Jossey-Bass
Higher and Adult Education Series

Contents

Preface

As a teacher of adults I live simultaneously in two educational worlds. In one, you might call it *Powertopia*, power is experienced as an enabling and equalizing force. Here people exercise power to make space for each other to speak, as they strive to understand another's point of view. Compassion is the quality valued above all other virtues, so Powertopia's citizens ensure no one is marginalized, diminished, or demeaned. Put colloquially, nobody gets screwed in this world. In the classrooms of Powertopia, power is exercised judiciously to support everyone's growth; egomaniacs are not rewarded for steamrollering and shutting down other learners; racial, class, and gender microaggressions are unknown; and people's minds are open to considering ideas and practices that threaten their own comfortable sense of identity.

This dreamlike version of Habermas's (1979) ideal speech situation where everyone strives for intersubjective understanding and is open to critical thinking doesn't, of course, exist. But it's what I'd like to see in place in my own classrooms even as I live in the second of my educational worlds, the real world. One set of toes, if not one of my feet, is always in Powertopia. Much of how I exercise power in the real world is governed by a desire to create Powertopia. I suspect that many teachers of adults have their own version of Powertopia lurking at the fringes of their consciousness, and measure their effectiveness as adult educators and trainers at least partly by how far they get in sneaking features of it into their real-world classrooms.

Whether or not there are any elements of Powertopia in your own world, you will always be faced with the reality of power. The one thing you can depend on in any adult teaching or training is that complex power dynamics are present. There is the power of your own positional title, the power you express because of your training, the power you demonstrate through the command of your subject or skill set, and the power grounded in your particular personality. Your students have the power to amplify or disable your intentions, the power to take learning in a new direction, and the power to make you feel powerful or powerless. The power differences that exist among students outside the classroom because of their class, race, gender, personality, and experiences will often quickly reproduce themselves inside the classroom unless you use your own power as the teacher to stop this happening.

As you teach a course or workshop, power constantly moves around the room, reconfiguring itself as it's exercised in new, or familiar, ways by different people. Sometimes situations develop in which power seems to be humming gloriously, lifting the energy in the room and taking everyone into new learning areas. At other times, power runs out of control and the class becomes a train wreck of bitterness, anger, or passive aggression. Student power, teacher power, institutional power, racial power, cultural power, and the power of the subject's grand narrative constantly intersect in ways that catch you by surprise. There is no such thing as a power-free adult classroom.

Powerful Techniques for Teaching Adults explores the dynamics of how power and adult teaching intersect. It begins with an analysis of power and looks at some common approaches (teaching critical thinking, using discussion, fostering self-directed learning, democratizing the classroom, and using the creative arts and film) held to be empowering for adult learners. It then explores how to teach against dominant power, even when students resist that invitation. Although power is the theme that runs through the book, this is not primarily an academic analysis. Instead, as the title clearly indicates, this is a book that deals with teaching techniques. I have tried to cram into its pages as many examples as I thought readers could stand of teaching exercises and activities. I offer them in the hope that readers can study them and decide if parts of them might fit into their own classrooms. As I make clear in the final chapter, I urge you to take bits of one exercise, combine them with bits of another, and add totally new wrinkles to my techniques. In providing as many examples of tips and tools as I have, my hope is that something, somewhere, seems relevant, so you can say (hopefully more than once) "I could use that, or something like it, in my own teaching."

Speaking of power, I have also tried to use my authorial power to write in a way that's reader friendly. I've written, coauthored, or coedited eleven other books for Jossey-Bass, some of which have sold well and have made money for the company, others that have won awards for scholarship and research. So I have amassed enough cultural and economic capital to write books in different voices. Some, such as *The Power of Critical Theory* (Brookfield, 2004), *Learning as a Way of Leading* (Preskill and Brookfield, 2008) and *Radicalizing Learning* (Brookfield and Holst, 2010), are more philosophically or academically inclined. Others, such as *The Skillful Teacher* (Brookfield, 2006), *Discussion as a Way of Teaching* (Brookfield and Preskill, 2005) or *Teaching for Critical Thinking* (Brookfield, 2012), are written chiefly for practitioners. *Powerful Techniques for Teaching Adults* is clearly in that second category. I use the first person throughout, pepper the text with personal anecdotes and asides, and keep the citations and references to a minimum. I hope that as you read the book you feel you're in a sort of conversation with me—though I admit, it's a weird sort of conversation where one person holds forth and another only listens.

Overview of the Book

In chapter 1 I describe how power manifests itself in all adult class-rooms and define a powerful technique as one that meets one or more of four conditions: it adapts itself to power dynamics, it empowers people, it teaches people about power, and it represents a responsible use of teacher authority. I then turn in chapter 2 to a project often described as empowering—using different methods and techniques to teach adults to think more critically. Critical thinking happens when learners question assumptions and explore different perspectives, particular those pertaining to the use of power. I explain how teachers can use their own power to model critical thinking through Speaking in Tongues, Assumptions Inventories, Point-Counterpoint, Structured Devil's Advocacy, and Questioning Strategies. I also present powerful learner exercises such as the Scenario Analysis technique and the Critical Conversation Protocol.

Adult educators often claim discussion to be the most adult of all teaching methods, partly because of its potential to disperse power democratically around the group. Chapter 3 proposes some specific exercises to ensure discussion is experienced as truly democratic and participatory, in other words, as empowering. I explain how to help learners establish their own ground rules, describe a Grading Participation Rubric I use, and offer conversational protocols such as the Circle of Voices, Circular Response, Conversational Roles and Moves, Hatful of Quotes, Snowballing, Chalk Talk, and the Appreciative Pause. I argue that democratic, participatory discussions do not happen by accident but must be planned for. The techniques in this chapter are some of the ones I've had most success with in my own teaching.

Self-directed learning is also often lauded as the method that most directly displaces teacher and institutional power, since it places the locus of control for decisions regarding the planning, execution, and evaluation of learning in the hands of the learner. This kind of empowering learning is held to be particularly suited to adults, principally because they are deemed to be more experienced and motivated than children and adolescents. Chapter 4 defines and illustrates self-directed learning, explains how it relates to power, and then reviews some ways to foster self-direction. These include the Learning Audit, Letter to a Second Self, and the Learning Journey Poster Session. I review approaches to developing informational literacy in Search Engine Selection, the Criteria Gallery, and Wikipedia Construction, and I explore how to conduct learning projects through Project Flow Charts, Practicing Learning Decisions, and Developing Emotional Fluency.

Adult teachers concerned with power frequently try to create more democratic classrooms and this is the concern of chapter 5. I define democracy as an ever-widening, inclusive conversation, an economic arrangement, and a struggle against dominant ideology. A democratic classroom should include multiple voices and perspectives, should recognize learners as decision makers, and should exhibit a responsible use of teacher power. Ways to democratize adult classrooms are explored in the chapter such as student governance, the Critical Incident Questionnaire, Newsprint Dialog, the Three-Person Rule, Structured Silence, Nominating Questions, and Who's the Expert?

My focus shifts in chapter 6 to teaching about power and tries to clarify why adults often resist teaching that encourages them to challenge dominant power. I describe how to set a tone to examine dominant power, propose a Power Calisthenics icebreaker, outline the Power Bus as a form of student introductions, and provide a creative simulation developed by community college instructor Gary Cale. I end by exploring how to use narrative and story and present techniques such as Coding the Story, Hunting Assumptions, the Power Trajectory, and Trawling for Hope.

The use of the creative arts to teach about power is explored in chapter 7. I examine the role of intuition through Intuitive

Critical Incidents and Word/Image Association. Different forms of collage are proposed such as Cultural Collage, Quilts of Power, Collaging Discussion, and Metaphorical and Analogical Collages. In theatrical approaches I describe some well-known approaches such as Forum Theater, Image Theater, Invisible Theater, and Culture-Jamming. The chapter ends with some daily power simulations such as Being Ignored, Microaggressions, and Marcuse Academy.

The final chapter 8 moves away from the emphasis on techniques to consider how any attempt to teach about power, and to harness its energy in a classroom, is always emotionally laden. I draw connections between emotion and power and review different ways we can survive the emotional demands of powerful teaching. These include recognizing what's emotionally important, monitoring anticipatory anxiety, cultivating empathic detachment, managing epistemological confusion, and nourishing the soul. I end the book with a discussion of how I have tried to use my own authorial power within its pages.

Audience

The chief audiences for this book are anyone who is interested in how adult teaching techniques intersect with the power dynamics of adult classrooms, anyone who believes education should empower learners, and anyone interested in getting adults to challenge dominant ideology. I would be so bold as to suggest this encompasses pretty much anyone who teaches adults in any setting! If power is omnipresent in all adult learning settings, then everyone who works in those settings should find something of interest in this book. As I was writing this book, I received requests about the techniques it demonstrates from practitioners as diverse as community and technical college instructors, corporate trainers, adult basic education tutors, university lecturers, social movement activists, military trainers, community group facilitators, seminarians, online

program designers, parent educators, health professionals, propri-
etary schoolteachers, and environmental activists. I believe that's
an accurate representation of the kinds of adult teachers who will
find this book helpful. Since all those people deal every day with
power dynamics in their classrooms, they all should find something
of interest in the book.

Acknowledgments

I n all my recent books, acknowledgments to the same people tend to crop up. Sue Huber, executive vice president at the University of St. Thomas, gives me consistent support; David Brightman at Jossey-Bass always encourages me to write personally to practitioners rather than to impress fellow academics; my family (Kim, Molly, and Colin) gracefully accept my need for solitude to write; and my band members (The 99ers—Erik and Christopher) take my mind off all things educational and allow me to come back to those things with renewed energy. So, this time to all of those people, I'll just say "thanks again."

About the Author

The father of Molly and Colin, and the husband of Kim, Stephen D. Brookfield is currently Distinguished University Professor at the University of St. Thomas in Minneapolis-St. Paul, Minnesota. He received his BA degree (1970) from Lanchester College of Technology (Coventry, UK) in modern studies; his MA degree (1974) from the University of Reading (UK) in sociology; and his PhD degree (1980) from the University of Leicester UK in adult education. He also holds a postgraduate diploma (1971) from the University of London, Chelsea College(UK), in modern social and cultural studies and a postgraduate diploma (1977) from the University of Nottingham (UK) in adult education. In 1991 he was awarded an honorary doctor of letters degree from the University System of New Hampshire for his contributions to understanding adult learning. In 2003 he was awarded an honorary doctorate of letters from Concordia University for his contributions to adult education. In 2010 Muhlenberg College awarded him an honorary doctorate of letters for educational leadership in the scholarship of teaching.

Stephen began his teaching career in 1970 and has held appointments at colleges of further, technical, adult, and higher education in the United Kingdom, and at universities in Canada (University of British Columbia) and the United States (Columbia University, Teachers College and the University of St. Thomas).

In 1989 he was Visiting Fellow at the Institute for Technical and Adult Teacher Education in what is now the University of Technology, Sydney, Australia. In 2002 he was Visiting Professor at Harvard University Graduate School of Education. In 2003–2004 he was the Helen Le Baron Hilton Chair at Iowa State University. He has run numerous workshops on teaching, adult learning, and critical thinking around the world and delivered many keynote addresses at regional, national, and international education conferences.

In 2001 he received the Leadership Award from the Association for Continuing Higher Education (ACHE) for "extraordinary contributions to the general field of continuing education on a national and international level." In 2008 he received the University of St. Thomas John Ireland Presidential Award for Outstanding Achievement as a Teacher/Scholar, and also the University of St. Thomas Diversity Leadership Teaching and Research Award. Also in 2008 he was awarded the Morris T. Keeton Medal by the Council on Adult and Experiential Learning for "outstanding contributions to adult and experiential learning." In 2009 he was inducted into the International Adult Education Hall of Fame.

He is a six-time winner of the Cyril O. Houle World Award for Literature in Adult Education: in 1986 for his book *Understanding and Facilitating Adult Learning: A Comprehensive Analysis of Principles and Effective Practices* (1986), in 1989 for *Developing Critical Thinkers: Challenging Adults to Explore Alternative Ways of Thinking and Acting* (1987), in 1996 for *Becoming a Critically Reflective Teacher* (1995), in 2005 for *The Power of Critical Theory: Liberating Adult Learning and Teaching* (2004), in 2011 for his book with John D. Holst, *Radicalizing Learning: Adult Education for a Just World* (2010) and in 2012 for *Teaching for Critical Thinking: Challenging Students to Question their Assumptions* (2012). *Understanding and Facilitating Adult Learning* also won the 1986 Imogene E. Okes Award for Outstanding Research in Adult Education. These awards were all presented by the American Association for Adult and Continuing Education. The first edition of *Discussion as a Way of Teaching: Tools and Techniques for Democratic Classrooms* (2nd ed., 2005), which he coauthored with Stephen Preskill, was a 1999 Critics Choice of the Educational Studies Association. His other books are *Adult Learners, Adult Education and the Community* (1984), *Self-Directed Learning: From Theory to Practice* (1985), *Learning Democracy: Eduard Lindeman on Adult Education and Social Change* (1987), *Training Educators of Adults: The Theory and Practice of Graduate Adult Education* (1988), *The Skillful Teacher: On Technique, Trust, and Responsiveness in the Classroom* (2nd. ed., 2006), *Teaching Reflectively in Theological Contexts: Promises and Contradictions* (coedited with Mary Hess, 2008), *Learning as a Way of Leading: Lessons from the Struggle for Social Justice* (coauthored with Stephen Preskill, 2008), and *Handbook of Race and Adult Education* (coedited with Vanessa Sheared, Scipio Colin III, Elizabeth Peterson, and Juanita Johnson, 2010).

1

The Essence of Powerful Teaching

I remember well my first week of teaching. I was employed as a part-time lecturer in liberal studies at Lewisham and Eltham College of Further Education in southeast London. Because the institution I was working for had the word *college* in its title, I assumed my students would be intellectually curious, motivated by a quest for truth and beauty. I also assumed things would be friendly and collegial, as befitted a college environment.

But that first week power came crashing into my world. The students (all apprentice plumbers, builders, or electricians) clearly had no interest in what I had to teach. They were there to learn a trade and any time they spent in being "liberalized" by yours truly was time they resented. So, they found all kinds of ways to disempower me. They would get out of their chairs and move around the room at will, shout at each other, refuse to answer my questions, poke fun at me, swear, and make jokes I didn't get. I was powerless to do anything about this. I tried to use humor back, tried to show them I was relaxed and "cool," a friend almost, and tried to appeal to their better nature. Nothing worked. There was no coercive power I could use, since there were no liberal studies exams they needed to pass, and their sponsoring employers resented students wasting their time with me. Soon I was pushed into trying to keep the students quiet and busy by creating classroom activities that that left as little opportunity for disruption (and discussion) as was possible.

I realize now that the students (who were fifteen or sixteen years old) were probably a little giddy with the fact that I had no formal power over them, only the power of persuasion. Maybe they were confused by the lack of boundaries and conspired to push me into acting in a traditional teacherly role. It probably didn't help that I was only five years older than they were and clearly a novice at my craft. One day during that first week a fistfight broke out between a White English boy and an Afro-Caribbean boy that I assumed was racially motivated. As I wrote in *The Skillful Teacher* (Brookfield, 2006) the thought popped into my head "What would John Dewey do?" (it may have been "What would R.S. Peters do?" Or "What would Alfred North Whitehead do?"). Nothing came to mind, and that was when I realized that the most difficult challenge of that first year's teaching was going to be to understand power—what the limits of my power were, how best to use that power, how to head off students' exercise of their own power to disrupt and sabotage, and how to deal with the power differences of racial identity among class members.

Over the years that concern with power has only intensified. If there's one thing I know about teaching adults it's that power is always in the room, constantly surfacing in surprising ways. I've had over four decades of experience since that first eventful week in 1970, but the same questions and dynamics perplex me as much as they did then. How can I ensure that my positional power as the teacher is being exercised responsibly? What do I do when students use the power of silence, negative body language, mockery, verbal hostility or overt noncompliance to sabotage me? How do I deal with power discrepancies among students when I suspect some students are speaking more and dominating the class because of the power they exercise in their roles outside the classroom? How can I teach students about the ways that dominant power and ideology constrain their lives, even as they embrace that power enthusiastically?

This book explores these and other related questions about how power, teaching, and adult learning intersect. I assume power is omnipresent in all adult learning situations in which someone is identified as the designated teacher. From adult higher education to corporate training, religious formation to social movement education, professional development institutes to community college classrooms, power dynamics endure. It doesn't really matter what the subject content is, teachers and learners constantly exercise power. I would argue that a recreational class on local history is as much informed by power dynamics as a critical theory class studying the concepts of hegemony and dominant ideology. You can't understand adult education or teaching without examining power. This is why experienced practitioners "often have sophisticated practical understanding of how power works, enough so that they are able to work effectively" (Wilson and Nesbit, 2005, p. 449).

Much of adult education purports to be about empowerment, about teaching for a particular kind of learning that involves adults developing skills, increasing understanding, and acquiring information that enables them to take all kinds of matters into their own hands (Archibald and Wilson, 2011). This kind of teaching is intended to nurture a sense of agency in people so that they feel confident in their abilities as learners and political actors. Of course empowerment, like power, is not a transparent, monolithic idea. Empowering people to learn the rules of the game so they can succeed in negotiating organizational politics is not the same as empowering people to reject those rules and seek to change the basic way organizations function. The whole notion of empowerment suffers from the confused belief that adult educators can "give" their power to learners. As teachers we can work to remove barriers and to help students develop knowledge, skills, and confidence, but only students can empower themselves. Empowerment, after all, can only be claimed, not given.

Anyone interested in empowering learners has to acknowledge that they are acting politically—in other words, to make power work on their behalf. The teaching I explore is meant to prepare people to participate in deciding how they will use the resources available to them and how they will act in the world. Because I work from a critical theory perspective (Brookfield, 2004), I am interested in ways learners challenge dominant ideologies such as capitalism, White supremacy, and patriarchy. From this perspective empowered people work to change the fundamental, structural aspects of their lives and communities. This project is described much more fully in my book with John Holst, *Radicalizing Learning* (Brookfield and Holst, 2010). In line with this project I was particularly pleased to be contacted by different groups involved in the 2011 Occupy Wall Street movement who wanted my suggestions on techniques and methods to institute horizontal decision making in their general assemblies.

I am also interested in helping learners feel powerful enough to change significant elements in their lives without necessarily changing the fundamental structures in which they function. So I hope students I teach will get more satisfying jobs, learn how to advocate for themselves and their families, get involved in local community organizations, and so on. We all have to live in this world while dreaming of another possible world (like Powertopia), and it does not seem philosophically contradictory to work in the present, with all its constraints and limitations, while simultaneously working for a radically different future. In fact I'd say this is life as a lot of us know it. Of course, putting elements of an imagined future into practice is the difficult bit.

The Omnipresence of Power

Power is the enduring reality of all kinds of learning settings. From rigidly controlled attempts to ensure that adults learn a skill in a highly precise manner with minimal opportunity for deviation or creativity, to informal enthusiast groups in which people gather to pursue a shared passion wherever it takes them, power is always there. We see power exercised when teachers move learners to engage with unfamiliar, and sometimes disturbing ideas, or when coaches, therapists, or mentors help people to understand how others see them. We see it when trainers encourage students to experiment with new skills or techniques, or when leaders attempt to change culture by modeling vulnerability, transparency, or risk taking. In all these examples there is a flow of energy, in which people's actions create reactions, people's choices have consequences, and the meanings people intend to communicate are understood in certain ways. But in all these examples there is also an inherent unpredictability. Actions produce unexpected results, choices lead to total surprise, and meanings are ascribed to words and phrases that are opposite to the ones intended. So though it's ever present, power manifests itself in multiple and contradictory ways, and it constantly disturbs any attempts to make teaching and learning fit some prearranged script.

Power is also present when teachers' actions get in the way of learning, as happens when they say they will do one thing (such as encourage all ideas to be expressed) and then do something entirely different (such as using sarcasm, ridicule, or shaming to make it clear which opinions they find noteworthy). My high school headmaster used his power in an overt and physical way when he caned me for entering school premises before classes started one freezing cold winter's morning in 1964. Educators and trainers can create the conditions in which people feel empowered to take chances, challenge authority, disagree, or come up with original analyses. They can also turn learning spaces into dead zones of mind-numbing busywork, in which people's creativity is exercised for the sole purpose of finding new ways to manage the boredom.

Adult learners exercise power when they suggest examples that clarify a concept or illustrate a principle, helping a discussion gather momentum. They support each other in powerful ways—building confidence, providing encouragement, and coming up with illustrations that explain complex ideas. Their power can also stop teachers dead in their tracks when they simply refuse to ask or answer questions. Every teacher knows the panic of ending an explanation, asking for questions, and being met by total silence. Does this mean students have understood everything or that they are completely confused? Are they just uninterested or are they intimidated? Is their silence an act of resistance or apathy? Are they initiating a performance strike or are they uncertain of what participation in class looks like? In a meeting leaders can similarly be stymied by a lack of participation. No matter how much positional authority you may enjoy, you can feel your "power" slipping away as you introduce a new agenda item at a meeting only to be met by averted gazes, slumped shoulders, or glazed eyes.

The reality of power is just as present online as in any other setting. Just because courses happen online does not mean that power relations are elided (Pettit, 2002; Jun and Park, 2003). Teachers have the power to set deadlines for student postings, to mandate how many postings constitute an acceptable level of participation, and to encourage or humiliate students through the way they comment on their contributions. In some ways a teacher's negative comment online has more enduring power than one made in the middle of a classroom discussion. The words are always there, frozen on the screen as a reminder of a teacher's disapproval. Students, however, have the power to evade and sabotage teacher's intentions by posting comments that are fabrications and in no way representative of their real opinions. They also have the power that their greater use of, and familiarity with, digital technology may give them.

Efforts to introduce more student-centered, empowering activities sometimes, in a teasing contradiction, underscore teachers' power. Telling students they have the power to decide when to call a break, how many absences may be taken in a semester, or to grade some assignments seems, on the face of it, to be empowering. But this is still an exercise of teacher power. After all, the teacher is the one creating the possibility that students can make these decisions. It's a fundamentally different dynamic when learners insist they need more breaks than you are providing because they know their energy level at the end of a hard day better than you do. It's even more striking when they leave a session en masse to get refreshment or to use the toilet, leaving you wondering whether or not to carry on with a classroom activity. In my own workshops, I time a break once an hour simply because if I don't adults will get up and take one anyway.

To take another example, Katherine Frego (2006) includes an Amnesty Coupon (which I have sometimes used) in her syllabus that students can redeem one time during the semester as an amnesty from an assignment deadline. If students never redeem the coupon, they gain extra points on their grade. Adults appreciate this kind of acknowledgment that life gets in the way of academic study. Yet, even a creative device such as the Amnesty Coupon clearly entrenches teacher power since the teacher is the one responsible for its design and implementation. I'm the one who puts the coupon in the syllabus and declares it to be legitimate. It's an entirely different dynamic if the adults I'm teaching come up with the idea and force me to consider it seriously.

Even in recreational adult education classes where enrollment and attendance are wholly voluntary, power moves around the room in unpredictable ways. A university noncredit or extramural course for adults has power present before students even arrive in the room. As Kenkmann (2011) describes, and as my own practice corroborates, teachers in such classes typically arrive early to rearrange the furniture, open windows, adjust thermostats, distribute materials, write on the board and position themselves close to the front desk or computer terminal. Even putting chairs into a circle and explaining to learners that you do this to displace power "in many ways reinforces power structures rather than undermines them, because it suggests that the teacher is the one who has power in the first place that can then be surrendered" (Kenkmann, 2011, p. 284).

As an adult learner, I have felt as foolish, ashamed, or angry in leisure classes as I have in the most rigidly controlled and mandated learning environments. In *Becoming a Critically Reflective Teacher* (Brookfield, 1995), I described my experiences in a class for adult nonswimmers where a teacher's inability to understand my fears stopped him from knowing what would help me learn, and where a fellow student's struggles allowed her to sense what would move me forward (wearing goggles). I should admit that recreational teachers have also inspired me to take risks and made me feel proud of my accomplishments. Sometimes it was because of a methodology they used, but more often it was because of who they were. By that I mean the way they exuded a quiet enthusiasm, displayed openness to criticism, or were humble about their accomplishments. I remember these things more vividly than any new skill they taught me. I shall argue throughout this book that modeling is one of the most powerful techniques that teachers use.

How Do Adult Teachers Think About Power?

Not only is the reality of power everywhere, but its rhetoric is everywhere too. One of the most frequently used words in the discourse of adult learning, *power* has three chief connotations. First, and most frequently, a powerful teacher or leader is often characterized as a person with charisma, wisdom, and presence—someone who can hold an auditorium in the palm of their hands or whose personality can fire people with enthusiasm for learning. These are the individuals who win teacher of the year awards and who feature in media portrayals of teachers. The power thought to be exercised here is usually the power to inspire.

In this discourse power flows overwhelmingly in one direction, from teacher to taught. The teacher motivates and inspires others by her presence. A powerful technique is understood in a similar way as a task, exercise, or activity that is so skillfully energizing that it cannot fail to activate students' enthusiasm, dispelling any resistance to learning they feel. Such a technique is imagined as a kind of elixir that, once drunk, turns apathy into engagement, hostility into eagerness. In *Learning as a Way of Leading* (2008), Stephen Preskill and I argued that this was the prevailing model of leadership in contemporary culture.

A second connotation of power is that it is a force used to intimidate, control, or bully. Whenever I feel I am being made to complete a meaningless task, simply because my teacher has told me I must do this or risk failing the course, I am in his power. I can, of course, exert my own power of noncompliance, but the consequences of doing this are usually worse than the boredom of having to jump through a particular teacher-prescribed "hoop." So many organizational behaviors are determined by edicts and requirements issued from above. In the universities in which I have worked, what I and my colleagues taught, and how we taught it, have been strongly influenced by the dictates of whichever accreditation agency had the power to award or withdraw the university's accreditation. The power here is the power of coercion.

Coercion, by the way, is not always a bad thing. Being coerced into making sure you treat people respectfully, don't privilege research over teaching, try to recruit employees who represent racial diversity, challenge groupthink, and allow learners time to think before they speak are all coercions I would endorse. Sometimes I use my authority as a leader or teacher to coerce my students or colleagues into examining ideas or practices they would much rather ignore. An example of this would be in leadership courses where I insist that the White students I teach explore the concept of racial microaggressions. These are the small behavioral tics and gestures (tone of voice, body language, choice of examples, eye contact, and so on) that Whites display without realizing how these diminish racial minorities. I don't like owning up to my racial microaggressions and my students often don't either. But I force the issue and insist that we cover this ground. Baptiste (2002) describes this as ethical coercion and points out that it is usually masked by blander language such as facilitation or encouragement.

The third way power is spoken of is particularly prevalent among trainers and educators of adults. This is the discourse of empowerment, where the point of learning is thought to be the development in learners of a sense of agency—a belief that they can accomplish something that previously had been considered unattainable or that had they had never even imagined. An empowered classroom is usually thought of as one where students decide what they wish to learn and how they are going to learn it. An empowered learner is deemed one who applies the new skills learned in class to take action in the world outside. Time after time in my career I have heard people say they wished to empower students, meaning they wanted them to feel more confident in their abilities and to see themselves as self-directed learners who could take responsibility for planning and conducting their own learning without a teacher's assistance.

These are laudable aims, but they are also complicated. For example, what if my students self-directedly decided to explore White supremacist ideology with a view to spreading racial hatred? What if the soccer teams I have coached decide the best way to avoid defeat is to keep all ten outfield players in the penalty box, pack the goalmouth, and then fake being fouled with a view to getting opponents expelled from the match? What if the staff members I supervise decide to tell students or colleagues who seem to be depressed to "snap out of it" and refuse their requests for help? Would I unequivocally support these aims because they helped students develop a sense of their own agency? Of course not! My own commitments, values, and ethics would stop me. I don't want the most loud-mouthed students or the most bigoted colleagues to feel even *more* confident. On the contrary, I want to disturb them, to force them to be silent sometimes so they have to listen to what others are saying. And I want to require them to show they have striven to understand a view that challenges them before they dismiss it.

As already mentioned, empowerment is not something teachers, professional developers, or leaders can *give* to students, colleagues, or followers; it's something students *claim*. And not everything that students wish to claim is desirable. Sometimes we have to insist and coerce, to stand our ground, and not give in to students' demands. This is one of the hardest lessons I have learned as an adult teacher. I used to think that a proper adult learning environment was one in which I found out what students wished to learn, or how they wished the class to proceed, and then taught that content or ran the class that way. And in certain situations I still feel that's true. But I realize that being adult-centered does *not* absolve me of making value-based choices. Sometimes it means trying to find out as much as I can about how my students are experiencing their learning and then using what I have discovered to help them engage with material I feel is worth the effort.

A Note on Sovereign and Disciplinary Power

Over the past three decades the work of the late French cultural critic Michel Foucault has had a significant influence in shaping how adult teachers think about power. Many practitioners, including yours truly, now concede that power is much more dispersed and slippery than they had previously thought. In particular, Foucault's notion of disciplinary power—the way we exert power on ourselves to make sure we keep within acceptable boundaries—is widely cited. I often hear adult teachers talk of working in the *panopticon* (a system that we can't detect or block in which we feel permanently under surveillance) and of how they make sure they don't cross limits for fear of being reported by students or colleagues who disagree with them. In my own case, I'm very aware that e-mail is not a private form of communication and that out there in cyberspace are watchers who, at some unknown point in the future, can retrieve anything I type on my keyboard.

Foucault argues that disciplinary power is the quintessential form of power in the information age and that it has replaced what he refers to as *sovereign power*—power exercised from above by an authority figure who doles out rewards and sanctions. Although I am persuaded by Foucault's notion of disciplinary power, I believe what he called sovereign power still exists everywhere. For me sovereign power is not a kind of power that has been superseded. It's alive and well in meetings where people disagree with something but don't want raise their concerns because a powerful administrator is present. There is nothing covert about this. They don't speak up because they don't wish to challenge a powerful figure in the room.

Go to any adult literacy center, corporate training session, professional development day, or online adult classroom, and you will see the enormous sovereign power teachers in those settings exercise over students. They make most, and sometimes all, decisions on what is to be learned, how that learning will be arranged, how success in learning will be judged, and what materials will be used to support such learning. They arrange the minutiae of interactions such as how the room will be arranged, when breaks will be called for and for how long, and whether or not the lights will be on or the blinds open. Certainly, students often push back, subvert, challenge, and sabotage this power. But it remains very real.

Of course those same teachers are themselves subject to the sovereign power exercised over them by accreditation agencies, professional codes or expectations, and licensing requirements. They have to deal with supervisors, senior colleagues in their departments, department heads, deans, vice presidents, tenure and promotion committees, and boards of trustees. They also face the sovereign power of institutional habit. As Hunt (2006) outlines, teachers of adults face structural and systemic constraints that limit their ability to teach in ways consistent with their philosophies. For example, a commitment to intensive individual feedback is stymied by being required to teach large lecture classes, a belief in collaborative work is torpedoed by a system that allows only for individual grading. If teaching authentically means staying true to the values you believe and espouse, then many of us are forced into a "long-term unconscious acceptance of inauthenticity as a condition of employment" (Hunt, 2006, p. 55).

So I believe sovereign power is undeniable and that at times it works in conjunction with disciplinary power in a seemingly unchallenged double-whammy. At other times it flourishes on its own. How many times have you tried to change some aspect of your institution's or organization's functioning only to be told, unequivocally and directly, "No!" In my own four-decade-long career I have been told at various times I can't use pass/fail grading, I can't have students defend their dissertations as a team even if they have written the document as a team, I can't deviate from the syllabus, I can't take students off-site for field trips, I can't team-teach a course because it's too expensive, and I can't dispense with grading on a bell curve.

My understanding of power has been immeasurably enriched by Foucault and his notion that power is complex and multilayered, that it often moves around a room in unpredictable ways, and that those in apparently subordinate positions sometimes have the power to push back and sabotage (as when students stay silent when you pose a question to a group). But I am in no way ready to believe that sovereign power doesn't exist. After all, when I was thirty-two and was fired, I didn't internalize a desire to be fired as a pleasurable way to support the institution and I didn't fire myself! No, it was a board of trustees who decided that in a time of newly imposed financial austerity they had the sovereign power to decide I was the most expendable member of staff.

What Does It Mean to Teach?

Having explored the idea of power at some length, I want now to turn to the other part of the title of this book—techniques for teaching adults—and say something about how I understand teaching. In popular culture, the image of a good teacher is usually that of a charismatic individual who, through a mixture of dedication, empathy, courage, and genius ignites the fires of learning in students and leaves a mark on their lives that endures over the decades. Think of films like *Mr. Holland's Opus, Stand and Deliver, Remember the Titans, Dead Poets Society, The Emperor's Club,* or *Dangerous Minds,* and you'll see what I mean. From my own view as a working teacher, these films have done me more harm than good. As a shy introvert I find media images of supremely heroic, energetic, and accomplished teachers very intimidating. A lot of the time I feel I'm just muddling through the day trying not to create a disaster. I often leave a class thinking I'm an amateur and feeling confused and tired. So I'm continually reminding myself that teaching should not be confused with charismatic performance.

To teach is to help someone learn. This may sound obvious, but for me it's a mantra that bears repeating every day. The point of teaching is to help someone acquire information, develop skills, generate insights, and internalize dispositions they did not know before. The incredible complexity of adult learners—the different ways they learn, the varied purposes they bring to learning, the cultural and political constraints they endure, and the multiple identities and backgrounds they exhibit—means we have to think of teaching in similarly complex terms. I suppose there are some who can stand in front of a group of learners and use their personal charisma to talk brilliantly about a topic or demonstrate a new skill flawlessly and superbly, but this is only one contextually determined act of teaching among endless possibilities.

When I write a syllabus that is designed to help students understand the terrain they are to explore and the resources that will help them in that exploration, I'm teaching. When I write a book like this, I'm teaching. When I draw up a list of discussion questions to provoke students into considering new perspectives, or when I create a video record of a skill demonstration, I'm teaching. When I call a break to keep energy levels high, I'm teaching. When I ask students to spend a period of class time silently reading a passage, I'm teaching. I could go on and on with this list but I hope you get the point. My favorite question to ask myself when I'm trying to decide among all the different options open to me about how I could spend my time in class is "How does this help learning?"

Thinking of teaching as helping learning implements the Ignation notion of *Tantum Quantum*—that context constantly alters how a practice is put into effect. As a teacher I work in very different ways depending on the context in which I find myself and the pedagogic purposes I'm pursuing. For example, in any particular week I move among the five perspectives Pratt (1998, 2002) identifies as influential in adult teaching. On Monday I may run a faculty development workshop on how to write a scholarly book proposal. Here I'm helping unpublished colleagues learn how to increase their chances of getting a book contract by taking them through the stages of writing a clear and persuasive proposal (what Pratt might call the transmission mode of teaching). On Tuesday I might be a consultant designing an executive development seminar to get business leaders to analyze their practice critically and identify blind spots in their decision making (what Pratt might call the developmental perspective).

Wednesday could see me inviting a colleague into my classroom so that she can observe how I run discussion sessions with the intent of adapting some of my strategies in her own teaching (what Pratt labels apprenticeship). Thursday I may work with a group of students who are on the verge of dropping out of a program and spend much of the session reassuring them that they have the ability to succeed (what Pratt describes as nurturing). The week may end on Friday with me running a session with a group of early childhood supervisors on recognizing racial microaggressions in their leadership practices or advising Occupy Wall Street groups on how to democratize their decision making (the social reform perspective).

It could also be that in the same class I teach informed by each of these five perspectives at different moments. As a recent summary of Pratt's *Teaching Perspectives Inventory* noted (Collins and Pratt, 2011), "effective teaching depends on context" (p. 259).

Now I have to own up and say I've probably never had a week in which all these events happened within the space of five days. But they have all happened within a few months of my writing these words. So how I teach at any moment on any day is strongly influenced by the purposes I'm trying to achieve and what I know about the people I'm working with. Some things do hold true, such as my belief that the most important knowledge I need to do good work is a constant awareness of how people are experiencing their learning, or my belief that I must always try to model whatever I'm asking learners to do. But exactly what I'll do, and the way I'll do it, varies with local circumstances. This is what Fenwick (2006) calls "poor pedagogy" "enacted in microrelations, in our ethical action in the immediate" (p. 21). When I do find myself in practice, some particular event—a provocative and disturbing question or a student's body language—may change radically the way I'm teaching in that particular moment.

So when I talk about teaching in this book I'm talking about any intentional act designed to help someone learn something. This certainly does include standing in front of a group and talking, but much of the time I'm teaching with my mouth shut (Finkel, 2000). At times I'm proactive in pushing students to engage with material that challenges them, while at other times I hang back and allow them to chart the course of learning. Sometimes I intervene to provide clarification and assistance, sometimes I let students struggle for an extended time. My intention always is to work skillfully to arrange the circumstances in which students will learn best. If I think this is most helped by my giving a lecture, then I'm happy to do that. But my starting point is always to ask myself what I want someone to learn and then to think of which approaches and activities will best help that happen.

Although this book is about techniques for teaching, I don't want to imply that teaching is only something that happens in formal educational institutions or something that is only done by people referred to as teachers, lecturers, or professors (Halx, 2012). Teaching happens in intimate relationships, families, recreational groups, communities, social movements, and all kinds of organizations. In fact, two books which I coauthored specifically focus on social movement teaching (Preskill and Brookfield, 2008; Brookfield and Holst, 2010). Teachers are called by many labels—facilitators, leaders, trainers, animateurs, counselors, therapists, or supervisors to name a few. Sometimes, particularly in intimate relationships, they have no special label; they're just friends, partners, siblings, or lovers who help us learn something about life. So I use the term *teacher* in a generic way throughout this book, and I apply it to the multiple contexts in which someone is intentionally helping someone else learn something.

What Makes Teaching Adults Distinctive?

This is a book about teaching adults, as against teaching children or adolescents. So a few words on what it means to work with adults are in order. I think that the methodology of teaching adults is not different in kind from that of teaching children or adolescents. Any differences that do exist in a particular situation are those of degree. Over my career, everything I've seen claimed as quintessential examples of adult teaching—such as emphasizing learner self-directedness, using dialog and discussion, working experientially, having learners construct the curriculum around their pressing concerns, getting students to ask critical questions, or creating classroom democracy—I've observed being done by teachers of children and adolescents. The best dialogic teacher I've ever seen worked exclusively with eight- to eleven-year-olds, and the most democratic classroom I've ever been in was in an American middle school.

When it comes to adult learners, it's plainly ludicrous to talk about teaching adults as if all adults across the planet represent a monolithic, generic category for which we can generate standardized techniques. In the *2010 Handbook of Adult and Continuing Education*, for example, Hansman and Mott (2010) and Boucouvalas and Lawrence (2010) explore the multiple variables present when considering adult learners, nothing less than the full diversity of humanity. Cultural tradition, class membership, racial identity, learning style, personality type, developmental stage, models of cognitive processing, previous experiences, people's particular brain chemistry, current ability level, readiness for learning—all these represent a bewildering set of learner characteristics. Then, add in the range of different settings in which learning happens—from programs to integrate Swaziland inmates into society after a jail term (Biswalo, 2011), to curricula in adult business schools (Love, 2011), online leadership programs for Newfoundland women (Clover, 2007), or peace education for women in Iraqi or Palestinian war zones (Mojab, 2010)—and it's clear that talking about adult learners as a unilateral group sharing similar characteristics is an essentialist absurdity. As English and Mayo (2012) appropriately observe, "an infinite range of disciplines and interdisciplinary studies constitute adult education's oyster" (p. 5).

So is there anything general we can say about teaching adults? I believe so. The first has to do with the reality of experience. As a general rule, the longer the time you spend on the planet, the more things happen to you and the more you interpret and give meaning to these experiences. That means adult students typically have a greater breadth and depth of experiences than younger students. But even this is obviously not a hard and fast truth. After all, a thirteen-year-old dropout who deals drugs and takes responsibility for rearing siblings, or a teenage refugee from a war zone who has had to survive on the streets in an alien culture, has had a much greater range of experience than someone who is forty years old, has lived in the same neighborhood, has smoothly progressed through schooling and into work in the same community, and has kept their beliefs intact.

One thing that marks adult teaching differently is an intentional focus on the diverse experiences learners bring to the classroom. Teachers of adults keep in mind the importance, wherever possible, of using learners' prior experiences to create connections to the new material being studied or the new skill sets being developed. You can do this with children, of course, but the greater variety and depth of experiences that many adults have had often means there are more opportunities for this to happen.

Second, across multiple learning contexts most teachers of adults try to set a tone of respect towards their learners. One of the most frequent claims I've heard from colleagues in the field is that they try to treat people as adults. When I ask what this looks like they usually reply by saying things such as "I don't talk down to my students," "I take learners' contributions seriously," or "my students teach me far more than I teach them."

Of course, talking about a tone of respect is hugely problematic. For one thing, what counts as respectful conduct varies enormously across cultural and organizational contexts. I grew up with the notion that interrupting someone talking was disrespectful and that good conversation resembled a series of monologues. But Alice Walker describes an African American speech pattern of people constantly interrupting each other in what she calls "gumbo ya ya" (Ampadu, 2004). Here interruption is a sign of attentive listening through making an immediate response in the middle of a comment. It's a respectful way of responding. In a Confucian influenced classroom (Lee, 2011; Sun, 2008; Wang and Farmer, 2008; Zhang, 2008), a respectful way of treating learners is to take pains to ensure that they have learned a skill in exactly the way the teacher intends, so as to ensure they can imitate or replicate this with little individual variation.

Most English language analyses of what curriculum should be taught to adult learners frame this issue in terms of adult roles and tasks. So an adult curriculum becomes one constructed around what any particular group contends are the distinctive roles and tasks people enact in adulthood. This is clearly culturally dependent. In my own case, I believe that a major task of adulthood is learning to create and sustain systems that encourage people to treat each other compassionately and fairly. So for me an adult curriculum—even if its focus is on helping people learn a very specific skill—in some way links to developing systems that stop an unrepresentative minority from having disproportionate control over resources that should be equally available to all. From this standpoint, a properly adult curriculum would teach skills that in some way allowed people to practice participatory economics (Albert, 2004, 2006) or democratic socialism (Brookfield and Holst, 2010). As Silver and Mojab (2011) document, the chance to teach this perspective has often been snuffed out as somehow being unpatriotic. If you believe, as I do, that a significant part of adult life is coming to understand how power operates, how dominant ideology shapes what seem to you to be "natural," "commonsense" ways of thinking, and how to subvert this process of ideological manipulation, then much of your curriculum will focus on teaching about power.

Fourth, and connected to the point above, adult teaching for me always has a distinct purpose of helping people learn how to exercise power on their own behalf. This is the tradition that is probably the most venerated in the English-speaking adult educational world, with the work of Myles Horton (Horton, 2003) and the Highlander Folk School in Tennessee, and Paulo Freire's (Freire, 2011) literacy work in Brazil and Chile being well-cited examples (see for example, McCormack, 2008; McDermott, 2007). Here the intent of teaching is to help learners understand how much they already know and how their experience, critically and collectively analyzed, can suggest responses to the problems they face in their communities, organizations, and movements. In interviews with Highlander participants, for example, Ebert, Burford and Brian (2004) describe how participants pooled their experiences to analyze the causes of community problems and generate helpful responses in their struggles. Workshop facilitators would occasionally interject with questions, but participants made the decisions on what to explore and how to explore it. Highlander challenges the notion that only professional experts have valid knowledge and explores "forms of knowledge people have that are not recognized or are erased by standard social science such as storytelling, theater, drawing, popular knowledge, so-called folk wisdom" (Hoagland, 2011, p. 97).

This fourth response to the question "What makes teaching adults distinctive?" has particular resonance for this book. Since the focus of the book is on teaching power, one of the themes we will explore is how people learn to exercise power on their own behalf and the role teachers play (if any) in this process. This exercise of student power takes different forms. Sometimes the teacher has deliberately set up the classroom to be an analog of democratic process. Students may respond well to this or view it with suspicion, wondering what game the teacher is playing. Sometimes learners will fight against what they see as an arbitrary use of teacher power and reject teacher authority, no matter how much teachers protest that this is being used for learners' benefit. Throughout I will try to illuminate the contradictions of this process of empowering learners.

Empowering learners to develop agency through self-directed or collaborative action are the kinds of phrases that spring frequently, but uncritically, from adult teachers' lips, including my own. Archibald and Wilson (2011) point out that with regard to empowerment in adult education "the concept's ubiquity is troubling, largely because power has often ironically been omitted from discussions of empowerment" (p. 22). As we shall see, any genuine attempt to live out the philosophy of empowerment quickly brings you up against the realities of external and hierarchical power. Susan Chase's (1995) classic study of women school superintendents, *Ambiguous Empowerment,* illustrates how the rhetoric of empowerment bumps up against the realities of male power as the freedom that is given with the left hand is quietly taken back with the right.

So What Is a Powerful Technique?

Now that I've argued for the ubiquity and complexity of power I feel a need to be more direct and offer my own understanding of exactly what comprises a powerful technique. As I use the term throughout this book, a powerful technique comprises four possible elements: (1) it takes account of power dynamics; (2) it supports learners claiming empowerment; (3) it illuminates how power works; and (4) it renders teacher power transparent and open to critique.

It Takes Account of Power Dynamics

First, a powerful technique takes into account the power relationships that exist in all adult learning environments. There are struggles over what should be taught, what counts as legitimate knowledge, what processes of learning are allowed, and how learning should be judged. A powerful technique is employed with an awareness of the power dynamics existing between instructors and learners and between learners themselves. From this point of view, it is not the technique that is inherently powerful but the intent of the user. Hence a technique becomes powerful when used with an intentional effort to understand how it intersects with power dynamics.

In this way, something as traditional as a lecture is a powerful technique if it sets out to challenge dominant ideas or explore a subversive body of work. Similarly, a teacher who leaves the stage and walks to the back of the auditorium where students are clustered and then proceeds to lecture from there is employing a traditional technique in a powerful way. Ira Shor (1996) calls this "lecturing from Siberia." He points out that most higher education classrooms contain a Siberia zone that is the point farthest away from the teacher. Students sit there so as to be unobserved and avoid participating. By locating yourself in Siberia, you upset the traditional power relations in the classroom.

A powerful technique always adapts itself to the realities of power dynamics. For example, discussion techniques are only effective when informed by an understanding of how power operates in the classroom and in the relationships between teachers and learners. A teacher who runs a discussion with no awareness of interstudent power dynamics may preside over an disengaged or proforma series of speech acts in which the most confident and extroverted students automatically move front and center and shut others down. Or, a discussion in which the leader consciously or unconsciously moves the conversation in a direction he wishes it to go is a counterfeit discussion in Paterson's (1970) terms. In both these instances, a lack of awareness of power sabotages the effectiveness of the technique.

It Supports Learners' Claiming Empowerment

Second, despite my cautions regarding the term *empowerment* earlier, a powerful technique is understood to be one that prefigures people claiming their own empowerment. By that I mean that it develops in them a sense of their own agency and a heightened self-confidence in their abilities as learners. A powerful technique is powerful not just because it is startling, engaging, or forcefully employed (which is how many texts use the term), but because it increases the learner's perceptions and enactment of being powerful. Kilgore (2004) captures what I mean when she defines powerful knowledge as "knowledge that is personally empowering and socially transforming" (p. 48). So much of adult learning philosophy focuses on the need to empower learners, and this book is one that explicitly ties this focus to specific teaching techniques.

As I've already pointed out, however, this is by no means a simple or unequivocal practice. There are contradictions and tensions in the realization of empowerment, which themselves surface the reality of power. At the root of empowering learners is the fact that this can never be done directly by the teacher. The most a teacher can do is try to remove barriers to learners' claiming their own empowerment and, as mentioned earlier, try to create the conditions under which learners realize and exert their own power. Using discussion protocols that create an opportunity for everyone to speak is one such approach. Another is to model a self-critical analysis of one's own ideas in front of students.

Sometimes learners claim empowerment in directions the teachers opposes. For example, I have often taught classes in which the students rebel against my using participatory approaches and ask me to lecture. I have also been told to stop asking students to think critically and to tell them the "answer" and the correct way of understanding something. Do I accede to these requests because they are an example of students claiming their own empowerment? No, I don't. But that then raises the question of how I judge what is authentic, desirable empowerment as against inauthentic or counterfeit examples. Throughout this book, I try to address these tensions by exploring when and how trainers, leaders, and teachers need to insist on their agendas, to insert themselves into apparently free-flowing discussions, or to live with being the focus of learner resistance. I will also try to illuminate instances in which attempts to empower learners are done in such a manner as to have precisely the opposite effect.

It Illuminates How Power Works

Third, a powerful technique is one that helps learners understand how power operates both in the microrealities of their daily relationships and practices, and in the broader organizations, communities, and movements in which they live. I wrote a whole book on this called *The Power of Critical Theory* (Brookfield, 2004) where I argued that a critical theory approach to working with adults would help them learn, among other things, how to challenge ideology, unmask power, and practice democracy. That book was intentionally a theoretical analysis with only a final chapter touching on the practice of teaching. In a sense the book you're now reading is the workbook for *The Power of Critical*

Theory, because it explores how to teach adults to understand the constraints and possibilities of power.

As we shall see, it is not just gatekeepers and those who benefit from an unchanged status quo in teaching who mount resistance to learning about how power operates. Learners themselves frequently turn away from the emotional and political tornado involved in studying power. Indeed, one of the most underresearched aspects of this kind of teaching is how teachers maintain sanity and resolve in the face of sustained hostility from students. As Somers (2011) notes, "experiencing personal attacks and having learners direct their emotional responses towards them, feeling inadequate, taking things personally, learning how to detach, feeling excited about the fact that students are learning and the overall need to feel protected are all common and understandable human reactions to the environment that these educators face" (p. 658). The final chapter in this book focuses specifically on how to negotiate the emotional territory of teaching against power.

It Renders Teacher Power Transparent and Open to Critique

Finally, a powerful technique is one where teacher power is transparent and open to critique. By that I mean that the teacher is exercising authority in a way that is clearly communicated and clearly understood by everyone involved. In adult education, this readiness to acknowledge teacher power, and to admit that teachers are pursuing an agenda, is often avoided for fear of seeming disrespectful, undemocratic, or authoritarian. We (and here I include myself) don't want to seem directive. Instead we want to believe we are the same as our students and that it's some sort of historical accident or purely a matter of serendipity that we just happen to be the teacher.

One of the ways we hide from ourselves the fact that we have power is by our use of language. We describe ourselves as facilitators and, as Kilgore (2004) notes, "to honor students we refer to them as *learners*, as if they weren't really subject to the teacher's pedagogical machinations at all" (p. 49). Of course those same "learners" usually see right through this sham. In a doctoral program emphasizing democratic student governance that I helped create, one of the students got right to the heart of the matter by telling me "your so-called democracy is hypocritical because you can always fail us," a comment that became the title of a paper that Ian Baptiste and I wrote exploring the contradictions inherent in trying to work democratically in a program within a hierarchical institution (Baptiste and Brookfield, 1997).

It's interesting that when we examine research documenting what students look for in their teachers, two of the most important behaviors are (1) regular and full disclosure of the expectations, criteria, and agendas that teachers hold, and (2) teachers laying out the rationale behind their actions and decisions. Both of these entail teachers making their power transparent. I have written at some length about this in *The Skillful Teacher* (Brookfield, 2006) so won't go into great detail here. But it's clear to me from that research that in most situations adult students are fully aware of the power that teachers exercise and just wish they'd be open and honest about it. We (and here, again, I mean me) can congratulate ourselves on how equally, respectfully, and collegially we're treating students, but they know full well that to some degree we have their fate in our hands because we decide whether or not they pass the course, and we also judge how smart they are by awarding a particular grade.

In my experience students are very adept at picking up on a teacher's biases and agendas early on and then feeding back whatever it is they think the teacher will approve of. This is essentially no different than the dynamic I've experienced of being a member of a task force or committee led by a powerful figure who opens a meeting by declaring that all views are welcome and that nothing is off the table, and then proceeds by his nonverbal gestures (eye contact, head nodding, grunts) to communicate exactly which contributions are appropriate and which are beyond the pale.

In the past I have often felt queasy about acknowledging that I have an agenda that I want fulfilled, preferring instead to believe

I am there only to help students realize their own learning desires in whatever way feels best to them. Occasionally it's true that I can work in this way. But that's only because I have already decided, on the basis of my knowledge of the group, that I like the directions they are taking and that I support their overall project, whatever that may be. On the whole I concur with Kilgore's (2004) argument that "what unfolds before us in the adult education classroom does so largely at our behest" (p. 48) and that an honest pedagogy (though she frames this as a postmodern pedagogy) "would be concerned with naming what makes us submissive and identifying what grants us power" (p. 48).

Naming and Clarifying Teacher Power

I ended the last section by asserting that a powerful technique is one where teacher power is transparent and open to critique. Given that an open acknowledgment of one's power and an invitation to critique this are not typical components of adult teaching texts, I want to say more about this as I end this chapter. If teachers are honest with students, they must acknowledge that they have considerable power. They have the power to define curricula, set evaluative criteria, and then use these criteria to decide the worth of student work. Teachers cannot pretend this difference doesn't exist and simply be friends with students, though they can treat them in a friendly, respectful, and collegial way.

There will be times in every teacher's practice when their agenda for learning is in direct conflict with that of the students. In such a case, it would be inauthentic for teachers to deny their identities by simply agreeing to do what students want. Being authentic involves staying true to one's agenda, being open and honest about this, and sometimes placing one's power behind this. This raises many complex questions—can a teacher be authentic yet practice ethical coercion? What power do students have to keep the teacher honest? Are authenticity and authority compatible? In this section

I wish to explore a central question—how do we exercise power in an ethical and responsible manner while being authentic, even as we face student hostility? In doing this I will draw on several educators whose work is informed by critical traditions, particularly Ian Baptiste, bell hooks, and Herbert Marcuse.

Grenadian-born adult educator Ian Baptiste (2000, 2001) is one who has considered questions of power and the justifiable use of authority at length. To Baptiste, adult educators often function as persuaders and organizers (in the sense that Gramsci [1971] used those terms) but choose not to acknowledge this. In Baptiste's view it is naïve, and empirically inaccurate, for adult educators to insist that their job is not to take sides, not to force an agenda on learners. Like it or not (and Baptiste believes most of us do not like to acknowledge this), adult teachers cannot help but be directive in their actions, despite avowals of neutrality or noninterference.

One of the most contentious aspects of Baptiste's writings is his insistence on the morality of coercion. He believes that adult educators cannot avoid imposing their preferences and agendas on learners, and that in certain instances it is important that they do this. Sometimes, in furtherance of legitimate agendas or to stop the perpetration of illegitimate ones, Baptiste argues that the adult educator must engage in manipulation, a word most teachers instinctively recoil from. To support his case, he describes a situation in which he worked with a number of community groups on the south side of Chicago to assist them in reviving an area ravaged by pollution and migration. As the neutral, independent facilitator, he was supposed to stay free of forming alliances with any of the groups involved. Citing his liberal humanist sensibilities, he describes how in trying to stay neutral "I succeeded only in playing into the hands of the government officials (and their lackeys in the community). They played me like a fiddle, pretending in public to be conciliatory, but wheeling and dealing in private" (p. 47).

In hindsight, Baptiste argues the experience taught him that in situations where there is a clear imbalance of power adult educators should take uncompromising stands on the side of those they see as oppressed. An inevitable consequence of doing this will be the necessity for them "to engage in some form of manipulation—some fencing, posturing, concealment, maneuvering, misinformation, and even all-out deception as the case demands" (pp. 47–48). He points out that if adult educators do admit that manipulation is sometimes justified, then an important learning task becomes researching and practicing how to improve one's manipulative capacities. Through studying ethically justified manipulation, adult educators can "build a theory that can legitimize and guide our use of coercive restraint" (p. 49).

Baptiste's analysis raises some troubling issues for my earlier assertion that powerful teaching involves a transparent acknowledgment of how I use my power. Most teachers would accept that sometimes one must conceal one's intentions from one's employers to ensure one is able to take risks, experiment, and generally work in critical and challenging ways. Much more contentious is the issue of whether it is ever authentic to conceal one's intentions from students. Yet, for teachers trying to teach critically by raising uncomfortable and challenging viewpoints in class, making full disclosure of their intentions in advance could easily undercut their project. Students who are ideologically predisposed to shut out an alternative perspective may simply decide not to show up for class when they learn that exploring this alternative perspective is an element of a course they are considering. The same could be said for employees told to attend workshops on racism or sexual harassment. So to be educationally effective—that is, to have people be ready to consider an alternative and troubling new perspective—instructors may need to keep concealed the fact that participants will be asked to do this until they (the teachers) judge students to be at a point of learning readiness for this.

Teachers may also wait to introduce new perspectives until they feel they have earned students' trust. But earning trust is not the end of the story. Even if the trust is earned at an earlier stage in a course or program, it may be that when teachers start to introduce the new perspective or activity the acquired trust will then be completely destroyed. In introducing previously unannounced and challenging material, teachers may find that students see this as a fundamental and surprising change of direction. In this situation those teachers will be seen as acting in ways that contradict their words, as fundamentally and troublingly incongruent.

Requiring students to engage with new and challenging material is certainly justifiable. In the case of mandatory workshops on racism or sexual harassment, few would openly argue that these are frivolous or unnecessary. Indeed, one could argue that the most valuable learning that people experience often happens when they are forced to consider perspectives, information, and realities they would prefer to avoid. This illustrates a wonderfully contradictory dynamic: attending assiduously to building trust and being transparent by making full disclosure in advance of one's agenda (which is something that is supposed to increase learners' openness to new learning) is often canceled out by the equally justifiable need to conceal significant information about the learning agenda (to avoid learners deciding prematurely to exit the activity). So the requirement that teachers make full disclosure is undercut by the need to keep the agenda concealed until learners are ready to confront difficult tasks.

There is another contradictory dynamic at play here where students' judgment of authenticity is concerned. For students a prime indicator of authenticity is the teacher's clear responsiveness to learners' concerns (Brookfield, 2006). Yet, students' long-term intellectual development sometimes requires that we refuse do what they ask, thereby risking appearing to be unresponsive to their wishes. For example, I know that when I'm trying to get students to think critically I must sometimes refuse to comply with their requests to tell them what is the correct view to hold on an issue or the right assumptions to follow in a certain situation. My refusal to tell them the "proper" way to think—in effect, to refuse to comply with their request for the right answer—appears to contradict the condition of responsiveness.

One theorist who has explored this dynamic is Herbert Marcuse (1965). Marcuse argues that it is educationally crucial that learners be exposed to alternative, often dissenting, ideologies and perspectives, even though they do not see the necessity for this. To him this is the practice of liberating rather than repressive tolerance. Marcuse argues that without knowing of the full range of options, viewpoints, or ideologies surrounding an issue, students cannot make a truly informed judgment as to which directions they wish to explore more deeply. One particular problem he identifies occurs when teachers appear to show respect for students by allowing them to determine the direction of learning.

When students have this option, Marcuse argues, they will usually choose curricular directions and learning activities that are familiar and comfortable. These directions and activities will be ones that have, in effect, been ideologically predetermined by students' previous histories and experiences. Students will choose learning projects that support and confirm prevailing ideology and steer clear of anything they sense is "deviant" or "left field." If we accept that learners need exposure to all available information and perspectives so that they can make informed choices about what to learn, then the teacher's duty (according to Marcuse) is to spend a considerable amount of time exposing students *only* to ideas and activities they would otherwise have avoided. This is the only way teachers can ensure students will be availed of the full range of perspectives and opinions that exist on any issue.

The African American feminist bell hooks also has much to say on the way in which a concern for being responsive to students' wishes brushes up against the inevitability of teacher power. For her the exercise of teacher power is often unavoidably, even necessarily, confrontational. In her judgment the teacher's position "is a position of power over others" with the resultant power open to being used "in ways that diminish or in ways that enrich" (hooks, 1989,

p. 52). She freely admits that sometimes the exercise of power to force people to confront their own uncritical acceptance and practice of dominant ideology is fraught with risk. To emphasize the commitment students should have to the learning of others, she lets students know that poor attendance negatively affects their grade. She also requires all to participate in class discussion, often by reading out paragraphs they have already written.

Such practices inevitably lead to negative critical comments by students, a fact that she admits has been difficult for her to accept. Because "many students find this pedagogy difficult, frightening, and very demanding" (hooks, 1994, p. 53), teachers who use it will be resisted, even disliked. Students may also elect not to take their courses. This is why hooks insists that the humanistic emphasis on having students perceive the classroom as a safe, positive, or congenial environment for learning is not always a good criterion to use in assessing teacher competence.

There are, of course, professional consequences to receiving poor evaluations, such as being denied reappointment, losing merit pay, or being refused promotion or tenure. If this is the case, then the institutional pressure is on for teachers to work in ways that students find pleasing and familiar. If, on the other hand, teachers insist on sticking to their guns and require students to engage with activities and ideas they would much rather avoid, they risk being labeled in course evaluations as at best unresponsive, at worst hostile or incompetent. In such a situation, the best a teacher can do is make sure that students are fully aware of why she is insisting on her agenda and refusing to comply with students' demands. After all, part of being trustworthy is to present as honest a picture as possible of one's agenda and convictions. So, although in the short term students might disagree strongly with a teacher's direction, they will believe the teacher to be honest if that teacher makes full disclosure as to why the direction is being pursued in the face of students' dissent.

The more fundamental and essentially irresolvable contradiction in being both authentic and true to one's agenda as a critical teacher arises when you are trying to bring students round to the point where they are willing to consider ideas and activities that previously they would have ignored or derided. As argued earlier, this sometimes involves a "softly, softly" approach in which the full import of your intentions is only gradually revealed. Such an approach may require that there be no early full disclosure of the teacher's intentions for fear that students would drop out of the course before being required to engage with new and threatening ideas. In such a situation, authenticity (if interpreted as full disclosure) and teaching for intellectual development (if understood as requiring students to stretch themselves in ways they would not themselves have chosen) may be directly at odds. After over forty years trying to resolve this contradiction, I have realized it is irresolvable—one of the ontological and practical contradictions that we have to live with even as our institutions pretend that teaching (defined as the sequenced, orderly managing of student learning to achieve predetermined outcomes) is always free of ambiguity.

Summary

In this chapter I have argued that teachers of adults, even in noncredit classrooms where there is no formal evaluation by teachers and no compulsion for students to attend, need an understanding of how power dynamics constantly intersect with individual and group learning. I have tried to define the terms I will be using throughout this book, and to address how even the most nondirective and low key facilitator always exercises power. In the next chapter, I look at a common adult learning process—learning how to think critically—that often requires the full force of teacher power to be employed before learners will take it seriously. It is also a teaching approach that usually is explicitly tied to learner empowerment.

2

Teaching for Critical Thinking

I have long believed that thinking critically lies at the heart of acting powerfully. If you know the assumptions you're operating under and are aware of different perspectives and possibilities, only then can you act in a way to further your own genuine interests. Acting this way is one important indicator of empowerment. Moreover, since becoming aware of your assumptions and finding out about multiple viewpoints happens best in groups, critical thinking can be understood as a social learning process that inevitably involves others. Since all groups exhibit constantly changing power relationships, this means critical thinking constantly intersects with power.

When people think critically they try to identify the assumptions that frame their thinking and actions, and they try to check out the degree to which these assumptions are accurate and valid. The chief way they do this is by looking at their ideas and decisions (intellectual, organizational, and personal) from several different perspectives. On the basis of this they then take what are hopefully informed actions.

What critical thinking looks like and how it's implemented varies by life context and academic discipline. In *Teaching for Critical Thinking* (Brookfield, 2012), I outline five interpretations of the process from the perspectives of analytic philosophy and logic, natural science, pragmatism, psychoanalysis, and critical theory. The rest of that book explores multiple approaches and exercises. In this present chapter, I understand the purpose of critical thinking as chiefly informed by critical theory and its method as chiefly informed by pragmatism. I present the bookends to a typical critical thinking sequence, beginning with modeling, following this with a Scenario Analysis exercise, and ending with the Critical Conversation Protocol.

As with any aspect of teaching, the most important knowledge we need to do good work is a thorough understanding of how students experience learning. Where learning to think critically is concerned, five themes repeatedly emerge from surveys of adults' experiences. First, students say they are helped when teachers model the process and when they draw students' attention to how that's happening. So one responsible and appropriate use of teacher power seems to be to describe your own processes of critical thinking in front of students, as well as opening yourself up to their critique, an approach that can itself feel empowering for them.

Second, learners say critical thinking is best developed in small groups where peers serve as critical mirrors, shedding light on assumptions that have never been checked and introducing new perspectives that have not been previously considered. It seems that students experience critical thinking primarily as a social learning process. As already mentioned, this means it intersects constantly with power dynamics. If you are going to be responsible for introducing group processes that try to uncover hidden, implicit, or tacit assumptions, and if you are hoping that students will generate different perspectives and interpretations, then you are going to be working with currents of power flowing around and within the group.

Third, students say they find it helpful to ground critical thinking in concrete experiences through case studies, critical incidents, simulations, and scenarios. Designing simulations is one explicit use of teacher power that can be helpful to students. Moreover, if the scenarios themselves focus on the use of power, then we have a multilayered situation in which (a) the content students are exploring is power, (b) the materials are designed by the teacher, reflecting her authorial power, and (c) the effective (and powerful) implementation of those materials involves teachers incorporating an understanding of the group's power dynamics.

Fourth, adults stress that the most significant moments in critical thinking happen when some kind of unexpected event or idea jolts them out of their comfort zone, what theorists of transformative learning call a "disorienting dilemma" (Mezirow and Taylor, 2009) and Vygotsky (1978) calls moving people beyond their "zone of proximal development." Creating these moments of dissonance is a clear use of teacher power, particularly when they involve students' being forced to deal with ideas and problems they would much rather avoid. For example, getting some White adults (myself included) to acknowledge their own commission of class, race, and gender microaggressions is something that many students would prefer to avoid. In these circumstances forcing the issue may require teachers to exert the full extent of their institutional, positional power.

Finally, when students look back on their learning journeys, they tend to view the trajectory of how they learned to think more critically as developmental. They say they prefer to start by practicing critical protocols in settings that are relatively nonthreatening before gradually bringing this process to bear more and more closely on their own life and experiences. Designing the sequence of exercises and judging when students are ready to move from one stage to the next is another exercise of teacher power.

Beginning with Modeling

Of the five themes that emerge from students' responses on what most helps them learn to think critically, the importance of teachers' modeling the process in front of them is the one that surprises me the most. At the beginning of my career, I believed I could measure my success as a teacher by how much my students *didn't* notice me, how much they forgot I was there. If they were learning without me saying or doing very much and if they mostly ignored my presence, then I felt I was teaching in the best way possible. I still believe this is very valid in many situations and that, in Finkel's (2000) terms, you can be very effective when you teach with your mouth shut. But when it comes to students' learning how to practice critical thinking, it seems they constantly look to us to see what the process looks like. Furthermore, because unearthing and questioning assumptions is often risky, it's important that teachers earn the right to ask students to do this by first modeling how they try to unearth and research their own assumptions. There's something essentially false about you asking a learner to do something that you haven't done first.

The modeling that students appreciate from teachers takes different forms. Most importantly, it seems that the more personal examples we give of how we try to think critically, the more students appreciate this. A teacher's early disclosure of a critical thinking experience can set a tone of openness that significantly influences students' readiness to explore their own assumptions. I often begin a session on critical thinking talking about my unwillingness to question my assumptions about the causes and treatment of clinical depression and how that prevented me from seeking help for my own depression. Or I will talk about how difficult it is for me to question my assumption that I have escaped any kind of racist, sexist, or homophobic conditioning. Describing racial or gender microaggressions I have recently committed is intended to encourage students to be willing to talk about such aggressions in their own lives.

Students also say that when it comes to a threatening activity like being asked to think critically about their long-held assumptions, it inspires confidence to see that teachers clearly have a plan for doing this, a set of reasons informing their actions. Speaking out loud about why you are introducing a particular classroom activity, why you're changing learning modalities, or why you've chosen certain readings demonstrates to students that you are a thoughtful, one might say critically reflective, teacher. Knowing that they are in the hands of such a teacher builds students' confidence. No one likes to think that the person leading them in an activity is making it up as she goes along with no forethought, reasoning, or previous experience. This is particularly the case when the teacher is asking you to engage in a risky learning activity, as is the case with practicing critical thinking. So explaining the reasoning behind your classroom actions and decisions is clearly a responsible use of power in students' eyes.

Having discussed two general elements in modeling critical thinking—using personal examples and explaining the reasoning behind your actions—let me review some specific modeling practices that students have picked out over the years as being helpful. All of these are designed to demonstrate either how to uncover and check assumptions or how to view knowledge and skills from multiple perspectives.

Speaking in Tongues

This activity is designed to show students how the same idea, facts, skills, or content can be interpreted in different ways. You begin by posting signs around the classroom corresponding to the number of different viewpoints you wish to consider. So, for example, if I were teaching a lesson on the intellectual traditions informing critical thinking, I might post five signs—analytic philosophy, scientific method, pragmatism, psychoanalysis, and critical theory. The activity starts with you standing in the center of the classroom and reviewing the content in the way it's generally understood. Hence, I might kick off by going over the definition of critical thinking given in the syllabus and examining how the University of St. Thomas (my employer) incorporates critical thinking into its mission statement.

You then move to the first sign you've posted and explain the content as if you were someone who only thought within that framework. So if I moved to the analytic philosophy sign, I would only speak about critical thinking as the construction and deconstruction of arguments and detection of logical fallacies. You then move to the second sign you've posted and give your understanding of the content as if you were solely concerned with that second perspective. So I would move to the scientific method sign and speak about critical thinking as the generation and testing of hypotheses and the application of the principle of falsifiability. The process would continue as I moved around the different stations. Students say that bringing in a simple spatial difference—speaking the language of a different theoretical paradigm when you are at a different station in the room—helps them realize that different perspectives can be taken on the same material.

A further variant on this exercise is to ask the class to generate questions about the topic after you've done your minireview at each of the stations you've posted. You can then respond to the same question in several different ways by going to two or three of the stations and responding in the voice of someone answering just from that perspective. Finally, when you have done this a couple of times in class you can add a further complexity. This time, you divide the class into groups and ask different groups to go and stand at the different signs. You then pose a question or raise an issue about the material, and you ask the groups to brainstorm for a couple of minutes on how they would answer the question or respond to the issue if they operated *only* within the framework represented by the sign they are standing by. The exercise ends with each group giving a summary of their responses.

Assumptions Inventory

In this exercise you get into the habit of stopping any presentations you make to compile, in front of the class, an Assumptions Inventory. This is, quite simply, an audit of the assumptions you hold that inform how you've just presented an idea, theory, or concept. It can be adapted to almost any subject or topic such as . . .

- Presenting your reasoning behind the way you've just presented a mathematical problem and demonstrated the solution

- Explaining how you've designed an experiment to measure velocity

- Describing how you discern the meaning of certain analogies used in a poem

- Summarizing the causal chain you've identified in a sequence of historical events

- Reviewing how a set of skills learned in a classroom can be applied to a real-life setting

- Justifying why you choose one theory over others as the best explanation for a particular phenomenon

At appropriate junctures you stop to distinguish between explicit and implicit assumptions informing your argument and to give examples of the most persuasive evidence for each of those assumptions. You also identify anything that's questionable about the assumption. Perhaps some assumptions are less evidence-based than others, or some have never been properly challenged. You also explain how and why your assumptions have changed and which you feel most or least confident about.

Point-Counterpoint

This activity is possible only if you are team-teaching a class. Essentially, it requires two or more people to analyze an idea or take apart a piece of content from discernibly different perspectives in front of the class. I usually team-teach once a year and the point-counterpoint moments are often the ones that students pick out as the most engaging parts of the course. This is where students see the faculty attempt to model what respectful disagreement and a critical analysis of each other's positions look like. This is extremely helpful if you are asking students to do these things as part of their own small group discussions.

Certain kinds of interactions are important to demonstrate when modeling Point-Counterpoint. Probably the most important is showing students how to pose questions that ask for evidence without attaching judgmental elements to them. Examples of these would be "Can you tell me more about. . .?," "Why do you think that's the case?," "What's the most convincing piece of evidence for that view?" or "How do you respond to Smith's research that challenges your position?" Other questions would seek clarification such as "If I understand you correctly you seem to be saying. . ." or "Can I just check that I've followed your argument correctly?"

Point-Counterpoint also allows you to show how you try to incorporate, or build on, your co-teacher's comments, which, in turn, emphasizes for students the importance of careful listening. You can strive to answer questions addressed to you by your teaching partner as fully and clearly as possible, and be ready to admit when you don't have an answer or when you need some time to think through what you want to say. When you disagree with a co-teacher's analysis, or you take a very different position on understanding a piece of content, you can say "I take a different view on this and here's why I think the way I do" or "My approach doesn't emphasize what you cover, here's my line of analysis." Often the greatest moments of delight that students note on their Critical Incident Questionnaires are when two instructors publicly disagree on something. This immediately gets their attention and wakes them up.

Structured Devil's Advocacy

This is a solo version of Point-Counterpoint. As part of your presentation you strive to spend some time presenting any arguments that counter your own assertions. A dramatic approach is to state your opening position while you stand in one part of the room and then to move to another part of the room, look back at where you originally stood, and then direct a second set of comments back at that spot as if you were speaking to the person (yourself) who was standing there. Here you deliberately state an alternative view, or you analyze the ideas you were just describing through a different research paradigm or a different theoretical framework. You are deliberately playing devil's advocate with the position you've just stated.

Structured Devil's Advocacy articulates a different perspective on what you've just said and opens up questions about it. You say things like "looking at this idea from another point of view we can see that . . ." or "here's a whole other interpretation of this argument that calls many of its central assumptions into question." You can model critical analysis by presenting counterarguments or rebuttals, in essence using the principle of falsifiability described by Karl Popper (1959/2002). When you do this you address your imaginary other self by name and say things like "Stephen, what you're omitting to mention is . . .," or, "Of course, Stephen, you could pursue a very different line of reasoning if you argue that . . ."

Ending Lectures and Discussions with Questions

Lecturers are often told that the golden rule of effective lecturing is to "tell 'em what you're going to tell 'em, tell em, then tell 'em what you've just told 'em." The problem with this rule is that it commodifies knowledge as a neatly bounded package of facts or concepts. Doing this is inimical to intellectual inquiry, particularly to the student's ability to make connections across subject areas and disciplines. Even more worryingly, ending with a summary of what's already been said establishes a sense of definitive closure, of the last word having been spoken on the subject.

I argue that good lecturers end their presentations by pointing out all the new questions that have been raised by the content of the lecture, and also by pointing out which of the questions posed at the start of the lecture have been left unanswered or been reframed in a more provocative or contentious way. This prepares students for the same practice in discussion where conversation sessions can be ended by asking students to volunteer the most pressing questions the discussion has raised for them rather than by asking for a summary of "what we've learned today in our discussion." If possible, lecturers should spend the last ten minutes of a lecture asking students to write down the questions the lecture has raised for them and then find a way to make them public. Students can be asked to speak their questions to the whole class, or they can be asked to share them with each other in small buzz groups of two or three. If they write them down, they can pass them to the lecturer and have the lecturer read out a random selection. As handheld devices become common in classrooms, students can send their questions anonymously and electronically to a classroom whiteboard for review. When I give a keynote speech, I like to have a Twitter feed projected onto a large screen next to my PowerPoint slides so participants can see a running stream of comments and questions.

Even if none of these things are possible, your own behavior of finishing a lecture with a list of new questions the lecture raises for you, or ending with an acknowledgment of the omissions, ethical dilemmas, and contradictions that challenge what you've just articulated, is a powerful piece of modeling. You should be warned, though, that initially students will probably be very critical of this approach. They will see your behavior of ending with questions or raising problems as unnecessarily confusing, as pulling the rug out from under their feet. Over time, as you consistently explain how doing these things is your best attempt to model the spirit of critical inquiry you are trying to encourage in learners, students' frustration will often diminish.

So What Do *You* Think, Teacher?

One of the classroom moments a lot of us dread is the question from students—"But what do *you* think, teacher?" If we are trying to get them to think critically about their own and others' assumptions about a topic, and if we are encouraging them to take responsibility for developing their own independent intellectual judgments, then we may feel that the last thing we want to do is tell them what our thinking is on the question that's been raised. The danger of doing this, of course, is that students will then take your response as gospel truth, as the "correct" way to think about a topic or problem. On the other hand, if we wish to model for students what we're asking them to do, it seems fundamentally contradictory not to be able to give our views on something. After all, we're asking students to tell us their emerging thinking—shouldn't students expect us to tell them ours?

My way through this is slightly convoluted, but it is one I use a lot and it has got me out of a lot of these "What do *you* think, teacher?" situations. Basically, I tell the students I will give them two or three answers to the question. One of them represents my true reasoning on the topic, the other one or two are plausible viewpoints but they don't represent my own thinking. I briefly explain my two or three responses, and then ask students to vote on which of my answers they feel really represents my own views. Students then form into groups based on which of the three answers they chose. I give them a few minutes to share with each other the reasons they have for believing my view was a, b, or c.

The whole class then reconvenes, and I ask each group to tell me what were the main reasons why they thought view a, b, or c represented my own thinking. I ask them particularly to talk about the assumptions they think I hold and to provide the evidence that prompted their choice. This is where students will refer back to the evidence I quoted in previous class meetings, or they'll point to the correspondence between one of my answers and what they've read in the textbook. When I've heard from the different groups, then I'll tell them which answer is the one I actually believe.

I like this exercise because I'm meeting students half way and showing them that I'm not playing a game where I hide my own opinions while asking for theirs, and then pounce on someone who says something that contradicts my beliefs. Students find out what I believe, but they have to work to do this. They have to trawl my past comments or review what they think course materials say before deciding what they think are my opinions. And then, of course, they have to provide reasons, assumptions, and evidence to support their choice. To me this exercise strikes a nice balance between telling people immediately what you think (which is consistent with you doing what you're asking students to do, but runs the risk of then having students ape your views), and avoiding their question entirely (which forces them to think it out for themselves, but contradicts the conviction that you should be willing to model, first, whatever you're asking students to do).

Scenario Analysis

Against the background of public and explicit teacher modeling of critical thinking, I usually recommend beginning a critical thinking sequence with the Scenario Analysis technique. Here you take a piece of material you are trying to teach and rewrite it as a description of an imagined event in which a fictional character is making a choice. Students are then asked to put themselves in the head of the character and try to identify the assumptions that character might be operating under. They give suggestions on how the character might check his assumptions, and then offer another way of looking at the scenario that the character clearly does not share. These scenarios are usually brief, from two paragraphs to a page. They are really bite-size case studies and, because of their brevity, are easy to fit into any class period.

This exercise can be adapted to almost every subject and topic by writing the scenario as a situation in which a fictional character is making a judgment about the correctness of how a chunk of content should be understood or a skill practiced. So, for example, you could write scenarios in which . . .

- A fictional chemist trying to understand the cause and effect relationship in a particular chemical reaction sets up an experiment to test what she feels is a plausible hypothesis. Students are asked to identify the reasoning behind the chemist's choice of her particular hypothesis and also encouraged to propose an alternative hypothesis that the fictional chemist could have chosen.

- A fictional mathematician formulating a mathematical proof adapts a protocol the students are familiar with to construct an equation. Students are asked to identify the reasoning behind the mathematician's adaptation of the protocol and to propose an alternative method of constructing an equation.

- A fictional psychologist studying a child with learning difficulties concludes the child is autistic. Students are asked to identify the assumptions the psychologist held when he made the diagnosis and how he could have checked these out. Students then suggest alternative diagnoses that the fictional psychologist could have made based on the information provided in the scenario.

- A fictional climatologist is researching greenhouse gas emissions and concludes from studying records of iceberg movement that global warming is a hoax (or a real threat). Students try to identify the piece of evidence the fictional climatologist took most seriously. They try to pose alternative assessments of the existence of global warming that the climatologist might have made had he focused on different information.

- A fictional triage nurse in an understaffed emergency room makes a decision about the relative seriousness of a patient's condition based on information he gathers from the patient. Students try to identify the information that they feel was most influential in the

nurse's diagnosis. They offer alternative plausible
diagnoses that could have been made if the fictional
nurse had focused on different information.

To illustrate what a Scenario Analysis exercise might look like,
let me give an example of one I've used in leadership training.

Scenario Analysis Exercise—The Anti-Racist Ground Rule

David is a White college teacher working on a campus that comprises 90 percent White European Americans. In recent months
the campus has experienced a number of racially motivated hate
crimes. Crosses have been burned, swastikas daubed on the Jewish
frat house, and racist epithets sprayed on the side of the building
housing the minority students' center. As a response to these events
the university has initiated a program of antiracist workshops involving students who have been identified as influential campus
leaders. The hope is that after participating in these workshops,
these leaders will spearhead an attempt to condemn and prevent
these racist acts.

The college has asked for faculty to volunteer to lead some of
these workshops. Although he has no experience working in this
area, David wants to do something to help, so he signs up. From
the few discussions he's led in the past concerning the dynamics
of race and racism, David knows things can get contentious very
quickly. He's seen discussions that have been designed to decrease
racism actually incite it and lead to minority students dropping out
of class.

To make sure that the antiracist workshops don't fall into the
same pattern of making the situation worse, David decides he will
institute a ground rule to guide conversation in the workshop he
will be running. His ground rule is that if a person of color discloses
an experience where they have been the target of racist speech or
actions, the White students should not try to convince the student that they misperceived the situation and saw racism where it

really didn't exist. One of the topics the workshop is supposed to address is racial microaggressions—the subtle and small gestures, remarks, and actions that Whites exhibit that people of color perceive as racist but that Whites don't recognize as such. David wants to make sure that White students don't dismiss examples of racism they are confronted with and that they don't try to maintain that such events are all in the heads of students of color. He believes that the ground rule that White students should not try to talk students of color out of their belief that they have experienced racism will help keep the group's focus on racial microaggressions.

1. What assumptions—explicit and implicit—do you think David is operating under in this situation? List as many as you can.

2. Of the assumptions you've listed, which ones could David check by simple research and inquiry? How could he do this?

3. Give an alternate interpretation of this scenario. A version of what's happening that is consistent with the events described but that you think David would disagree with.

Typical Assumptions Students Believe David Holds

1. Workshops are a good response to hate crimes.

2. The students chosen to participate in the workshops are people whose voices carry weight with other students in the broader campus community.

3. Students will change behavior if their racism is pointed out to them.

4. The ground rule will protect students of color from further racism.

5. Students of all races will observe the ground rule.

6. Students of color will appreciate the ground rule.

7. White students are unaware of their racist actions.

8. David is nonracist

9. David has the authority to insist the ground rule is observed.

10. The ground rule will decrease racist thoughts and feelings in White students.

11. Talking about racism can be done calmly.

12. White faculty members are the people best qualified to lead the workshops.

Ways That David Could Check These Assumptions That Students Often Propose

1. Study how other campuses have responded to hate crimes and the effectiveness of any antiracism workshops they have instituted.

2. Ask students of color how they feel about the proposed ground rule.

3. Ask students across campus to nominate the most influential student leaders.

4. Ask faculty who have experience in these kinds of workshops their opinion of the ground rule.

5. Review antiracist workshops run at other campuses and find out what exercises and approaches worked best.

6. Ask community leaders in the area how they have responded to racism in businesses and government agencies.

7. Institute some form of anonymous ongoing evaluation to see if the ground rule is having the effect intended for it.

8. Ask faculty colleagues of color their opinion of the ground rule.

Alternative Interpretations Students Often Give

1. The ground rule will lead to White students feeling they have been labeled as racist before they have had the chance to contribute to a discussion. It will increase their feelings of

resentment and harden their resolve not to take the workshop seriously.

2. The students of color will perceive the ground rule to be condescending and patronizing, because it implies they are unable to stand up for themselves when pointing out examples of racial microaggressions.

3. The ground rule itself is a racial microaggression because it springs from an unarticulated assumption that Whites are the "saviors" of people of color.

4. The ground rule is primarily designed to make David feel better about himself and to increase his own feeling of self-importance. It is designed to allow him to congratulate himself on his own antiracist righteousness.

5. The workshops will be perceived as a public relations exercise by students of color who will view them as exercises in image manipulation designed to make sure enrollment doesn't suffer.

Several observations need to be made about the Scenario Analysis technique. The first is that it is a social learning exercise, one in which students work in groups to focus on uncovering and checking assumptions by viewing them through different perspectives. Although the exercise begins with each student individually completing the three questions about the scenario, it is in the group sharing that the real learning occurs. Students come to realize they need others to help them see things they've missed, a major reason why students' preference for learning critical thinking through social learning was emphasized earlier. The exercise works best when different students identify assumptions that come as a surprise to their peers and when they propose widely varying explanations of what could be happening in the scenario.

The second point is that this exercise also builds on an insight students offer of how they best learn critical thinking; in this case through a concentration on specific experiences. The scenario focuses on a concrete situation, and students find it much easier to hunt assumptions when there is a specific experience to explore. Scenarios can be written in more complex ways by adding multiple characters who all have to make choices and giving more nuanced information that complicates their options. Third, it's important to stress is that there is no right or correct answer to any of the questions. Telling students this at the outset takes a lot of the pressure off their shoulders. Now they don't need to worry about whether their understanding of the scenario is the proper or "correct" one.

In fact I usually tell students that the more assumptions and interpretations they generate, and the more different ways they propose for the fictional characters to check those out, the better. The intent of the exercise is to provide an introductory engagement in the critical protocol of unearthing and checking assumptions by viewing them through different perspectives. Because it is not the students' own reasoning at stake, and because all the attention is on the fictional character's assumptions and interpretations, students are mentally freer to participate than if we began with an example from their own lives. Even if the scenario happens to be close to one the students have experienced, there is no pressure on the students to disclose that fact. All they are being asked to do is be a mental detective regarding the thinking of a fictional individual.

What is the instructor's role in a Scenario Analysis? Well, she usually writes the vignette and runs the exercise, essentially coordinating the different responses that groups come up with in their discussions. In the later phases of this exercise, instructors do offer judgments and clarification. When students suggest different ways the actors in the scenarios could check out the accuracy of their assumptions, these have to be within the range of possibility. When proposing alternative interpretations of the scenario, it is the teacher's job to probe why the students came to their alternative interpretation and to ask for information from the scenario that justifies the interpretation.

In fact this third part of the exercise—offering alternative interpretations—is usually the one that students find it hardest to complete. What often happens is that they offer alternative recommendations for action, telling the character how they should behave differently, rather than giving an alternative interpretation of what's happening that fits the brief facts given. I usually have to stress that the one thing students doing Scenario Analysis should *not* do is offer any advice to the fictional characters as to how they should resolve their situation differently. This is very deliberate on my part. Unless I specify very clearly that no advice should be given, the students will spend the bulk of their time discussing what David should do. Removing that possibility from the exercise means (theoretically, at least!) that students will focus all their attention on assumptions and interpretations.

In passing, I might add that the same dynamic is true of teachers. Get a group of teachers together over coffee, tea, or beer, and as soon as one of them brings up a problem they're facing and asks for help, the first thing the other group members will do is start telling the teacher in trouble what to do. What is skipped over is the critical scrutiny of how the teacher has framed the problem, whether or not it's the real problem to focus on, what assumptions the teacher brings to understanding and resolving the problem, and the different approaches that could be taken to addressing it. This is why critical conversation groups focus not on brainstorming solutions to problems, but rather on understanding what assumptions teachers hold about their problems, and what different understandings of these problems can be generated.

Critical Conversation Protocol

The Critical Conversation Protocol is an activity that should be placed towards the end of a critical thinking program since its complexity makes it a far more intimidating experience than a Scenario

Analysis. A critical conversation is a focused conversation in which someone is helped:

1. To come to an awareness of the assumptions she is operating under.

2. To investigate whether these assumptions are well grounded.

3. To look at her reasoning and actions from different viewpoints.

4. To think about the implications of the conversation for her future actions and thinking.

In a process of structured critical conversation I suggest that people think of playing one of three possible roles—storyteller, detective, or umpire. The storyteller is the person who is willing to make herself the focus of critical conversation by first describing some part of her thinking, practice, or experience. The detectives are those in the group who help her come to a more fully informed understanding of the assumptions and actions that frame her thinking, practice, or experience. The umpire is the group member who has agreed to monitor the conversation with a view to pointing out when people are talking to each other in a judgmental way. She also keeps the group focused on the discrete stages in the exercise.

All participants in the group play all three of these roles at different times. The protocol is so rich and complex that it happens several times, but each time the roles switch so participants have the chance to be the storyteller at least once, the umpire at least once, and the detectives several times. The idea is that if this is done multiple times, the behaviors associated with each role gradually become habitual.

The exercise has five discrete stages to it and the person chosen to be the umpire has the responsibility to make sure the stages are followed in sequence. The umpire is mostly a non-speaking role. She interjects only if the group is going off track or if she judges that someone is breaking the ground rules for the exercise. Here's how the activity proceeds . . .

1. The Storyteller Tells the Tale (10 minutes)

The conversation opens with the person who is the storyteller describing as concretely and specifically as possible an incident from her learning that for some reason was a problem. In the natural sciences, this could be an experiment that, to the storyteller, went disastrously and puzzlingly wrong. In the humanities, it could be an aesthetic engagement with art, philosophy, or literature in which the student was the only person to experience a work of art or set of ideas in a particular way that set her off from the mainstream. In social sciences, it could be a theoretical paradigm that the student was unable to understand or one that once understood seemed to have no application to the content it was supposed to explain. In fields of applied studies, it could be a nurse or a teacher who was faced with a serious dilemma that seemed to have no clear resolution.

The learning incident is one that is recalled because it was particularly frustrating. Most probably it is an incident that leaves the teller somewhat puzzled by its layers and complexities. The storyteller describes the incident in her own words and without any questions or interruptions. Her colleagues, who are in the role of detectives, attend to her remarks very carefully. They are listeners with a purpose.

The detectives are trying to identify the explicit and implicit assumptions the storyteller holds about what are supposedly correct ways of understanding the problem she discloses. Some of these will be general assumptions about the procedures used to judge whether or not knowledge can be trusted in the discipline. Some will be about how a good scholar should behave or what a correct intellectual protocol or research methodology looks like. Some will be more specific to the particular topic, assignment, or action described. These will have to do with the choices the storyteller made and the actions she took. The detectives are listening particularly for assumptions the storyteller holds about what counts as legitimate knowledge. They listen also for assumptions that are hegemonic;

that is, ones that seem admirable and useful to the storyteller but that actually work against her best interests.

The detectives are also asked to imagine themselves inside the heads of the other researchers or learners in the story (if there are any) and to try to see the events through their eyes. If this is an incident involving only the learner, and no teachers or other students were involved, the detectives try to think of different intellectual orientations in the field that might help deal with the confusion the storyteller is recounting. If possible, the detectives make mental or written notes about plausible alternative interpretations of the story that fit the facts as they hear them but that would come as a surprise to the storyteller.

2. The Detectives Ask Questions About the Event (10 minutes)

After the storyteller has finished speaking, the detectives are allowed to break their silence to ask her any questions they have about the events she has just described. The detectives are searching for any information that will help them uncover the assumptions they think the storyteller holds. They are also looking for details not provided in the first telling of the story that will help them relive the events described through the eyes of the storyteller or through the eyes of the other participants involved, if there are any. This will help them to understand these events from the different participants' perspectives.

The ground rules they must observe concern how they ask questions of the storyteller. They can only ask questions that request information (Can you say more about. . .?, Can you explain again why you decided to. . .?) not questions that pass judgment (Are you seriously telling me that you. . .?, Why on earth would you. . .?). Their questions are asked only for the purpose of clarifying the details of what happened. They must refrain from giving their opinions or suggestions, no matter how helpful they feel these might be. Detectives should also ask only one question at a time. They must avoid asking multiple questions masquerading as a single request for information. They should not give advice on how the storyteller should have acted.

As the storyteller hears the detectives' questions, she tries to answer them as fully and honestly as possible. She also has the opportunity to ask the detectives why they asked the particular questions they put to her. The umpire points out to the detectives any examples of judgmental questions that they ask, particularly those in which they imply that they have seen a better way to respond to the situation. An example of such a question would be one beginning "Didn't you think to. . .?"

The umpire brings the detectives' attention to the ways in which their tone of voice and body language, as well as their words, risk driving the storyteller into a defensive bunker. Essentially the umpire serves as the storyteller's ally, watching out for situations in which the storyteller might start to feel under attack.

3. The Detectives' Report the Assumptions They Hear in the Storyteller's Descriptions (10 minutes)

When the incident has been fully described and all the detectives' questions have been answered, the conversation moves to the assumption reporting phase. Here the detectives tell the storyteller, on the basis of her story and her response to their questions, what assumptions they think she holds.

This is done as nonjudgmentally as possible, as a reporting back exercise. The detectives seek only to state clearly what they think the storyteller's assumptions are, not to judge whether they are right or wrong. They are asked to state these assumptions tentatively, descriptively, and nonjudgmentally, using phrases like "It seems as if. . .," "I wonder if one assumption you might be holding is that. . .?," or "Is it possible that you assumed that. . .?" They state only one assumption at a time and do not give any advice about the way the learner *should* have understood or responded to the incident described. The umpire intervenes to point out to detectives when she thinks they are reporting assumptions with a judgmental overlay.

4. The Detectives Give Alternative Interpretations of the Events Described (10 minutes)

The detectives now give alternative versions of the events that have been described, based on their attempts to relive the story through the eyes of the other participants involved, or to understand the learning event through alternative intellectual paradigms. These alternative interpretations must be plausible in that they are consistent with the facts as the storyteller describes them. When appropriate, detectives should point out how power or hegemony plays itself out in the different interpretations they are giving.

The detectives are to give these interpretations as descriptions, not judgments. They are describing how others involved in the events might have viewed them, not saying whether or not these perceptions are accurate. They are speculating how the learning event might look when viewed from a different intellectual framework, not saying that this is the one the storyteller should have used. They should not give any advice here.

As the storyteller hears these alternative interpretations, she is asked to let the detectives have the floor so that they can state their case as fully as possible. After they have described how the situation might look through the eyes of other participants or from a different intellectual vantage point, the storyteller is then allowed to give any additional information that would cast doubt on these interpretations. She is also allowed to ask the detectives to elaborate on any confusing aspects of why they are making their interpretations. At no time is she expected to agree with any interpretations the detectives offer.

5. Participants Do An Experiential Audit (10 minutes)

Finally, the ground rules cease to be in effect any longer and the detectives can give whatever advice they wish. The storytellers and detectives state what they have learned from the conversation, what new insights they have realized, what assumptions they have missed or need to explore further, what different understandings they have as a result of the conversation, and what their reflection means for their future actions. The umpire gives an overall summary of the ability of participants to be respectful listeners and talkers and also gives her perspective on the story.

Although this is a heavily structured and artificial exercise, the intent is for these dispositions to become so internalized that the ground rules outlined above eventually become unnecessary. And, although I've presented this as a neatly sequenced exercise with five discrete stages, the reality is that, of course, it isn't! As the conversation proceeds past the designated question period, the detectives think up new questions that they want to ask that will help them tell the storyteller what her assumptions are and offer her new perspectives. So the assumption giving and the alternative perspective reporting periods are always peppered with questions.

In my experience using this with thousands of different participants, the most frequent job the umpire has to do is step in when people give advice in the guise of asking questions, reporting assumptions, or providing alternative perspectives. We are so culturally conditioned to move straight from being told the problem to providing the solution, that the intermediate stages of critical analysis are completely forgotten. Yet problem solving can be done uncritically, as when no one asks whether the problem we're spending time solving is the real problem at issue or in whose interests is it that the current problem be solved. Critical problem solving tries to unearth the assumptions that frame why someone sees something as a problem, it tries to unearth the assumptions informing how people take action to solve the problem, and it constantly explores different perspectives that have not previously been considered.

I have used this process in multiple settings: at retreats to help a group of practitioners come up with new ways of responding to wearyingly familiar problems; in faculty conversation circles in schools, colleges, and seminaries; and in community action groups.

It has been used in nursing education training and in leadership workshops for corporations. I have also used it as a way to shake up meetings. It seems to be infinitely adaptable and is really very simple to use, providing the ground rules are clearly understood and enforced.

One caveat needs issuing, however. I would never use this without first doing a teaching demonstration of how the process works, in which I play the roles of facilitator, umpire, and storyteller. When I do this I carry three different baseball caps with me. I wear red when I'm the umpire, because I need to put a red light on to stop detectives from being judgmental, bombarding the storyteller with questions, and offering advice. I wear a green one when I'm playing the role of storyteller, because I've received the green light to tell my story. And I wear an orange one when I'm in role as facilitator, to signify pausing to take questions about how the exercise should proceed, explaining next steps in the activity, laying out initial ground rules, and so on. Critical Incident Questionnaire (CIQ) responses from students have consistently reported that the teaching demonstration is invaluable in helping students understand the intricacies of the process and alerting them what to watch out for. It also, of course, is consistent with what students tell us about the importance of teachers' modeling for them what critical thinking looks like.

Summary

Critical thinking is something most teachers would probably say they were trying to encourage in their students. An emphasis on this process crosses the liberal and radical traditions in the field of adult education, though which intellectual tradition teachers work within frames exactly how they define this process. I have tried to outline how teachers can use their power to model critical thinking across disciplinary boundaries and to give examples of introductory and advanced activities that seem to me to be adaptable to different topics and subjects. One of the things that is clear about critical thinking is that it is a social learning process. Consequently, dealing with emerging power dynamics in learning groups is going to be particularly important for teachers trying to teach critically. In the next chapter I examine in more detail the place of discussion in adult education, and I describe how adult teachers can use discussion to engage students emotionally as well as cognitively.

3

Using Discussion Methods

Discussion, not lecture, is the adult education teaching method used most uncritically. When I've asked teachers I've observed why they used it, they often say something like "Well, I'd lectured for a while, so it was time to get the students to participate by having a discussion." This "talk for talk's sake" rationale is one I have adopted myself. There's also the vague feeling that in getting students to talk the teacher's power has been displaced in the room and that now a degree of democracy is in place. Of course, the students know teacher authority is as present as ever, and they also know that interstudent power dynamics are now in play. In one way there's a curious equality of passive listening during a lecture. But in a discussion, the power differences among the students due to their different racial identities, class memberships, cultural backgrounds, genders, and personality characteristics quickly manifest themselves. The usual extroverted suspects, who are often from the dominant culture and possess the cultural capital of an academic vocabulary, move front and center to shape the conversation while others lapse into a familiar silence. As English and Mayo (2012) write, "the question becomes; Who dialogues with Whom and from what position of power or subordination?" (p. 62).

In my own experiences as a student, I knew very well that classroom discussions were not power-free zones, but psychodynamic, emotional battlegrounds. I don't think I'm alone here. So many people have been burned by participating in discussions that were touted as free and open but that in fact were guided to a predefined end point by the facilitator. Others feel they have wasted too much time in discussions that were uncontrolled and went widely off the point, probably because one member strong-armed the group with no opposition from the teacher. Far from greeting discussions with eager anticipation for the engagement that lies ahead, I often find that adults' shoulders sag with momentary deflation when I tell them we're moving into discussion.

This picture of asymmetrical power relations and frustrated energy doesn't usually show up in many adult education analyses of discussion. Instead, it's usually lauded for a mix of pedagogic and political reasons. Pedagogically, discussion is held to engage learners in participatory learning, which helps them come to a deeper understanding of the topics considered. Politically, discussion is supposed to provide an analog of democratic process, a space where all voices are heard and respected in equal measure. Adult educators of the last two decades have often invoked Habermas's ideal speech situation—which to many is exemplified in the rational discourse of respectful open discussion—as the organizing concept for good adult educational practice (Brookfield, 2010).

The Power-full Reality of Discussion

As a learner I rarely found participating in discussion the liberatory, democratizing experience I heard it proclaimed to be; rather, I experienced it as a competitive ordeal, the occasion for a Darwinian style survival of the loquaciously fittest. Participating in discussion became translated into a series of power plays and verbal sallies. It was a form of competitive intellectual besting in which those who said the most, or made the most brilliantly articulate and insightful comment, claimed an appropriate triumph. We knew we were engaged in the same kind of name-dropping that grips guests at an academic cocktail party as they struggle for recognition and status.

Our participation was framed by the need to speak as often and intelligently as we could, thereby impressing the teacher with how smart we were. The idea that we might be involved in a group creation of knowledge never occurred to us. It was also very clear that those who did well in discussion were those who brought the appropriate cultural capital to the occasion—a wide-ranging vocabulary, a confident manner, an ease at speaking in public, and an expectation of being listened to and taken seriously.

Upon moving into employment as a beginning adult educator in1970s England, I was then firmly initiated into a professional ethic that held discussion in the highest esteem. From Freire's *Pedagogy of the Oppressed* (1970) to Paterson's article on "The Concept of Discussion" (1970), readings of varying ideological hues in my diploma in adult education courses clearly implied that all good adult educators sooner or later turned to discussion as a natural methodological choice. On working in Canadian, and then American, adult education, I found dialogical approaches to be similarly venerated and associated with the legacies of Moses Coady, Myles Horton, and Eduard Lindeman, all valorized figures in each country.

As someone committed to the field, I put aside my personal memories of unsatisfactory discussions and embraced the method. One of my assumptions in doing this was that the more experience I had in running discussions, the more creatively improvisational my practice would become. I assumed that as the years passed I would become better at walking into an adult education setting, sensing the mood of the group, and coming up with some probing, deeply provocative questions on the spot. There would be no need to prepare because my pedagogical alacrity would carry me through any class. Power never really reared its ugly head in this fairytale land of my imagined future practice.

The exact opposite has turned out to be the case. The longer I use discussion methods the more I plan, prepare, and create conversational protocols. This deepening emphasis on the structure of discussion is because I realize how power suffuses every discussion group I've ever been involved with. On the surface of a typical adult classroom, it might look like democracy is in place. The chairs are arranged in a circle so everyone can see everyone else. Since the teacher's chair is part of the circle, you couldn't pick her out at first glance. People are talking, so open exchange seems to be happening. And if the teacher says very little, we can assume the students have forgotten she's there, correct? Well, not really. One of the hardest lessons I have had to learn as a teacher is that my power is always present as a determining influence in every discussion, even if I say nothing.

Michel Foucault's (1980) much celebrated work on the microdynamics of power has helped me understand better how power operates in a discussion session. Foucault argues that in every sphere of human interaction judges of normality survey proceedings to make sure that the appropriate standards for behavior and regimes of truth (the procedures for determining which knowledge is legitimate) are in place. In a discussion students are aware that a judge of normality (the discussion leader) is always watching their behavior to ensure that people are participating in the conversation in a suitable manner.

Teachers tacitly operationalize what counts as appropriate participation and how it will be recognized in any number of ways. Through the judicious use of invitational eye contact, they confer the message that now a particular student can make a comment. With a nod of approval, they register that a student has made a particularly insightful comment, and with a grimace they visibly yet silently condemn another comment as obviously asinine. They deploy a range of subtle, nonverbal behaviors to signify approval or disapproval of participants' efforts, which serve to clarify exactly what are the teacher's discussion norms. Through frowns, smiles, sighs of frustration or pity, grunts of agreement, disbelieving intakes of breath at the obvious absurdity of a particular comment, they communicate to the group when members are close to or moving away from these norms.

Unless teachers specifically do something to prevent it, learners typically interpret teachers' injunction to "participate" as meaning that they should jump in at every opportunity to capture the teacher's attention and register the fact that they are frequent contributors. Participation becomes a verbal blood sport, and those who are most confident and have the greatest intellectual capital wield the greatest power. Participants may throw into the discussion terms, concepts, theories, and names in a desperate effort to sound knowledgeable and profound, often irrespective of whether or not these contributions actually enhance the conversation. When a teacher asks a student a question, it is rare for that student to stay silent while she thinks about her response; to do so is too risky for it could be seen as a sign of intellectual unpreparedness or cognitive sluggishness. I have never even seen a student in a discussion ask for a minute or so to think about a response to a teacher's question, yet this is surely a reasonable request. A good question needs time for a response.

An Example of Teacher Power in Action: The Unwitting Diktat

A while ago I was running a discussion-based course with the awareness of how patterns of domination structured by participants' race, class, and gender can emerge in discussion groups unless a deliberate intervention is made to prevent this happening. I didn't want anyone (in particular, males, Whites, or middle-class students) to take up a disproportionate amount of airtime, so I raised this issue early in the course. Students seemed to agree with the need to equalize the chance to contribute to the discussion and suggested a number of ways this might happen: for example, by posting a charter for respectful discourse on the wall at the start of each class session, by appointing a different student each session to watch out for people who are trying to say something but not being noticed, or by doing a regular circle of voices exercise. I airily threw a suggestion into the mix to the effect that we could have a "three-person rule" whereby once you've said something you don't speak again until at least three other people have spoken (unless you're explicitly asked to say something by another member of the group). There was no particular response to my three-person rule, so I dropped the idea.

Six or seven weeks later as I read the usual end of week anonymous Critical Incident Questionnaire responses for that week's class, I was astounded. Out of eighteen completed forms there were five mentions of how students were finding it increasingly difficult to speak in the group and how they thought I, the teacher, was continuously stifling discussion. I was staggered. Here I had been priding myself on my awareness of the traps of antidemocratic discourse and my sophistication in democratic process. Yet it seemed that I had created exactly the opposite state of affairs. Far from students feeling relaxed about participating, they declared themselves to be inhibited from speaking by my apparently arbitrary exercise of teacher power.

The next class session I asked the students to suggest possible reasons why some of them might have written on their CIQs that they felt inhibited. It emerged that several of them had been slavishly following the three-person rule since the time I had airily mentioned it (and then assumed it had been rejected). What I believed had been an off-the-cuff suggestion that had fallen flat on its face had been heard by them as a diktat, a teacher imperative. As a consequence they had been strenuously monitoring their own speech and feeling frustrated at the constraint I had imposed on their pattern of participation.

The vignette above illustrates how a teacher's power map of a discussion-based classroom can be entirely different from the one students are reading. In the rest of this chapter, I introduce some discussion practices deliberately designed to challenge the norm that discussion trophies go to those who speak the most and sound the smartest, and to democratize participation. I do believe that discussion offers an opportunity for temporarily upsetting the usual power relations that students experience and that teachers can use their own power in a judicious way to equalize the opportunity for participation.

Developing Bottom-Up Ground Rules

Many problems that typically plague discussions such as people talking too much, discussions going off track, or a discomfort with prolonged silence can be partly alleviated if the group has generated some ground rules to govern how it functions. This became apparent to me early on in my career as a lecturer/organizer (that was my official job title) working with community groups. Every community has its power brokers, opinion leaders, and living historians who, unless a deliberate attempt is made to frustrate this process happening, will automatically set the agenda for community projects. In this sense, community groups are no different from formal classrooms in which the acknowledged confident and strong personalities will move to front and center stage.

Below is an exercise designed to help groups in different communities, organizations, and movements research their own previous experiences as discussion participants in order to generate their own conversational road map.

Instructions to Participants

1. Think of the best group discussions you've ever been involved in. What things happened that made these conversations so satisfying? Make a few notes on this by yourself. (five minutes)

2. Think of the worst group discussions you've ever been involved in. What things happened that made these conversations so unsatisfactory? Make a few notes on this by yourself. (five minutes)

3. Meet with three of your peers and take turns in talking about what made discussion groups work so well for you. Listen for common

themes and shared experiences of what conversations looked like when they went well for you. (ten minutes)

4. Then talk about what made discussion groups work so badly for you. Again, listen for common themes and shared experiences. (ten minutes)

5. For each of the characteristics of good discussion you agree on, try and suggest one thing a group could do to ensure, as much as possible, that this characteristic is present. Be as specific and concrete as you can. For example, if you feel that good conversation is cumulative and connected, with later themes building on and referring back to earlier ones, you could propose a rule whereby every new comment made by a participant is prefaced with an explanation as to how it relates to or springs from an earlier comment. (ten minutes)

6. For each of the characteristics of bad discussion you agree on, try and suggest one thing a group could do to ensure, as much as possible, that this characteristic is avoided. Be as specific and concrete as you can. For example, if you feel that bad conversation happens when one person's voice dominates, you could propose a rule whereby no one is allowed to follow a comment they have made with another comment until at least three other people have spoken (the three-person rule). (ten minutes)

7. As a whole group we will reconvene, and people can post or report out their suggestions for ground rules. We will then decide which to try out.

Participation Grading Rubric

One of the typical ways teachers in formal education settings try to get discussion going is by declaring that participation in the course counts towards the overall grade or mark awarded. This will certainly induce speech among those most concerned with getting good marks, but it often has little to do with democratic discussion. Instead, it turns discussion groups into the kind of glad-iatorial arenas mentioned earlier in which participants verbally slug it out to gain recognition and affirmation from the teacher. Some-times the frequency of a student's verbal contributions—almost re-gardless of their lucidity or relevance—becomes the criterion for judging participation. Furthermore, unless the pattern of participa-tion is deliberately disrupted in the first couple of meetings of the course, the pecking order is firmly established by the third meet-ing. This pecking order is powerfully self-fulfilling; the longer a stu-dent remains silent, the more intimidating becomes the prospect of speaking.

Because so much student behavior in formal education settings is determined by the grade, I have tried to make a virtue of this ne-cessity by developing a grading rubric that I use to teach students my own discussion norms. I want them to realize early on that the most important part of participation is listening, not talking. A good dis-cussion participant is someone who links contributions, asks ques-tions of others, builds on comments, and raises questions. I publish this rubric in the course syllabus in the hope of displacing the norm that participation means grabbing the verbal spotlight.

Instructions to Students

20% of your grade for this class is based on your participation in dis-cussion. Participating in discussion does not mean talking frequently or showing everyone else what you know or that you have studied a lot. Good discussion participation involves people trying to build on and synthesize comments from others and on showing appreci-ation for others' contributions. It also involves inviting others to say more about what they are thinking. Some of the most helpful things you can do are call for a quiet interlude, bring a new resource to the classroom, or post an observation online. So there are multiple ways quieter learners can participate.

Below are some specific behavioral examples of good participation in discussion:

Ask a question or make a comment that shows you are interested in what another person says.

Ask a question or make a comment that encourages another person to elaborate on something they have already said.

Bring in a resource (a reading, web link, video) not covered in the syllabus that adds new information or perspectives to our learning.

Make a comment that underscores the link between two people's contributions and make this link explicit in your comment.

Use body language (in only a slightly exaggerated way) to show interest in what different speakers are saying.

Post a comment on the course chat room that summarizes our conversations so far or suggests new directions and questions to be explored in the future.

Make a comment (online if this is appropriate) indicating that you found another person's ideas interesting or useful. Be specific as to why this was the case.

Contribute something that builds on or springs from what someone else has said. Be explicit about the way you are building on the other person's thoughts. This can be done online.

Make a comment on your CIQ that prompts us to examine discussion dynamics.

When you think it's appropriate, ask the group for a moment's silence to slow the pace of conversation to give you and others time to think.

Make a comment that at least partly paraphrases a point someone has already made.

Make a summary observation that takes into account several
people's contributions and that touches on a recurring theme
in the discussion (online if you like).

Ask a cause and effect question—for example, "Can you
explain why you think it's true that if these things are in place
such and such a thing will occur?"

Find a way to express appreciation for the enlightenment you
have gained from the discussion. Try to be specific about what
it was that helped you understand something better. Again
this can be done online if this suits you better.

Circle of Voices

Early on in a discussion-based course it is a good idea to introduce
students to a number of exercises designed to equalize participation
and to teach students that listening, appreciating, and synthesizing
are just as crucial to good discussion as making brilliant original
contributions. For students unused to discussion or for those
introverts who find talking in public an excruciating ordeal, an
orientation or induction period is particularly appreciated. Such
a period comprises a scaffolding experience, a time when students
learn a series of protocols where the ground rules for participation
are clear and the intimidating need to come up with impromptu
contributions is removed.

The Circle of Voices is one such protocol that students can learn
on the first day of class that will help orientate them to participating
in democratic discussion. This is one of my most favorite discussion
protocols, and one I use a great deal at the beginning of a group's
time together. It has two basic purposes. The first is to give everyone
a chance to contribute on a topic before any premature consensus
emerges. The second is to teach the importance of active listening so that a discussion can develop organically, constantly looping
back to, building on, and extending earlier contributions.

Participants form into groups of five and a question for discussion is announced. Groups are allowed up to three minutes silent time to organize their thoughts and to come up with responses to the question. During this time they think about what they want to say on the topic once the circle of voices begins. This silent preparatory time is crucial to this and to so many other discussions intended to provoke critical thinking. Yet the dominant classroom practice of discussion is to announce a question and then ask for immediate responses. If people are to do something as complex as try to uncover assumptions and generate new perspectives, they need regular periods of quiet processing or silent contemplative time.

After this silent period the discussion opens with each person having a period of uninterrupted airtime of no more than a minute. During this time each speaker can say whatever she wishes about the topic at hand. While each person is speaking no one else is allowed to interrupt. People take their turns to speak by going around the circle in order, which removes from participants the stress of having to decide whether or not they will try and jump in after another student has finished speaking.

After the initial circle of voices has been completed and everyone has had the uninterrupted chance to make their opening comments, then the discussion opens out into a more free-flowing format. As this happens, a second ground rule comes into effect. Participants are only allowed to talk about another person's ideas that have already been shared in the opening circle of voices. Participants cannot jump into the conversation by expanding on their own ideas; they can only talk about their reactions to what someone else has said in the opening round. The only exception to this ground rule is if someone asks a group member directly to expand on her ideas. This second ground rule prevents the tendency toward grandstanding that sometimes afflicts a few articulate, confident individuals.

I have used this exercise in multiple settings both within formal organizations and in social movements. Universally people say they appreciate the directions, mostly because they hear from people that usually don't speak up. Extroverts also often say that the exercise makes them realize how much they dominate conversations without being aware that's happening.

Circular Response

The Circular Response exercise is a way to democratize discussion participation, to promote continuity of conversation, and to give people some experience of the effort required in respectful listening. It was developed by Eduard Lindeman (Brookfield, 1988) in the 1930s as part of his efforts to democratize conversation among community groups and to help them focus on two or three shared concerns instead of trying to pursue multiple agendas. Although somewhat similar to the Circle of Voices, it adds another layer of complexity, since in the opening round participants have to respond extemporaneously to the previous speaker's remarks.

The exercise begins with either the leader posing a question to the group for discussion or with a group member suggesting a topic and the group agreeing to the question or topic. Participants form into circles of ten to twelve, and the conversation begins with a volunteer who takes up to a minute to say whatever she thinks about the topic concerned. After the minute is up, this first discussant yields the floor to the person sitting to the discussant's left, who speaks for a minute or so. The second speaker is not free, however, to say anything she wants. She must incorporate into her remarks some reference to the preceding speaker's message and then use this as a springboard for her own comments. This doesn't have to be an agreement—it can be an expression of dissent from the previous opinion. It can also be an expression of confusion where the second discussant identifies some aspect of the first speaker's remarks that she finds difficult to understand. The second speaker could also talk about how the first speaker's comments cover such unfamiliar ground that she is left with no conversational opening, or how her experiences or thinking are completely at odds with the first comments.

After a minute or so, the second discussant stops speaking, and the person to her left becomes the third discussant who follows the same ground rule to refer to some aspect of the preceding speaker's message as the springboard for her own comments. Following this pattern, the discussion moves all the way around the circle. Each discussant must ground her comments in reference to something the previous speaker has said. The process ends where it started—with the opening speaker. Only this time the opening speaker is responding to the comments of the person who spoke before her. When this first round of conversation is over, then the group moves into open conversation with no more ground rules. Questions can be asked about opening contributions, clarifications sought or offered, and new ideas introduced.

The interesting thing about this exercise is that the eleventh or twelfth person to speak has no inherent advantage over the first or second contributor. The twelfth person cannot sit in reflective luxury rehearsing a perfect contribution, because she has no idea what the eleventh person is going to say until that person speaks. Whenever I have used this exercise, I invariably observe that in the first round of conversation heads lean in as each person sees how their contribution to the discussion is responded to. This is really an online threaded discussion happening synchronously in a face-to-face classroom. Unlike an online classroom, however, you don't need to wait for hours or days to see what someone will do with your comment.

Circular Response is not an introductory discussion exercise in my opinion. There is often high anxiety around the prospect of having to speak in a way that responds immediately to another's contribution. To help ease this anxiety, I always say that speakers can take a few moments to think about their response; they don't have to spring straight into speech after the previous speaker has stopped talking. I also make it clear that it is fine to say that you can't think of a response to the previous speaker's comments; but if you do this, then you need to say why you're having difficulty making a connection. Is it because you have no experience that fits the previous speaker's? Are you unfamiliar with the language or terminology used? Do you find some of the argument hard to follow?

Conversational Roles

Assigning roles to students might be something you'd imagine they would experience as constraining to conversation, a limiting exercise of teacher power. In fact classroom feedback consistently underscores how much students appreciate being given some sort of guidance on what kinds of speech acts teachers are looking for. They say they often find it helpful to know at the outset of a discussion the sort of conversational role they are required to play. Knowing that they have a particular task to fulfill seems to remove some of the performance anxiety created by the invisible norm whereby participation is seen as making frequent and impressive displays of their knowledge. Practice in playing different conversational roles helps create opportunities for the more tentative students to speak, thereby building their confidence. Any roles assigned must, of course, be alternated so that everyone takes their turn. It is an abuse of this exercise to assign the quietest role to the most vociferous student each week. A number of commonly used conversational roles are given below.

Problem, Dilemma, or Theme Poser

> This participant has the task of introducing the topic of conversation. She draws on her own ideas and experiences as a way of helping others into conversation about the theme.

Reflective Analyst

> This member keeps a record of the conversation's development. Every few minutes or so she gives a summary

that focuses on shared concerns, issues skirted, and emerging common themes.

Scrounger

The scrounger listens for helpful resources, suggestions, and tips that participants have voiced as they discuss how to work through a problem or situation. She keeps a record of these ideas and reads it out before the session ends.

Speculator

This person listens carefully for any emerging consensus. When she hears this, she tries to offer alternative viewpoints that have not been raised. This keeps groupthink in check and helps participants explore a range of different interpretations.

Detective

The detective listens carefully for unacknowledged, unchecked, and unchallenged biases that seem to be emerging in the conversation. As she hears these, she brings them to the group's attention. She assumes particular responsibility for alerting group members to concerns of race, class, and gender. She listens for cultural blindness, gender insensitivity, and comments that ignore variables of power and class.

Questioner

This participant identifies questions that arise during the discussion and tries to pose ones not already asked.

Umpire

This person listens for judgmental comments that sound offensive, insulting, and demeaning, and that contradict ground rules for discussion generated by group members.

Textual Focuser

> Whenever assertions are made that seem unconnected to the text being discussed, this person asks the speaker to let the group know where in the text the point being made occurs.

Evidential Assessor

> This student asks speakers to give the evidence for empirical generalizations that are stated as self-evident fact but that actually seem more like opinion.

Synthesizer

> This person attempts to underscore links between different contributions.

These roles are often hard to play so it's enormously helpful if students can see teachers modeling what each of these looks like. In team-taught courses, different instructors can take turns playing different roles and can let students know exactly which role is being played at any particular moment.

Conversational Moves

An alternative to assigning conversational roles is to use the Conversational Moves exercise developed by my sometime teaching partner Steve Preskill. Steve pastes a number of conversational moves (speaking directions) on 3x5 cards and then randomly distributes these among participants at the beginning of a discussion session. When I've used this technique, my moves parallel the criteria for good discussion participation published in the course syllabus.

Students privately read the move on their card and are asked to practice their move at some point during the discussion that follows if a suitable opening occurs. Students shouldn't become obsessed with making their move, as this is not always possible. But they should have the move at the back of their mind as something to do if opportunity allows. When the discussion is over, the entire list of moves is distributed so people can see the wide variety of ways that discussion participation can be recognized. If they wish to, participants can recap how they tried to make the moves they were allocated.

Specific Moves

Ask a question or make a comment that shows you are interested in what another person says.

Ask a question or make a comment that encourages another person to elaborate on something they have already said.

Make a comment that underscores the link between two people's contributions.

Use body language to show interest in what different speakers are saying.

Make a specific comment indicating how you found another person's ideas interesting or useful.

Contribute something that builds on or springs from what someone else has said.

Be explicit about the way you are building on the other person's thoughts.

Make a comment that at least partly paraphrases a point someone has already made.

Make a summary observation that takes into account several people's contributions and that touches on a recurring theme in the discussion.

Ask a cause and effect question—for example, "Can you explain why you think it's true that if these things are in place such and such a thing will occur?"

When you think it's appropriate, ask the group for a moment's
silence to slow the pace of conversation and give you and
others time to think.

Find a way to express appreciation for the enlightenment you
have gained from the discussion. Be specific about what it
was that helped you understand something better.

Disagree with someone in a respectful and constructive way.

Create space for someone who has not yet spoken to
contribute to the conversation.

Quotes to Affirm and Challenge

This exercise is designed to make it easier to begin discussions that
are grounded in students' prereading of an assigned text. Ask students to bring to class two quotes they have chosen from an assigned
text they have all read to prepare for the class. The student should
chose one quote because the student wishes to affirm it. The other
is one the student wishes to challenge. Students form small groups,
and each member takes a turn to propose the quote they wish to
affirm and the reasons for doing this.

The quote to affirm does not have to be defended as empirically
true. Sometimes a participant will propose a quote because it con-
firms a point of view she holds or because it supports what her intuition or experience tells her is accurate. Sometimes she feels the
quote states the most important point in the text, or she chooses
a quote because it contains a crucial new piece of information or
different perspective. At other times the quote is affirmed because
it is rhetorically rousing or expresses an idea so lyrically or transparently. When everyone in the small group has proposed a quote
to affirm, the group then chooses one to report back to the larger
class. During this whole class discussion, each group explains why
it was that they chose their particular quote.

The quote to challenge activity follows the same procedure only this time students choose a quote that they disagree with, find contradictory, believe to be inaccurate, or consider reprehensible and immoral. The quote to challenge is then reported back to the class along with the rationale for its choice.

Hatful of Quotes

The Hatful of Quotes exercise aims to make the mandated act of contributing to discussion as stress-free as possible. Prior to the discussion of a text, the teacher prints onto separate slips of paper multiple copies of five or six different sentences or passages from the text to be discussed. In class she puts these into a hat and asks students to draw one of these slips out of a hat. Students are given a few minutes to think about the quote they have picked and then asked to read it out and make some comment on it. The order of contribution is up to the students. Those who feel more fearful about speaking usually go last and take more time to think about what they want to say. Because the same five or six quotes are used, students who go later will have heard their particular quote read out and commented on by those who spoke earlier. So even if they have little to say about their own interpretation of the quote, they can affirm, build on, or contradict a comment a peer has already made on that quote. This exercise is a good way to create a safe opportunity for everyone to speak. Those who are diffident get to say something, thus building confidence for subsequent contributions.

Snowballing

Students uncomfortable with even small-group participation can be drawn into this, and then into whole class discussion, through the process known as Snowballing. This exercise progresses from individual solitary reflection through to a discussion involving the whole class. The process begins by students individually and silently spending a couple of minutes jotting down their thoughts about an assigned discussion question. After this reflective beginning, students then form into pairs and spend about five minutes sharing and discussing each other's ideas.

When the five minutes are up, each pair then joins another pair to form a quartet. The quartet conversation opens with each pair sharing a question they raised, a difference they noted in their conversation, or a new insight that suggested itself. After ten minutes the quartets join another quartet to form octets. Again, the octets begin their conversation with each quartet sharing a question they raised, a difference they noted, or an insight that suggested itself in their conversation. After twenty minutes the octets join other octets to form groups of sixteen and again, share a question, difference, or insight. In a class of around thirty-two the class ends by each group of sixteen joining the other for a final conversation. Through snowballing a class of thirty-two students that began with private, silent reflection ends up in whole-class discussion.

Chalk Talk

This exercise was introduced to me by Steven Rippe, a student in an organizational development class I taught at the University of St. Thomas. He, in turn, learned it from Hilton Smith (2009) of The Foxfire Fund. Chalk Talk is a silent and visual way to engage in discussion without speaking. It takes as long as it takes and it's over when it's over. I've used it mostly in ten-minute bursts as a reflective preparation for spoken conversation. It can also be a good way to unearth the concerns of a wide range of organizational members before building agendas for change. Here's how it works:

1. The leader writes a question in a circle in the center of the board—for example "What power dynamics might stifle our

project before it gets off the ground?" She places several sticks of chalk by the board.

2. She then explains this is a silent activity and that when people are ready they should write a response to the question on the board. They are also free to write responses to what others have written, to pose questions about comments already posted, to answer questions posted, to draw lines between responses on different parts of the board that seem to connect, or between startlingly different responses to the same question, and so on.

3. Whenever they feel ready, people get up and write something in response to the original question or to subsequent comments that are posted. Sometimes there are long silences or pauses between postings.

4. The facilitator also participates by drawing lines connecting comments that seem similar or contrasting, by writing questions about a comment, by adding her own thoughts, and so on.

5. When a suitably long silence ensues, the facilitator asks if people are done. If the activity is over, then the class moves into speaking about the postings on the board.

I like Chalk Talk for several reasons. One is that it has never badly misfired! Another is that it always produces far more contributions than throwing the question out to the whole class and asking for comments. Often well over half the group post something in a five-minute Chalk Talk session, compared to the 5 or 10 percent of students who would have dominated a whole-class discussion. It also honors silence and allows introverts to order their thoughts before posting. Of course, those same introverts may feel inhibited about writing something while everyone is watching. But since there are usually several people up at the board writing simultaneously, this is not too much of a drawback.

The Appreciative Pause

Thinking critically in discussion—with all the performance anxiety students feel about speaking extemporaneously, thinking on their feet, having to sound smart, and so on—is emotionally exhausting as well as intellectually demanding. This is why the last activity I mention—the Appreciative Pause—is so necessary.

One of the least practiced behaviors in discussion is to show appreciation for how someone has contributed to our learning. The Appreciative Pause is a technique that focuses deliberately on this behavior. One way the confidence to claim empowerment can be developed is for students to show each other how peer feedback has helped them identify and check assumptions, come to greater understanding, open up new lines of inquiry, and so on.

The Appreciative Pause works as follows. At least once in every discussion the instructor calls for a pause of a minute or so. During this time the only comments allowed are from participants who acknowledge how something that someone else said in the discussion (*not* the instructor) has contributed to their learning. Appreciations are often given for:

A question that suggests a whole new line of thinking

A comment that clarifies something that up to then was confusing

A comment that opens up a whole new line of thinking

A comment that helps identify an assumption

A comment that provides helpful evidence

A comment that identifies a gap in reasoning that needs to be addressed

A new idea that is intriguing and has not been considered before

A comment that shows the connection between two other ideas or contributions when that connection hasn't been clear

An example that helps increase understanding of a difficult concept

This can easily be done online by establishing an Appreciation Board, where students only post comments outlining how their peers have helped them progress with their learning. Comments accumulate over time to give a permanent record of the things peers have done that have been particularly appreciated. This can be reproduced for future courses to let new students see the importance of peer support and critique, and it can also prompt some new exercises that teachers can experiment in using.

Summary

Throughout this chapter I have argued against the idea that simply having students talk somehow equalizes power relations in the adult classroom. I have urged that teachers of adults need to intervene to create conversational structures that require attentive listening and that prevent articulate or egomaniacal participants from dominating the conversation and setting a premature agenda. I believe teachers of adults should use their power to create periods of reflective silence, to institute opportunities for everyone to speak early on, and to require people to build on previous contributions. Because of this you might think I'm a proponent of guided discussion. In fact, the reverse is the case if guided discussion means bringing the conversation to a predefined conclusion. That kind of discussion is a thinly disguised masking of teacher power.

Although I think it's necessary to guide conversational processes by insisting that all have an opportunity to speak, that silence be honored, and that inconvenient viewpoints are not shut down prematurely, I believe that guiding discussion to a predetermined end point of understanding is an example of counterfeit discussion as defined by Paterson (1970). Inherent in the concept of democratic discussion is the idea that you never know where you are going or where the conversation will end up. It might be cleaner and simpler to allow only comments that take the conversation to a specific finale, but if you do this you are engaging in structured dialog or Socratic questioning, not discussion. Both of these are legitimate teaching methods for helping students learn concepts in a particular way, and I use both of them myself, but they're not the same as discussion. Genuine discussion resists being corralled, which is part of the reason it is, by turns, both frustrating and exciting.

In the next chapter I turn to an approach—fostering self-direction—that, on the face of it, seems to be very far from a discussion-based approach to teaching. As we shall see, however, self-directed learning usually involves significant collaboration and requires students to learn how to incorporate discussion-based approaches into a broader learning effort. It also has the potential to create the conditions under which students claim empowerment.

4

Fostering Self-Directed Learning

When I think of empowered learners, I think of people doing things for themselves, making things happen by their own initiative. I think of self-directed learning in much the same way, as people deciding that they need to know something and, in the absence of anyone being available to teach them, attempting to learn it for themselves. DIY (do it yourself) is the heart of the punk ethic, for example (Furness, 2012). Sometimes I picture this happening individually, sometimes as part of a group effort. So for me the terms *empowered learners* and *self-directed learners* conjure up very similar images. This is why a book on powerful teaching techniques has to deal with self-directed learning.

But if the definition of self-directedness is that there is no teacher present, how can you talk about teaching it? Well, I have two responses to that question. First, as we shall see, in a lot of self-directed learning efforts there are often phases when learners use external teachers to teach them specific elements that move the overall project forward. Second, and this connects self-directed learning to the broader theme of teaching for empowerment, there are many things classroom teachers can do that help prepare the ground for adults to conduct self-directed learning projects outside any particular course.

What is Self-Directed Learning?

A TV commercial for Phoenix University that was running while I was writing this chapter celebrated learners studying on airplanes, buses, in factory cafeterias, on the bleachers at a Little League game, and so on. This is often how self-directed learning is thought of—isolated individuals working flexibly to further their education and training, fitting study in around the demands of work, home, and community.

But this is not self-directed learning, it is *self-regulated* learning (Bembenutty, 2011), in which students have some choice in determining how they will achieve institutionally approved objectives. A recent volume on self-regulated learning defines it as students' "capability to engage in appropriate actions, thoughts, feelings, and behaviors in order to pursue valuable academic goals while self-monitoring and self-reflecting on their progress toward goal completion" (Bembenutty, 2011, p. 3). This kind of self-regulation often has a degree of flexibility I support—giving learners the opportunity to decide when they will read set texts, complete set assignments, make mandatory postings, or demonstrate how their prior experience is equivalent to institutionally mandated skills. I like, as a general rule, to give students some choice over which of several study options they wish to pursue or to negotiate aspects of curricula with them. But I would not call it self-directed learning. Self-directed learning is learning in which decisions around what to learn, how to learn it, and how to decide if one has learned something well enough are *all* in the hands of learners. To use a fashionable formulation, the key question is where does the locus of control lie?

If self-directed learning is conceived as a process in which the key decisions around what and how to learn are in the hands of learners, then it quickly becomes apparent that self-directed learning is neither antipedagogy nor inherently isolating. Someone in charge of decision making may well decide that for a particular element in a learning project they need to place themselves temporarily under the direction of a teacher. For example, when forced (temporarily) to be a lead guitarist I asked another band member for advice. He told me to learn how to play some basic scales so I could then choose how to construct a particular guitar solo. I went on You Tube and followed the instructions in videos that had high viewer ratings. In this example, being self-directed meant seeking direction from both teachers and peers, yet the decisions regarding the overall direction and execution of my learning still remained in my hands.

It is no accident that the idea of self-direction has engaged the attention of adult educators in the United States. As a representation of how learning optimally occurs, the concept fits very much the American ideology of rugged individualism. Self-direction underscores the folklore of the self-made man or woman who succeeds against the odds through the sheer force of individual efforts. This is the narrative surrounding adult learner of the year awards bestowed on those who pull themselves up by their bootstraps to claim their place at the table of stories and voices. St. Clair (2004) outlines the hold that the myth of aspiration has on adult educators, and I contend that there is no more potent myth than the Eurocentrically inclined idea of new frontiers of learning being conquered by individual pioneers, boldly going where no man or woman has gone before.

Self-directed learning is at the heart of adult education, but how it is defined and practiced says much about the politics of the field. The prevailing view is one interchangeable with self-regulated learning: a process of helping adults acquire predefined skills, knowledge, and dispositions by allowing them to pace when and how to work. Self-directed learning is lauded for its being able to fit the individual circumstances of learners who are, for various reasons, unable or unwilling to attend institutional classes. This viewpoint is well represented in the *International Journal of Self-Directed Learning*, where articles regularly examine the effectiveness of self-directed approaches for helping learners acquire predetermined skills and negotiate predetermined curricula. Typical articles are those exploring self-directed learning methods in secondary school classrooms (Carmichael, 2007), geriatric care courses (Park et al., 2006; Park, Candler, and Durso, 2006), military college training (Gabrielle, Guglielmino, and Guglielmino, 2006), physics and chemistry courses (McCauley and McClelland, 2004; Thompson and Wulff, 2004), and among primary school students (Mok, Leung, and Shan, 2005).

From my standpoint, this is self-paced learning rather self-directed learning. If self-directed learning is undertaken because *learners*, not experts or authorities, see it as necessary, then it is potentially one of the most radical traditions in the adult education field. In my opinion, it is by definition anarchic and uncontrollable—people deciding what and how, to learn for themselves and to hell with what institutions say they should be learning. To be truly self-directed is to be empowered—to decide what is most important to you, how you want to go about learning it, and when you're done. The learning is done not to earn grades but because it has to be done if people are to lead meaningful lives.

Personal Illustrations

Let me illustrate my idea of self-direction by talking about three of my own self-directed learning projects. The first has to do with learning about race and racism. About twenty years ago a White colleague of mine—Elizabeth Kasl—challenged me by telling me my understanding and practice of teaching adults was race-blind. She told me (in gentler terms than the ones I'm using) that teaching as if the racial identity of teachers and students was not an issue was blinkered and naïve, and that I was committing daily racial microaggressions. I disagreed, but her comments planted a nagging seed of doubt, mostly because I admired her and assumed her judgment could be trusted. So eventually I decided that a major self-directed learning project for me should be to examine if and how the ideology of White supremacy—the belief that Whites are naturally best equipped to assume authority because they possess superior intelligence and leadership qualities—had nested itself in me.

There wasn't any workshop on how to do this at my own institution, so I had to work out on my own whom I should talk to, what I should read, and so on. One of the ways I did this was to draw on my knowledge of critical theory and the microrealities of power (Brookfield, 2004) to explore the ways I regularly commit racial microaggressions; that is, the small, daily acts of exclusion, stereotyping, and marginalizing of colleagues and students of color. As well as reading about this (Sue et al., 2007), I also talked to colleagues of color (Peterson and Brookfield, 2007; Sheared et al., 2010).

What makes this an example of self-directed learning is that the decisions regarding what and how to learn ultimately rested with me. This is not to say that other people weren't involved. After all, the impetus to learn these things had come after some disturbing conversations with Elizabeth. But just reading about this kept my understanding at the level of a wholly cognitive, rational analysis so I felt I needed to have long conversations with colleagues, peers, and students. Only by doing that could the raw emotional dimensions of how racism is perpetuated crash into my world. I needed people to direct me to useful resources, both human and material, and to help me process, chew over, make sense of what I was learning about racism on a general level and my collusion in it on a personal level. One of the hardest parts of this project was realizing that I needed to appreciate that racist instincts, impulses, and thoughts are so deeply embedded in me that the best I can hope for is to stop them from completely taking over in certain situations.

Another self-directed learning project I conducted in the last few years was learning how to cope with my own clinical depression. This was been more of an intrapersonal learning project as I found few fellow sufferers I could talk to, and it involved technical and emotional kinds of learning as well as developing the inter-personal skill to talk about a stigmatized topic (Brookfield, 2011). Here I copiously read self-help books and tried many of their recommendations having to do with exercise, meditation, and cognitive-behavioral therapy. When it was clear that none of those had much effect, I decided to seek psychiatric help and to consider medication. After a bump or two finding a psychiatrist, I was treated by one whose directive approach worked well for me. Under his direction I experimented with different medications before finding a combination of drugs that stabilized me. Now the cognitive-behavioral therapy scripts work much better for me. This is a good example of a project in which the learner chooses to place himself under expert authority for a period of time.

Finally, a few years ago my band, The 99ers (http://www.the99 ersband.com), were lucky enough to persuade Spinout Records (http://www.spinoutmusic.com/) in Nashville, Tennessee, to release our first album. We decided to record this in my basement so, in short order, I had to buy a portable twenty-four-track recording studio, learn how to operate it, learn how to buy affordable but quality microphones, learn how to record different instruments and vocals, and then how to mix the different percussion, bass, guitars, and vocals tracks together. I am something of a technophobe so this presented a real challenge. But I studied the manual that came with the studio assiduously, did a lot of trial and error learning, typed specific questions I had into online search engines, and talked to local DJs who directed me to engineers who could answer specific questions.

It's striking to me that in all three of these projects I used other people as resources and sounding boards. In doing this I was typical, at least according to research in this area. Peters and Grey (2005) summarize a stream of research documenting how collaborating with others is an integral element in self-directed learning. Recent empirical studies of self-directed learning among graduate students (Davis et al., 2010), community leaders (Phares and

Guglielmino, 2010), school principals (Guglielmino and Hillard, 2007), and executives in philanthropic and nonprofit organizations (Liddell, 2008; Ziga, 2008) all stress the importance of learning networks and using peers as sounding boards regarding the progress one is making. It is not an oxymoron to speak of collaborative self-directed learning (Moore et al., 2005). There is no contradiction at all in deciding you need others to get advice, check your progress, and help you troubleshoot or suggest new directions.

How Self-Directed Learning Relates to Power

Any time decisions about what learning is, how it should be conducted, and who should evaluate it are removed from the control of accredited teachers and institutions, a challenge to formal power is in place. At its heart, self-directed learning is about power and control—who has the power to decide what should be learned, what counts as legitimate knowledge or curricula, and who controls how these are explored. One reason the ideas of self-direction appeals to so many adult educators is because it represents a break with authoritarianism and educational totalitarianism. It means that control over the definitions, processes, and evaluations of learning rests with those who are struggling to learn, not with external authorities. The belief that through self-direction adults can gain increasing control over their lives (however naïve this belief might subsequently turn out to be) is an emancipatory belief. This is why as a graduate student I was so taken by Gelpi's (1979) view that "self-directed learning by individuals and of groups is a danger for every repressive force, and it is upon this self-direction that we must insist. . . radical change in social, moral, aesthetic and political affairs is often the outcome of a process of self-directed learning in opposition to the educational message imposed from without" (p. 2).

I have developed this argument more extensively elsewhere (Brookfield, 2000, 2007) so won't go into in depth here. Suffice it to say that issues of power and control, particularly regarding the definition of acceptable and appropriate learning activities, are always endemic to self-direction. Who defines the boundaries of intellectual and practical inquiry is always a political question, and self-direction places this decision squarely in the hands of learners. This was a cardinal principle of Myles Horton's work at the Highlander Folk School (Horton, 1990). Through the experience of making decisions about what was to happen at Highlander, participants learned democratic process. Horton argued that this process was indivisible; it couldn't be hedged around with facilitator-imposed constraints: "if you want to have the students control the whole process, as far as you can get them to control it, then you can never, at any point, take it out of their hands" (p. 136). As with the Highlander process, so with self-directed learning: who controls the ways and directions in which adults learn is a political issue highlighting the distribution of educational and political power. Who has the final say in framing the range and type of decisions to be taken, and who establishes the pace and mechanisms for decision making, reveals a great deal about where power really resides.

Andruske's (2000) study of self-directed learning as a political act illustrates this point well. She studied twenty-one women on welfare—often portrayed by right-wingers as scroungers with no initiative who spend their time leeching off the state—and concluded that "women's self-directed learning projects result in women becoming political agents . . . seeking to regain control and power over their lives as they navigate social spaces and social structures in their everyday worlds" (p. 14). Andruske's subjects engaged in complex legal research and policy analysis that brought them into direct conflict with bureaucrats and policy administrators such as welfare officials. They quickly learned that such officials would not as a matter of course inform welfare recipients of potential benefits, necessitating considerable research by claimants. So part of being self-directed was challenging the structures that controlled the flow of information in their communities and fighting for access to resources to improve their lives.

Fighting for the resources needed to conduct self-directed learning is, indeed, a political act that challenges dominant power. As a learner, I may come to a clear analysis of the skills I need to develop in order to do or learn something but be told repeatedly by those I approach for necessary resources that, while my plans are good ones, the budget cuts that have just been forced on my organization and community mean that priorities have changed, and my plans are now rendered useless. If this is the case, then sooner or later I am bound to realize that the problem of blocked access to resources is not just one of individual personalities (the myopic, anal-retentive, bureaucratic administrator constantly trying to thwart me) but also one of structural constraints.

If I need the physical equipment for a self-directed learning effort I have planned, and I'm told by those owning or controlling such equipment that it is unavailable to me for reasons of cost or because of other prior claims, this immediately raises an awareness for me of who owns the means of educational production. If I decide to initiate a self-directed learning project that involves challenging the institutional hegemony of a professional group (for example, physicians or lawyers), I may find that medical and legal experts and their professional organizations place insurmountable barriers in my path in an effort to retain their position of authority. So being self-directed can be inherently politicizing as learners become aware that the resources necessary to conduct their learning projects successfully are differentially distributed across society and often in the control of gatekeepers unwilling to relinquish their monopoly on information or facilities.

It may also be the case that I decide I want to learn something that I consider essential for my own development, only to be told that the knowledge or skills involved are undesirable, inappropriate, or subversive. A desire to explore an alternative political ideology is meaningless if books exploring that ideology have been removed from the public library because of their "unsuitability," or, perhaps more likely, if they have never been ordered in the first place. In a blaze of admirable masochism I may choose to undertake a self-directed learning project geared towards widening my understanding of how my practice as an educator is unwittingly oppressive and culturally distorted. Yet I may well find that the materials I need for this project are so expensive that neither I, nor my local libraries, can afford to purchase them. In this regard it is ironic—an example of Marcuse's (1965) idea of repressive tolerance—that critical analyses of adult education have their political impact effectively neutered by being hard to obtain from publishers or priced well beyond the pockets of those who could most benefit from reading them.

Five Caveats

Lest I fall into the trap I identified at the beginning of the chapter of uncritically celebrating self-directed learning, I want to add five caveats or objections to what I've been saying before I delve into practice.

Self Direction as Controlling

First, it's possible to understand self-directed learning in a very different, and much more controlling, way than the way I have portrayed it. Following Foucault's (1980) analysis of disciplinary power—power exercised by individuals to keep themselves in line—it is plausible to see the technology of self-directed learning (such as student learning contracts) as a highly developed form of surveillance. From this viewpoint, learning contracts can be understood as a sophisticated means of monitoring the content and methodology of learning without the teacher needing to be physically present. That the exercise of disciplinary power can be furthered through self-directed learning is illustrated in a book on creating self-directed classrooms where the "self-directed plan of discipline ... a written plan negotiated between the teacher and student" (Areglado, Bradley, and Lane, 1996, p. 66) is the means by which "self-directing behavior becomes self-discipline" (p. 63).

Counterfeit Self-Direction

Second, I should acknowledge that my analysis does not address the problem of counterfeit self-direction. By that I mean a self-directed learning effort where you believe you are in control of an authentically generated project, but in fact you are acting out an ideologically manipulated desire. For example, learning to control your emotions—as if emotions are aberrations getting in the way of reason—represents a Eurocentric Enlightenment way of being. Many could argue that trying to control our emotions as if they are taps to be turned on and off at our behest is psychologically harmful. Learning how to be more competitive to gain a market advantage and outsell or outperform the competition is a common organizational project. Yet such a project represents an unquestioning internalization of capitalism. Learning how to be popular, how to gauge what is the best way to win influence, or how to please all reflect dominant notions of what counts as successful. A young woman who learns how to hide her intelligence and fake an interest in sports in order to appear desirable to men is engaged in a self-directed learning project, but it's hardly one that is in her best interest. So one element of analyzing any self-directed learning effort is inquiring into the degree to which it represents and has been framed by dominant ideology and is therefore against our true interests.

Questioning the Self

Third, the notion of the self at the heart of self-directed learning is itself highly questionable. Self-directed learning rests on a modernistic concept of the self. A self-directed learner is seen as one who makes free and uncoerced choices from a smorgasbord of enticing possibilities. The choices the learner makes are held to reflect her desire to realize the strivings, dreams, and aspirations that lie at the core of her identity. So self-directed learning clearly depends on there being a self to do the learning. This views each individual learner as self-contained and internally driven, working to achieve her learning goals in splendid isolation. The self is seen as a free floating, autonomous, volitional agent able to make rational, authentic, and internally coherent choices about learning while remaining detached from social, cultural, and political forces.

Ehrenreich (1990) writes that in this conception of individualism "each self is seen as pursuing its own trajectory, accompanied by its own little planetary system of values, seeking to negotiate the best possible deal from the various 'relationships' that come along. Since all values appear to be idiosyncratic satellites of the self, and since we have no way to understand the 'self' as a product of all the other selves—present and in historical memory—we have no way of engaging each other in moral discourse, much less in a routine political argument" (p. 102). Critical theory questions this notion of a core self, arguing instead that identities are always embedded in history and culture, and that the self is always socially formed (Brookfield, 2004). Postmodernism also dismisses the notion of a core authentic self, positing flexible positionalities that change according to situational factors (Bagnall, 1999). A tenet of postmodernism (though postmodernists reject anything as fixed as tenets) is that the same person can behave in radically different and contradictory ways depending on the context. We can all be compassionate saints or genocidal devils depending on the situations we find ourselves in.

Self-Direction for Disempowerment

Although the examples of self-direction I have given are mostly positive, it is not uncommon to decide self-directedly to learn how to hide, even silence, oneself. In Alfred's (2001) research into how immigrant British Caribbean women learn to negotiate American culture, she describes how her subjects learned to silence their voices for fear of being misunderstood and how they learned to seek marginality, to hide so as not to be noticed in adult classrooms. As an introvert I hated to participate in discussion seminars in college so I learned to keep my mouth shut for fear of sounding unintelligent. In dealing with depression during my "secret" years (before I went public about my condition), I learned many strategies of deception that allowed me to explain why I couldn't meet deadlines, appear at conferences, or take trips without ever referencing the true reason. In these instances people are working in a self-directed way to develop certain skills and knowledge, but one could hardly view them as empowering.

Mixing Self- and External Direction

Finally, it is important to emphasize that while we can talk of self-directed learning as one of a range of possible ways of developing skills and knowledge, it is more problematic to talk of self-directed learners as if they were an entirely separate category, monolithically and unilaterally self-contained. The truth is that all of us are at times more self-directed in our learning, and at other times more externally directed. In an area in which I feel I know the layout of the territory I want to cross, I can be self-directed with far more confidence than in a project where I feel a total novice. Because I enjoy academic writing and find it relatively stress-free, I have never needed to take a course on scholarly writing for publications. Similarly, because songwriting comes easy to me, I'm fine with studying other songwriters' tricks and have never thought to enroll in a composition workshop.

But when it comes to learning how to use online tools to engage students I need someone to take me through a step-by-step explanation of a new software program or platform. The decisions regarding how I integrate that tool into my teaching may be my own (and therefore self-directed), but in order to know the possibilities of the tool and how it can be manipulated, I need a lot of initial external direction. So most learning projects involve alternating episodes in which self- or external direction is predominant.

Fostering Self-Directed Learning

This section is written for adult classroom teachers who want to help their students develop the confidence and ability to conduct self-directed learning efforts outside formal institutions. I believe there are things we can do inside institutions that can help students learn something outside them. In this sense, part of adult teaching involves reducing students' reliance on educational institutions when they decide they need to learn something. Whatever the educational level of adults I have taught, whether they are studying pre-college study skills or doing doctoral degrees at Harvard, my intent is to help them expand their repertoire of learning practices and increase their awareness of their strengths and weaknesses as learners. By so doing, I hope they are better placed to learn independently of a formal program.

Building Self-Confidence

A considerable amount of research has been conducted on the connections between self-efficacy and self-direction. In other words, a propensity to be self-directed is connected to a belief that you are capable of conducting such learning effectively (Hoban and Hoban, 2004; Ponton et al., 2005a; 2005b). One crucial preparatory step to encourage self-directed learning is to build confidence in those who feel that because of their age ("you can't teach an old dog new tricks") or social location ("learning is not for the likes of me") mastering a new set of skills or coming to understand complex ideas is something they aren't cut out for. Teachers who work with students across the lifespan often say that helping students become lifelong learners is an overarching agenda for their practice. So part of being a teacher in formal settings is working to help students develop the confidence to feel they don't always need an institution or teacher to help them conduct important learning. Some ways I try to do this are described below.

The Learning Audit

The Learning Audit is an instrument to let students see that although they may think no learning is happening in a particular course, over a period of time they are taking microsteps to develop skills and acquire knowledge. It comprises three questions that are regularly posed (maybe every two or three weeks) to students about their participation in a course. These questions are. . .

What do you know about the subject that you didn't know this time two weeks ago?

What can you do in this subject that you couldn't do two weeks ago?

What can you tell or demonstrate to someone about this subject that you couldn't have told, or demonstrated two weeks ago?

As students complete these I ask them to hand them to me so I can see how they feel they're moving forward, and then I return them to the students at the next class. Over the course of a semester students collect a series of audits. As part of their final learning portfolio for the course, I ask them to read through these and compile an inventory of the skills and information they feel they've developed over the term.

The intention of the Learning Audit is to convince students that, contrary to what they might believe, they are actually making small incremental gains. My hope is that this counters their belief that learning is beyond them and helps them realize that they are making progress and moving forward. This helps build a self-image as a learner that, in turn, contributes to their belief that learning is something they can do outside of a formal classroom.

Demystifying Learning

For adults whose time in formal schooling has been a sustained experience in being told they are mediocre and that significant learning is beyond them, the word *learning* takes on an aura of a mysterious phenomenon, a world that exists beyond their comprehension. So part of normalizing learning, bringing it into their worldview, is to strip learning of its aura of being something that only highly credentialed people can do. Two ways teachers can do this are through autobiographical disclosure and by helping learners construct an inventory of their own everyday cognition.

Autobiographical Disclosure　How a particular teacher incorporates an autobiographical disclosure of their own learning is obviously shaped by what constitutes their autobiography. In my own case I use several approaches. First, I often start a new course or program with a general autobiographical introduction detailing my own struggles with formal schooling. As I outlined in *The Skillful Teacher* (Brookfield, 2006), I have a history of mediocre performance as a learner. I almost failed to progress beyond age sixteen in high school, failed my university entrance exams at eighteen, graduated with a poor undergraduate degree from the college of technology that finally accepted me, and failed my master's degree exam. Starting the first class of a course with this disclosure is repeatedly described by students as a very effective way of keeping their own anxieties in check. If I made it through to a point where I'm now qualified to teach them, they conclude, then there is hope for them.

Second, I try to be open about my own struggles as a learner around particular subject matter. So when I teach critical social theory—an area rife with impenetrable scholarly jargon—I keep talking about how difficult it is for me to understand the topic, how my head hurts, and how after reading the same paragraph over five times I am no clearer about what it means. When I teach basic study skills courses, I talk about how I struggled to develop these same skills. When I run a faculty institute on recognizing racial microaggressions I lead off by describing my own struggle to recognize my own commission of such aggressions.

Third, I try always to introduce a new unit or module of study with an autobiographical illustration of how my knowing this material, or acquiring this skill, played itself out in some aspect of my own life. This could be in terms of my life as a scholar (how reading interviews with Foucault were much more helpful in my understanding his ideas than reading books he authored) or a more practical illustration from my work (how Foucault's work helped me understand how some of my own practices were experienced by students as surveillance).

Recognizing Everyday Cognition—Jeopardy *and* Mastermind   *Everyday cognition* is a term initially popularized by researchers Rogoff and Lave (1999) to refer to the knowledge and skills people develop in everyday situations (parenting, relationships, workplace roles, community organizations). One way to strengthen the self-confidence needed to undertake self-directed learning is to help learners appreciate the store of practical knowledge they have developed without consciously being aware of involvement in any kind of sustained learning project. For example, students can be invited to share their passions via *Jeopardy* (a US TV show) or *Mastermind* (an old UK show) quizzes.

I used to find out my students' passions (football, guns, soul music, clothes, dancing, beer, militia memorabilia) by asking them on the first night of class what they would like to be in life if they had the talent and freedom to choose anything. I then used their responses as the basis for organized class quiz games. The class would be divided into teams and would be asked general questions about the topics of the course, alternating with specialist questions based on their passions. My intent was to help them realize they already knew a lot and could do a lot, even if they had never taken an academic course after dropping out of high school.

Providing Exemplars

A very helpful way of convincing people that they can conduct a self-directed learning effort is to bring exemplars to a class. By exemplars I don't mean famous figures such as Harriet Tubman, Rosa

Parks, Susan B. Anthony, Nelson Mandela, or Wangari Maathai. I mean, rather, people who are as close to the students' own experiences as I can find who have themselves conducted self-directed learning projects. By inviting these individuals to class to talk about the ways they became knowledgeable or skilled, I can give students models that are accessible and understandable. Seeing how people just like them have conducted self-directed learning may convince them it is a possibility for them too. If bringing exemplars to class isn't logistically possible, then video-streaming comments from them online is an option.

Understanding Your Own Instinctive Preferences and Habits

Another way teachers can help learners prepare to undertake self-directed learning is to help them to become aware of their own instinctive learning preferences and habits. I use these terms rather than learning style, because they refer to a learner's personal history of choices and actions. (Learning style is a term for me that deals with information processing and brain chemistry.) In interviews with highly self-directed adults regarding the barriers that interrupted their learning projects, Guglielmino and others (2005) explored how personal learning habits were significant factors in stopping learning in its tracks. I would contend that being aware of your learning preferences and habits is crucial if you are to avoid falling into ruts when learning outside of formal education.

Some of the components of understanding your learning style are the following:

- Knowing what learning methods usually work best for you—this helps you decide what a good initial starting point might be

- Knowing what kinds of tasks typically cause you the most difficulties—this stops you from quitting prematurely when confronting such tasks

- Knowing when your instincts are to be trusted and when they should be disregarded—as when, for example, you don't seek out expert help because you believe you can accomplish everything on your own

- Understanding some of the typical rhythms of conducting learning projects—this helps you recognize temporary (as against permanent) setbacks

Critical Incident Questionnaire

One way that adult teachers can help students become aware of their preferences and habits is by asking them to review the Critical Incident Questionnaires (CIQs) they have completed over a period of several weeks. The CIQ can be downloaded for free at my home page (http://www.stephenbrookfield.com) where you can also read case studies of its application. It's a one-page response sheet that asks students five questions about their weekly experience of the class. Because it's anonymous I trust the responses more than those where students identify themselves. I always return the completed response sheets to the students by laying them on a table during a class break and asking them to retrieve their copies as I'm out of the room getting tea.

At the end of the course I ask students to go back over all their completed CIQs and to look for common themes. What were the kinds of classroom activities they found most engaging or distancing? What actions that I or their fellow students took did they find most helpful or confusing? What surprised them? I then ask them to provide me with a brief statement of what they've learned about themselves as learners having reviewed ten to fifteen of their completed CIQs. What kinds of learning activities are they drawn to and what do they avoid? Which tasks do they find most challenging and which do they accomplish easily? Are there certain kinds of resources they find more congenial than others? What have they learned about their own emotional responses to learning? How do they deal with disappointments and struggle? How did they judge when they needed to ask for help?

This paragraph of self-reflection is a required element in the final course portfolio the student submits to me. If it isn't handed in, then the student automatically gets a grade of incomplete for the course. My agenda here is to use my power to force students to know themselves better as learners, so that when they decide to conduct important self-directed learning efforts outside of class they do so with an enhanced awareness of what are their habitual preferences. The more they know what works and doesn't work for them, the better placed they are to plan their projects. The more awareness they have of their own emotional responses and rhythms, the more they are able to withstand moments of frustration, weather periods of demoralization, and know how to reactivate enthusiasm.

Letter to a Second Self

The *Letter to a Second Self* is an end of semester activity in which learners write to themselves as if they were another student. The student is asked to try and step outside of herself and imagine she is giving advice to an imaginary second self on how best to conduct a new learning effort. This learning is based on what she has found out about her own preferences and habits during the current course of study. I provide prompts for these letters such as. . .

- Here's the things you should watch out for

- Here are some approaches likely to be most helpful to you

- When you feel stuck you might want to try

- What's probably going to work best for you is. . .

- Make sure you. . .

- When you feel down or demoralized you should. . .

- Don't try to. . .

The intent, as with the CIQ reflection, is to get students to think about the big picture of their own learning efforts. I want them to see themselves as skilled technicians of learning, adults who know how best to conduct the nuts and bolts of self-directed learning efforts in ways that build on their strengths. But I also want them to develop some kind of emotional intelligence so that they keep the inevitable highs and lows of learning in some sort of perspective.

Poster Session—My Learning Journey

A more visual approach to helping adults develop some self-awareness is to schedule one class as a poster session in which students depict visually the journey they have taken over a semester. I stress that words are to be kept to a minimum and that I want people to use images—including abstract images—to represent how they negotiated their learning activities. I supply students with large newsprint to draw on, plenty of colored markers, pens, rulers, scissors, and tape. They also receive magazine photographs, cloth scraps, and other textured materials for creating a mixed-media collage creation, if they so desire. It's important that students know that abstract drawing with no attempt at representation is fine. I don't want this to turn into a test of artistic ability.

The students then hang their poster on the wall and put a blank sheet of newsprint by each one. They are then told to wander around the room looking at all the posters and to write down any questions they have about the images they see on the posters. They also add comments or interpretations of the images. After a time students then return to their original poster to read what others have written in response. I'll then open the class for discussion and reactions to the exercise. The theme of the discussion is "What does my poster teach me about who I am as a learner?" We talk about what their poster means for how they will conduct future learning efforts in a self-directed manner.

Chalk Talk—"I Learn Best When. . ."

The Chalk Talk exercise is one of my favorites as a classroom teacher, mostly because it democratizes participation very quickly and because it provides a graphic representation of where a group of people stands on an issue. In Chapter 3 I explained how the process works. When students do Chalk Talk around the prompt "I Learn Best When. . ." the board quickly fills up with very varied responses. After ten minutes it is typically full, and I call the exercise to an end. I then invite the students to look first for common clusters of responses, and we talk about what those tell us. We then turn to outliers—comments that are important but that don't comprise a cluster—and we discuss how those represent alternatives we need to examine. My intent is to get students to understand the range of potential approaches to learning that are available to them. As we discuss the pros and cons of the different approaches revealed, I ask people to think how they could incorporate new methods and strategies the next time they conduct a self-directed learning effort.

Developing Informational Literacy

The explosion of the Internet and its obvious use as a resource for self-directed learning has led to an interest in the opportunities and challenges it provides (Rager, 2006). In his analysis of how the Internet changes self-directed learning in rural communities, Hiemstra (2006) notes how rural users become skillful at evaluating web pages and negotiating search engines, and how Internet use becomes central to their life decisions. The same could probably be said for users in suburban and inner city communities. We now need to think of social media and the Internet as opportunities for participatory civic engagement (Black, 2012).

Teaching basic informational literacy goes beyond computer usage, of course, to encompass all kinds of information retrieval—from libraries, from other people, from mass media, and so on. Adult educators working in formal systems have multiple opportunities to teach informational literacy in a way that will be useful for learners who conduct self-directed learning outside the formal system. If you are interested in reading how I teach adults to read texts critically you can read chapter 6 of *Teaching For Critical Thinking* (Brookfield, 2012). Below I will focus on Internet analysis.

Search Engine Selection

A beginning exercise is to give learners a topic of interest to them—how to pass examinations, for example—and tell them to use different search engines to generate information about this topic. Students use two or three search engines (Google, Yahoo, and so on) and are then asked to choose the one that generated the most useful links. Once a tally of student votes has been taken, the different engines are discussed in turn. Students supporting each search engine say what it was about that particular engine that caused them to decide it was most useful—speed of response?, number of links?, ease of negotiation?, clarity of link descriptors?, relevance of top hits?, breadth of links open to retrieval?, and so on. The teacher then works with the students to discuss which criteria for judging search engine utility make the most sense to them, and how those criteria might be applied in a self-directed learning project totally unrelated to the student's formal curriculum.

Web Credibility—"The Criteria Gallery"

Another exercise is to choose a general topic of interest such as dealing with stress and to present four or five web pages exploring that particular topic or problem. Students are told to evaluate which of the four or five they would choose as being the most useful in helping them conduct inquiry on the topic outside class. Five minutes is allotted for students to work independently and choose one of the web pages. They then form into small groups and share their choices with each other and the reasons why they felt a particular web page would be the most helpful in a self-directed learning effort. I ask them to put on newsprint the top three or four reasons the group agreed were important in determining why they chose the pages they did and also to post one or two reasons for choosing pages that were only mentioned by one person.

When the posters are hung around the walls we have, in effect, a "criteria gallery." Students see which criteria are most frequently used by their peers when deciding to use a website to guide learning, and they also see some of the outlier reasons that have been offered. As a class we then discuss which would be the most accurate criteria to be deployed when assessing websites' utility for different kinds of self-directed learning projects such as. . .

- How to learn about breast cancer treatment

- How to oppose a neighborhood zoning decision

- How to set up a terrarium

- How to establish a charter school based on Islamic cultural values

- How to organize a mass demonstration

- How to create a cactus garden

- How to mobilize an "Occupy Anytown" community

Wiki Construction

One of the hardest things I confront as a teacher of adults is to develop in students the awareness that Wikipedia is not always to be trusted; or, more specifically, that it is not to be trusted as an objective source of information collated by experts who have no axe to grind. On a simple level you can do this by comparing Wikipedia entries that differ in regards to multiple citations, clarity of expression, breadth and depth of detailed information, coverage of multiple contrasting views, self-critique and caveats, and so on. What is harder is to get learners to evaluate critically what looks to be a credible Wikipedia entry.

One quick way to teach people to be skeptical about the objectivity and accuracy of a Wikipedia entry is to get them involved in constructing—that is altering—a fictional entry. I begin by creating a wiki on the course Blackboard page dealing with a topic we have reviewed in the course. I then ask students to add valid information to this wiki but also to add something they know to be false and present it in such a way as to appear entirely credible. Students make statements they know to be untrue and then back these up with fictional citations in sources that sound legitimate. After a suitable period I ask for challenges to the wiki postings.

When the class convenes we talk about the ways they have constructed their wiki and, if we're in a "smart" classroom, students navigate the entry on screen to show the class their erroneous contributions, and they describe the tricks they used to get this information to appear legitimate. They then remove any erroneous claims or information they have entered.

The point of this exercise is twofold. First, I want students to appreciate just how easy it is to post information online that looks credible and to increase their skepticism about its supposed objectivity. Second, I want to train them in recognizing spurious entries in Wikipedia. It's my own personal contribution to keeping Wikipedia credible and legitimate. I am a fan and user of Wikipedia as well as a contributor to it and want it to remain a valuable educational tool. My assumption is that if my students know how easy it is to fabricate a supposedly credible addition to their own wiki, they will be on the lookout for the same kinds of tricks used in an actual Wikipedia entry.

Designing Learning Projects

Finally, classroom teachers can help students develop some of the technical learning skills that will be helpful in future self-directed learning. Any assignments that ask students to take responsibility for at least part of their learning can add to a learner's repertoire of skills. Of course, a teacher giving you options to choose from, or encouraging you to be personally creative in deciding how to go about learning or demonstrating something, is not an example of self-directed learning. For that to happen the student would need to be in charge of deciding what and how to learn. But in order to make good decisions on the mechanics of how to learn, it helps to have had some experience with using different learning approaches in a formal setting.

Project Flow Charts

If students have an individual or group project they are required to accomplish as part of completing a course or program, teachers can help them decide what is manageable within the time they have available. One way is to develop a flow chart that starts with the completed project and then works back through the calendar to what will be the planned starting point. The final project is broken down into its constituent tasks, and these are then matched against the chunks of time available to the student on the flow chart. When students realize that their final project goals are way too ambitious given the time they have allotted in the weeks leading up to the completion date, they invariably redefine what the project goals are to make them manageable, or they reframe the project in a significant way. The flow chart helps students to see how a broad overall objective can be realized in small incremental chunks. Teachers can help students see that breaking an intimidating learning prospect into bite size daily or weekly tasks helps keep up morale and momentum.

Practicing Learning Decisions

The nuts and bolts of any self-directed learning project are the daily microdecisions learners make about what to do next. To the extent that teachers assign projects that place significant responsibility for these decisions in the hands of students, they are helping them undertake future self-directed learning outside the academy. So even if the boundaries and focus of a project have been set by the teacher (thereby disqualifying it from counting as self-directed learning) students still have the chance to practice learning decisions. Such decisions might include:

- When should I work solo and when should I seek out collaborators?

- If I use collaborators, how am I going to judge who will be most helpful?

- How do I know which is the best book to read when several are available?

- How can I use the Internet to accomplish my objectives?

- How do I keep the focus on what's integral to the project and what's superfluous?

- How do I break a large task into a series of manageable minitasks?

- How do I devise a realistic schedule and hold myself accountable to it?

Emotional Fluency

Emotion is central to learning, not something added to it or something that interrupts it. The decision to learn is in part emotional, fueled by a feeling of urgency, a desire to reduce anxiety, or a wish to experience the pleasure of confidently moving forward. We experience learning emotionally—feeling the chill of recognition, the joy of understanding, the pride of accomplishment, the shame of embarrassment, the self-loathing of failure, and the tired demoralization of not being able to "get it." In classroom learning, which is a social phenomenon, there is pleasure or anger at how a teacher or peer responds to you, frustration that someone can't understand your point, or gratification at being asked a question that shows someone has understood your point exactly.

Adult educators have recently focused much more on the emotional dimensions of learning (Dirkx, 2008), though Bierema (2008) usefully cautions against the danger of emotion "work"—manufacturing emotions one doesn't really feel as part of job responsibilities. I think of emotion work every time I enter a store to hear a "greeter" cheerfully call out "How are you?" fabricating a completely manufactured interest in my well being. Emotional fluency in self-directed learning is the opposite of emotion work. It is recognizing that emotional responses are integral to learning and coming to understand how these manifest themselves. Part of emotional fluency focuses on a meta-awareness of how emotions are moving through us, a noticing of an altered state of being. This is especially helpful when we're feeling demoralized, frustrated, and confused because things aren't proceeding as we'd hoped. Part of it also focuses on ensuring that the conditions that produce the most pleasurable states of feeling in a learning effort are conditions we attempt to reproduce whenever possible.

There are multiple ways of teaching emotional fluency. One is to include testimony from learners who are further ahead in a learning journey on the ways that emotions manifested themselves in their learning. Hearing others name emotions we are experiencing is helpful to our being able to keep our ups and downs in perspective. Video streaming testimony in online classes or having previous students visit your classroom and talk about how they experienced the course are two possibilities. Another is the Letter to Successors technique (Brookfield, 1995) in which students finishing a course write brief letters to future students passing on whatever information they feel it's important for new students to know about the class. In my experience these letters focus far more on the emotional aspects of learning than on the technicalities of how to complete assignments. I publish these letters (with their author's permission) on the course home page the next time I teach the same course to a new group of students.

Summary

Self-directed learning in the way I define it is part of the field of adult education that resists compartmentalization. It represents nothing less than the full range of learning that people decide they need to conduct to get through their lives. Learning how to cope with bereavement and illness, learning how to deal with being fired, learning what comprises true friendship, or how to build a lasting relationship are examples of self-directed learning all of us sooner or later undertake. Most community-based learning is self-directed as we try to manage the conflicting interests of different community groups or fight against outside interests that try to take our community away from us. And, of course, the full panoply of recreational and vocational learning, which for those of us stuck in unsatisfying jobs is what brings true meaning to our lives, is usually self-directed. Finally, the deepest spiritual engagements are often self-directed quests for meaning. In all these self-directed projects, we do not work alone—friends, peers, family, colleagues, and experts all contribute to our learning. But in the final say it's we who decide.

5

Democratizing the Classroom

Adult education has firmly embraced the democratic ideal. To describe an act of practice as democratic is to confer on it the adult educational "Good Housekeeping" seal of approval. Of all the ideas espoused as representing an authentic adult educational tradition, the idea that its practitioners should work to make their practice and the world increasingly democratic is the most powerful. The words *democracy* or *democratic* are often used to justify and defend whatever practice adult educators subscribe to, serving as a kind of scriptural signaling. They are invoked to signify the progressive credentials of the speaker. This is what in philosophy is called a *premature ultimate*, a term that, once invoked, has the effect of stopping any further serious discussion of its exact meaning. Describe one's practice as democratic and there is a chorus of agreement, a massed nodding of heads. If we answer a question about our practice by replying that we did something because it was democratic, then the conversation often comes to a full stop. The word is so uncritically revered in adult education that it has become almost immune to critical scrutiny.

Yet the idea of democracy is malleable and slippery, with as many particular definitions and interpretations as it has utterers. It can be invoked so frequently and ritualistically that it becomes stripped of any significant meaning. Only by trying to live out the democratic process do the contradictions of this idea become manifest. As a way of beginning this chapter, then, I need to address what I mean by democracy.

Defining Democracy

For me, a democratic system exhibits three core elements: (1) its participants engage in a constant discussion of how best to organize the community's affairs; (2) available economic and other material resources are shared by all, rather than being controlled by a disproportionate minority; and (3) a major task is to identify and challenge ideological manipulation, so that militarism, racism, White supremacy, patriarchy, ableism, and heterosexism are confronted and dismantled. These three defining characteristics are pretty lofty and intimidating and, of course, they are never fully realized. So teaching towards democracy is always a work in progress (Ayers et al., 2010).

For teachers there is a clear educational task implied by the first condition of democracy, namely that its members engage in a continuous, ever-widening conversation about how to organize social, economic, and political affairs. To be democratic, this conversation must be as inclusive and wide-ranging as possible involving widely different groups and perspectives. It must also be one in which people are able to make decisions based on full knowledge of the situations in which they find themselves, full awareness of the range of different possible courses of action open to them, and the best information about the potential consequences of their decisions. In Habermas's (1996) terms, democratic discussion occurs in its most fully realized form in an ideal speech situation that allows all participants full access to all relevant knowledge pertaining to the issues discussed. Mezirow (1991) used this element of Habermas's work to develop his theory of transformative learning, and it informs his conviction that adult educators need to ally themselves with social movements that seek to secure people's full access to the knowledge that affects how they might live.

Teaching democratically according to this notion focuses on creating conversational forms that are as inclusive as possible and fighting any vested interests concerned with blocking access to relevant information. When an organization or structure seeks to privatize knowledge and keep it the province of professionals, this also inspires adult educators to fight to make this knowledge available to all. Such was the raison d'être of much of Ivan Illich's (2000) and, within adult education, John Ohliger's (Grace and Rocco, 2009) work. A democratic decision draws its legitimacy from the fact that all fully informed stakeholders have been involved in the conversation leading to it. How that decision is arrived at varies according to who has the greatest stake in it. This is the argument of Albert's (2004, 2006) work on participatory economics or *parecon*. In parecon the chief decision makers involved in a situation are those who are most affected by the consequences of that decision.

The second condition of democracy is that it is an economic as well as political arrangement. Democracy is not just a political form involving voting procedures and structures of representation, but an economic one requiring the abolition of vast disparities in wealth, the equalization of income, and the placing of all forms of resources under common control. This is why democracy and socialism are intertwined. Important elements of democracy include many of the things that Franklin Delano Roosevelt called for in his 1944 State of the Union Address, sometimes called the "Second Bill of Rights" (Sunstein, 2006). These include the right to a good education, a decent job and livable wage, adequate food and clothing, acceptable medical care, and some protection from the ravages of old age. A socialist economy in which the populace as a whole controls the production and distribution of goods and services (as against control by an unrepresentative, privileged elite) is the most democratic economic arrangement possible.

In adult education one of the best articulations of this idea is W.E.B. Du Bois's "Basic American Negro Creed" (Du Bois,

1971) that was part of a work commissioned by an offshoot of the American Association for Adult Education and then not published (Guy, 1993; Guy and Brookfield, 2009). Leading according to this notion of democracy entails working to further the interests of organizations, groups, and movements that are trying to establish co-operative economic forms. Du Bois's creed linked the advancement of African Americans and the abolition of racism to socialism. The sixth element of his creed states baldly, "We believe in the ultimate triumph of some form of Socialism the world over; that is, com-mon ownership and control of the means of production and equal-ity of income" (DuBois, 1971, p. 321). This equalizing of work and wealth is urged as "the beginning of the rise of the Negro race in this land and the world over, in power, learning, and accomplishment" (p. 321). This equalization is to be achieved through taxation and through "vesting the ultimate power of the state in the hands of the workers" (p. 321), a situation that will be accompanied by the working class demanding their "proportionate share in administra-tion and public expenditure" (p. 322). Du Bois ends the creed with an expansive appeal to people of all races to join in fighting White supremacy and creating socialism. In his words "to this vision of work, organization and service, we welcome men (sic) of all colors so long as their basic subscription to this basic creed is sincere and proven by their deeds" (p. 322).

The third element of my understanding of democracy is that it is a struggle against ideologies that exclude disenfranchised groups from full and equal participation in civil society. These ideologies would be those of White supremacy, class superiority, patriarchy, homophobia, ableism, and so on. Western industrial societies purport to be completely open democracies in which all have equal opportunity to flourish, yet they are actually highly unequal societies in which economic inequity, racism, and class discrimination are empirical realities. The way this state of af-fairs is reproduced as seeming to be normal, natural, and in-evitable (thereby heading off potential challenges to the system) is through the dissemination of dominant ideologies. For me democracy can only flourish if these ideologies are challenged and then replaced. From this third perspective, adult education for democracy involves subverting and destroying elements of dominant ideology.

Adult Education and Democracy

The American adult educator Eduard Lindeman tried to take the understanding and analysis of democracy beyond ritualistic invocation. To Lindeman (1987) *democracy* was "one of the grandest words in the whole of human language" (p. 137) but also one of the least understood and most abused by hypocrites. He believed that most people "are democratically speaking, illiterate; they do not know how to operate in and through groups" (p. 150). This meant that they lacked the skill to deal respectfully with difference, live with unresolved conflicts, and accept that proposed solutions to complex social problems should always be viewed as temporary, as contingent. Lindeman believed democracy was present when "ultimate power resides in the people, in the collectivity" (p. 147) so that between people a relationship of "power with"—"to be so related to you that our powers will be multiplied" (p. 144)—replaced that of "power over." He stressed, though, that democracy was not just a set of discourse patterns or decision-making protocols but that it also required an economic leveling. Political democracy required economic democracy, a point later emphasized repeatedly by Horton. For Lindeman (1987) "democracy will remain a grisly joke, but an ironic joke, unless we learn how to make it operate in an era of economics" (p. 144).

At its root, Lindeman saw living democratically as an adult learning process. It required its participants to study and become increasingly adept at practicing a number of democratic disciplines. These included learning to honor diversity, learning to live with the partial functioning of the democratic ideal, learning to avoid the trap of false antithesis (where we are forced to choose between either/or, mutually exclusive options), learning to accept the compatibility of ends and means (where we avoid the temptation to bypass the democratic process in the interests of reaching speedily a decision regarded as obviously right and necessary), learning to correlate the functioning of social institutions (health, education, and social services) with democratic purposes, learning collective forms of social and economic planning, learning to live with contrary decisions, and learning to appreciate the comedy inherent in democracy's contradictions. For Lindeman, then, learning democracy was a central task of adult life.

What tasks should adult educators focus on where learning democracy is concerned? One might be to explore how adults become aware of and learn to live with the contradiction of subscribing both to freedom and democracy. As Baptiste (Baptiste and Brookfield, 1997) argues, democracy necessarily limits the exercise of freedom: "The freedom of interacting beings must be reciprocally regulated if their interactions are to be judged as being just. Ethical freedom is relative freedom" (p. 27). Living in association with others only works if we adjust our actions to take account of their presence. So in order to ensure equity democrats must restrict the range of behaviors in which people can freely engage. This means adults must face the difficult task of learning to live with contrary decisions, a task that Lindeman (Smith and Lindeman, 1951) identified as an important democratic discipline. They must also learn to be alert to the tyranny of the majority exposed by J. S. Mill (1961). In a famous passage from *On Liberty* (published in 1859) Mill contended that when society mandates certain ways of thinking as democratically agreed or as desirable common sense, it "practices a social tyranny more formidable than many kinds of political oppression ... it leaves fewer means of escape, penetrating much more deeply into the details of life, and enslaving the soul itself" (p. 191). This analysis of the oppressive control a majority can exercise in a democracy echoes Gramsci on the all-pervasive nature of hegemony and Foucault on power as inscribed in the choices and actions of everyday life.

Another of democracy's adult educational tasks is to investigate the general problem of how adults learn to live with the element of contingency inherent in the democratic process. Contingency—the acceptance of all understandings and solutions as partial, provisional, and continuously open to review and renegotiation—is often associated with postmodernism, as Bagnall's (1999) analysis of postmodern ideas, *Discovering Radical Contingency*, implies. Yet its roots are in pragmatism and that tradition's emphasis on continuous inquiry and experimentation as integral to democracy. Learning to live with this contingency is learning to accept that democracy is always a partially functioning ideal.

Learning democratic process involves cognitive analysis (why is democracy not working and under what conditions can it best be encouraged?), emotional intelligence (how do we learn to recognize and accommodate the inevitable frustration we feel as we try to organize for democratic purposes with people who are different from us and have different agendas?), communicative competence (how do we communicate across racial, class, and gender differences in the pursuit of the collective good?), technical skill (how do we learn ground rules to ensure all voices are heard? How do we make use of the Internet to document inequities in wealth and power, or to put grassroots groups separated by geographic distance in touch with each other?), and the development of ontological wisdom so that our faith in democratic possibilities is not crushed by events or experience. More generally, part of learning democratic process is dealing with the distortions to that process that inevitably are produced by the differential power possessed by community members based on their race, class, and gender. It also involves learning to break with Eurocentric patterns of communication and to introduce silence as an integral part of learning and careful and attentive listening as an integral part of discussion.

What Is a Democratic Classroom?

Building on the foregoing analysis, it seems to me a democratic classroom contains three intersecting elements. First, it must structure opportunities for the widest possible range of voices to be expressed and the widest possible range of learning practices to be included. Second, a democratic classroom should be one in which, wherever possible, decisions should be made by those most affected by those decisions, that is, the learners themselves. Third, where possible and appropriate, a democratic classroom should focus on incorporating unfamiliar perspectives, challenging dominant ideology, and on ideas and practices that have up to that point been largely unquestioned. Let me say something about each of these in turn.

Multiple Voices and Perspectives

The emphasis on involving multiple voices in a democratic process is relatively uncontroversial. Most proponents of working democratically would find it hard to argue against the idea that we should hear from as many people as possible on an issue. This emphasis on broadening participation so as to hear from everybody is something Stephen Preskill and I returned to again and again in our book *Discussion as a Way of Teaching* (Brookfield and Preskill, 2005). Not surprisingly the subtitle of this book is *Tools and Techniques for Democratic Classrooms*. So one feature of a democratic classroom is bound to be exercises, protocols, and activities that enable as many people as possible to be heard.

But a democratic classroom should not just hear from people in speech. It must also find ways to involve the contributions of those who are less drawn to speaking or less comfortable with writing. This means the regular use of visual and graphic modes of expression and frequent opportunities for silent communication. A democratic classroom is one where, by definition, there are not just many different opportunities for students to participate, but also many

different ways for them to be involved. Hence, democratic teachers use multiple methods and approaches because they understand
that students' different learning habits and preferences require this
variety.

There is a major complication regarding this emphasis on multiple voices—the danger of a discussion or analysis remaining at a
relatively superficial level because the effort to have everyone contributing means that a topic or issue is never the subject of an in-
depth analysis by two or three participants. I see this problem all the
time at academic conferences where question and answer sessions
are mostly brief exchanges on a variety of disconnected topics. The
presenter avoids getting into long conversations with one or two
questioners because this precludes others from having their questions asked and responded to.

Yet, a sustained engagement with a very different perspective is
often best achieved by two or three knowledgeable and committed
individuals having a public conversation on an issue while others
silently observe. Indeed, given that dominant ideologies and conceptions structure most people's thinking, one of the best ways to
help students break with their usual patterns of thought is to have
two people with very different views on something go back and
forth on it while others are silent. Sometimes democracy requires
replacing the emphasis on multiple voices with one on having a
paired exchange of unfamiliar perspectives.

Decision-Making Processes

A second feature of a democratic classroom is that it is one in
which decisions, wherever possible, are made by those most affected by those decisions, that is, by the learners themselves. I often
quote Myles Horton's dictum that at the Highlander Folk School
"decision making was at the center of our students' experiences"
(Horton, 1990, p. 152) so that through the experience of making decisions about what was to happen at Highlander, participants learned democratic process. This means that a democratic

classroom should be one in which students are making the majority of decisions about what they will learn, how they will learn it, how they will demonstrate what they have learned, and how that learning will be judged, assessed, and evaluated.

This emphasis on student decision making raises three complications. First, what if the majority of substantive decisions lie within the purview of external authorities, as is the case with accreditation or licensing agencies? As a trainee professional, I may decide I don't need to know certain things, but if I don't know them then I will fail my licensing exam and be unable to practice. For decision making to be meaningful it must be about something substantive.

Second, what if different members of the group express different, even contradictory, preferences for what is to be learned? Do we go with a simple majority so that those who share interests always win out over individual and divergent preferences? That doesn't seem fair or democratic.

Third, what if students have insufficient knowledge of the alternatives open to them, or if they are unfamiliar with the intellectual territory to be explored? It's hard to argue that a student's best interests are being served if she has the sole decision-making power about something where she has very little knowledge. This would be the equivalent of saying that a patient who knows nothing about a serious medical condition should have more decision-making power regarding diagnosis and treatment than a skilled and experienced practitioner.

Incorporating Unfamiliar Perspectives

This third element of a democratic classroom is evident when learners are urged to explore unfamiliar and often challenging perspectives. This is at the heart of Habermas's (1996) discourse theory of democracy, the idea that a decision only has democratic legitimacy if it has been reached after every possible relevant viewpoint and every possible piece of pertinent information has been considered. Habermas argues that we can establish an ideal speech situation—a set of conditions under which democratic discussion optimally takes place—that can guide the way we set up group conversations on important community issues and decisions. Although not a strict parallel with Lindeman's democratic disciplines, these ideal speech conditions contain the openness to new perspectives and the willingness to suspend one's own convictions temporarily that Lindeman also stresses. To Habermas it is important that we understand how decisions are arrived at democratically because people will only perceive decisions as credible if they are arrived at in this manner.

If exposing learners to unfamiliar perspectives is at the heart of a democratic classroom, then this means teachers must sometimes go against students' wishes and insist that they consider perspectives and viewpoints from very different, often critical, perspectives. This is where democracy and critical social theory intersect. A democratic classroom is one that should focus constantly on challenging settled consensus, majority views, and taken for granted ideas. This means that students and teachers will be concerned to challenge dominant ideology and learn how to uncover the ways power and knowledge are always intertwined, as Foucault (1980) would have it. Foucault argued that every group and subculture establishes a regime of truth—a set of procedures for determining which knowledge is established legitimately. A democratic classroom would be one that was concerned with uncovering the regime of truth in a particular topic, subject, or discipline and asking who benefitted the most from its existence.

There is, of course, a major problem with this third condition of a democratic classroom. What if in the desire to have students engage with unfamiliar perspectives teachers expose them to ones that are harmful or lunatic? Should a teacher designing a unit on race include far right, Aryan doctrines using the argument that they are outside the mainstream? Should a teacher in an introductory biology class give equal class time to creationism as she does to evolution? The libertarian viewpoint says that there should be no censorship of knowledge and that students should have the democratic freedom to make up their own minds on any issue, no matter how outrageous, harmful, or unsubstantiated a teacher may feel their position to be. This is one of many reasons why I am not a libertarian. Ultimately, I believe in situations where learners are novices or unfamiliar with what knowledge is out there, the exercise of teacher power comes into play.

Teacher Power

For some adult educators, teacher power is the fly in the ointment of many democratic classrooms. It is seen as undemocratic, a blatant contradiction, for teachers to insist on agendas and purposes they deem important in the face of student disinterest or resistance. For a teacher to refuse to budge seems like an authoritarian and unresponsive stance, totally at odds with democratic notions of adult education.

But a moment's thought quickly exposes this fallacy. If we lived already in a democratic world where all had equal access to all relevant knowledge on any particular topic, then teachers acting this way could be considered undemocratic. But we don't live in such a world. In our world—or at least in mine—dominant groups control the flow of information and define what counts as legitimate knowledge. In university tenure hearings, articles in which someone tells their personal story are seen as much less credible than those that follow an experimental design and use a control group to consider the influence of particular variables. In medicine, homeopathy has lowly status, and patient-centered communication skills are seen as much less important than scientific diagnostic skills.

In like fashion, adult educational centers, classrooms, and programs exist in a world of asymmetric power relations. Some members of the class are used to being heard and taken seriously because of how they speak or look, while others are used to remaining silent. What is considered "common sense" at any time or place, or in any subject, usually supports the status quo. Groups exercising dominant control in any community—including academic and scholarly communities—usually ensure that viewpoints that challenge their legitimacy are silenced or marginalized. The guardians of the regimes of truth do not want legitimacy to attach itself to anything critical of that regime.

So if we are to have a democratic classroom that meets the third condition of democracy by ensuring that students are exposed to unfamiliar and challenging viewpoints and perspectives, then this challenge has to come from somewhere—or, rather, from someone. And that someone is often the teacher. To be truly democratic, adult teachers sometimes have to exercise what Baptiste (2000) describes as ethical coercion. In other words, they are required to coerce—to force—students to engage with materials and ideas those students would prefer to avoid. To shy away from this task because it goes against the wishes of the majority is to neglect the democratic imperative. This is why the exercise of teacher authority is in no way contradictory to the democratic process.

Democratizing Adult Classrooms

In this section I want to explore a number of specific techniques that I have used to democratize classrooms. All of these in some way try to exemplify the three conditions of democracy I outlined earlier. But, equally, all are inevitably partially functioning ideals, working better at some times, and failing totally at others.

A World Divided into Thirds

Probably the most frequent, and often legitimate, objection that teachers have to the idea of working democratically is that their special expertise, experience, and training means they have far more knowledge than the students. Hence, the argument goes, to allow students to make curricular or methodological choices is ludicrous. In effect this allows the uninitiated to deepen their ignorance by studying material that is safe, unchallenging, or irrelevant. This is the very argument I made at the end of the last section in my discussion of teacher authority.

But as I said earlier, working democratically does not mean giving up your convictions as a teacher about the kinds of things students need to learn and the best ways to go about learning it. My rough-and ready-guide to balancing my insistence on what I deem is nonnegotiable, along with my commitment to working democratically, is to divide my world into thirds, as explained below. Of the available decisions about what happens in a classroom, I see roughly one third as being solely the province of the teacher, one third solely as the province of the learners, and one third being negotiated by both parties. Here's how that works.

The Teacher-Controlled Third

Teachers have total control over one-third of the curriculum and use it to cover what they consider to be the core and nonnegotiable aspects of the subject. They use this third to push the students beyond their comfort zone to learn difficult and challenging material. One third of all course resources are controlled totally by the teacher, usually in the form of required texts. Her control also extends to methods of teaching and methods of evaluation. For one-third of the course time she decides what will happen. She has power over how students will be assessed or graded for 33.3 percent of the total points available.

The Student-Controlled Third

Students have total control over one-third of the curriculum. Typically they use their control to study whatever aspects of the subject most interest them and to tailor the curriculum to their own circumstances. As part of this approach, the teacher must agree to do her best to teach whatever the students nominate. She also agrees to read whatever resources the students decide are necessary to cover the material. During the course students can choose the activities for one-third of the time, and 33.3 percent of the total points available for the course are self-graded.

The Teacher-Student Negotiated Third

In this third, both parties negotiate what will happen. The students suggest things that they wish to explore that are not part of the student-controlled third, and they nominate resources for further study. The teacher outlines what she can cover over and above the nonnegotiable elements contained in her third of the curriculum. She explains to students what she has to offer and how she could go about covering that material. Conversations take place as students accept, reject, or modify different elements of what the teacher is offering, and teachers do the same regarding students' suggestions. The means by which the 33.3 percent of possible points in this section are awarded is also negotiated.

Of course, in reality this neat division into thirds never works exactly. Given the partially functioning nature of democracy, it would be naïve to expect a precise compartmentalization of curriculum, methods, or evaluation. In my experience a typical student response is to tell the teacher "you make the decision for us; just do what you think is best." Students rightly sense that negotiating what will happen in a course will be complex and time-consuming. As adults they have so much going on in their lives, and they have made so many sacrifices to get to class, that the last thing they wish to do is waste time in democratic negotiation. "Just tell us what we need to know so we can pass this course, get trained to do this job, and get out of here as quickly and cheaply as possible" is something I hear time and time again.

In democratic negotiation, teachers have to respect students' wishes; so if this is what students tell you to do, I feel you have to honor that request—but with two caveats. First, I try not to agree to student requests for me to make all the decisions immediately, but hold my ground for a while as I share with them how students in previous courses found it useful to take control over some part of what happened. If possible, I'll begin a course with a brief, fifteen-minute First Day Alumni Panel (Brookfield, 2006). Students who have taken the course previously come back to the first session of the new course and pass on any advice they have on how the new students can get the most out of it. If that's not possible, I'll share the Letters to Successors that students in the last version of the course wrote for those who will follow them (Brookfield, 1995).

Second, I try to ensure that maybe a month into the syllabus there is some way that students can revisit their decision to have me be in sole control of what happens. I need to check in at least once a semester to see whether or not they now feel they'd like more say in what and how they're learning.

Student Governance

For students to be involved in making decisions about what and how to learn usually requires that they constitute themselves as a decision-making body that can express their wishes to teachers. This is often the most time-consuming and fractious part of trying to create a democratic classroom. Students who have nothing in common other than their desire to complete a particular course or program as quickly and cheaply as possible will usually have very different expectations for how a course should function and variable preferences on how learning should happen. I have been involved in two extensive attempts to institute a negotiated curriculum. One is in the doctoral program in adult education at National Louis University (Chicago), which I helped design and that, at the time of writing, is due to close in 2015. The other is the doctoral program in critical pedagogy at the University of St. Thomas that I also helped to design. That lasted for ten years before being merged with a doctoral program in educational leadership in which I also teach.

Even in these two programs in which applicants had signed up and committed themselves to doing doctoral work in a manner that explicitly tried to realize democratic practices, the students often had great difficulty reaching agreement, even failing to agree on how decisions should be made. The frustrations occasioned by trying to reach agreement led to a kind of "democracy fatigue," and a desire for the faculty to "tell us what to do and how to do it." The adult education doctoral program at National Louis University has had a history of its participants— both teachers and students—writing pieces that analyze this ongoing experimentation (Baptiste, 2001; Baptiste and Brookfield, 1997; Bronte de Avila et al., 2001; Colin and Heaney, 2001; Ramdeholl et al., 2010). These studies raise difficult questions such as "how could our decision making be truly democratic when the loudest or most articulate voices often dominated? How could we hope to avoid the contaminants of dominant culture—competitiveness, self-interest, chauvinism—when these are deeply embedded in our lives?" (Ramdeholl et al., 2010, p. 60).

Another experiment worth noting is Ira Shor's use at the City College of New York of the After Hours Group, a small group of students from a course who had the time and inclination to meet Shor after class and serve as a conduit for the concerns, requests, and frustrations of the rest of the students (Shor, 1996). In her collection of stories from The Open Book, an adult literacy program in Brooklyn, New York, Ramdeholl (2010) also describes initiatives that that program took, such as appointing literacy learners as teachers, creating a decision-making *Student Teacher Council* (that had mixed success), regularly publishing students' work, and having students as the majority voice on committees making hiring decisions regarding new teachers.

For the rest of this chapter I want to describe some specific techniques that I use in my own teaching to democratize my classrooms.

The Critical Incident Questionnaire

The Critical Incident Questionnaire (CIQ) is a technique I have already alluded to in the previous chapter. It is a single-page form I hand out to students once a week at the end of the last class of the week. It comprises five questions, each of which asks students to write down some details about events or actions that happened in the class that week. Its purpose is not to ask students what they liked or didn't like about the class, though that information inevitably emerges. Instead students are requested to focus on specific events and actions that are engaging, distancing, confusing, helpful, or surprising. Having this highly concrete information about particular events and actions is much more useful than reading general statements of preferences. The CIQ can be downloaded for free at my home page (http://www.stephenbrookfield.com) where you will also find case study examples of its use (Adams, 2001; Glowacki-Dudka and Barnett, 2007; Keefer, 2009; Phelan, 2012).

The CIQ takes about five minutes to complete, and students are told *not* to put their name on the form. If nothing comes to mind as a response to a particular question, they are told to leave the space blank. They are also told that at the next class I will share the group's responses with them. The five questions on the form are:

1. At what moment in class this week did you feel most engaged with what was happening?

2. At what moment in class this week were you most distanced from what was happening?

3. What action that anyone (teacher or student) took this week did you find most helpful?

4. What action that anyone took this week did you find most puzzling?

5. What about the class this week surprised you the most? (This could be about your own reactions to what went on, something that someone did, or anything else that occurs.)

Students are given the last five minutes of the last class of the week to complete this form. As they leave the room, I ask them to leave the CIQ on a chair or table by the door, face downwards. After I have collected the CIQ responses at the end of the last class of the week, I read through them looking for common themes. For a class size of thirty to thirty-five students this usually takes about twenty minutes. I look for comments that indicate problems or confusions, particularly if they are caused by my actions. Anything contentious is highlighted, as is anything that needs further clarification. Major differences in students' perceptions of the same activity are recorded as well as single comments that strike me as particularly profound or intriguing. These themes then become the basis for the questions and issues I address publicly the next time we're together.

At the start of the first class of the next week I spend three to five minutes reporting back to students a summary of the chief themes that emerged in their responses. I tell them I've conducted an elementary frequency analysis and that anything that gets mentioned on three or more forms (which usually represents approximately 10 percent of the class) will be reported. I let them know that I reserve the right to report a single comment if I find it to be particularly revealing or provocative. I also say that the only comments I will *not* report publicly are those in which students identify other students in a disparaging way. I inform students that if such comments are included on the form I will either reframe them as general observations or problems the group needs to address, or communicate them in a private, confidential conversation with the student concerned. Such conversations are usually with students who are reported on the CIQs to be dominating the class or generally throwing their weight around in an obnoxious manner.

If I have the time I will type up a one- or two-page summary and leave copies of this on students' chairs for them to read as they come in. Most times the pressure of other work means I give a verbal report. If students have made comments that have caused me to change how I teach, I acknowledge this and explain why the change seems worth making. I try also to clarify any actions, ideas, requirements, or exercises that seem to be causing confusion. Criticisms of my actions are reported and discussed. If contentious issues have emerged, we talk about how these can be negotiated so that everyone feels heard and respected. Quite often students write down comments expressing their dislike of something I am insisting they do. When this happens I know that I must take some time to reemphasize why I believe the activity is so important and to make the best case I can about how it contributes to students' long-term interests. Even if I have spoken this case before, and written it in the syllabus, the critical incident responses alert me to the need to make my rationale explicit once again.

Using the CIQ doesn't mean that I constantly change everything I'm doing because students tell me they don't like it. We all have nonnegotiable elements to our agendas that define who we are and what we stand for. To throw them away as a result of students' opinions would undercut our identities as adult educators. For example, I won't give up my agenda to get students to think critically, even if they all tell me that they want me to stop doing this. I will be as flexible as I can in negotiating how this agenda is realized, but I won't abandon it. I'll ask students to suggest different ways they might show me that they're thinking critically. I'll also vary the pace at which I introduce certain activities and exercises to take account of students' hostility, inexperience, or unfamiliarity with this process.

But for me to abandon the activity that defines who I am as an adult educator would mean that I have ceased to have the right to call myself one. So if students use their CIQ responses to express a strong opinion that challenges what you're trying to do or how you're trying to do it, you owe it to them to acknowledge this criticism. But you don't owe it to them to abandon entirely your rationale for teaching. What you need to do is make your own position known, justify it, and negotiate alternative ways of realizing your aims.

I have found the CIQ an excellent technique for unearthing power dynamics that would otherwise remain hidden from view. Knowing they have anonymity, students will disclose feelings and perceptions that they would be reluctant to speak in class. Sometimes these comments have to do with my use or abuse of my power. At other times they are about student-student power dynamics. Still other comments are intrapersonal, as students describe how surprised they are about their resistance to or acceptance of classroom activities they had previously disliked or favored. Because every person's voice carries equal weight on the CIQ, it means that the usual patterns of participation are disrupted. Through the CIQ, the quietest student in class has the same potential influence on proceedings as does the most confident or articulate.

The CIQ provides a map of where the whole learning community is on an issue, and not just the perceptions of those who feel comfortable speaking. I use it as one way to help equalize power in the class, to make sure all voices are expressed and reported out, and to draw a chart of the class's emotional geography. Nothing has been so successful for me in surfacing power imbalances in class and in helping a class identify racism, sexism, homophobia, and ableism that then needs addressing. It takes a courageous student to speak up in class on these issues, not knowing how a teacher or other students will respond. But knowing that the CIQ is anonymous, people will write honestly about painful, intense conflicts that otherwise would remain buried and unaddressed.

Chalk Talk

I have already discussed this technique in chapter 3 on discussion methods and also referred to it in chapter 4, so I will not say too much about it here. One of the reasons I love this technique is for its democratic dimension. In a very short time it produces contributions from far more people than would have been offered had I thrown the same question out to the whole class and asked for comments. As with the CIQ, the quietest student has as much power as the most articulate and verbose. The technique allows for multiple people to post simultaneously, something which can't usually happen in discussion because it is too distracting to have five or six speaking at once. The technique also meets the first condition of a democratic classroom, that of using different visual and silent ways of eliciting participation that do not privilege speech.

I have found this technique to be especially suited to the beginning of a new teaching module or to the first phases of a group project. In a very short time it produces a cognitive map of what are the main currents of thought in a group, the most provocative disagreements, and the outlier positions that need to be incorporated. Photos of the chalk talk graphic that I take and put on the course home page are returned to again and again over the course of the semester as a way of making sure the whole range of concerns are kept in mind, and to stop the interests of the most verbal moving front and center by default.

Newsprint Dialog

This is another mostly silent technique that I have used in multiple contexts—in academic classes, in staff meetings, in organizational retreats and in community forums. In 2011 a union educator put me in touch with the facilitation committee of Occupy Wall Street in New York, and I suggested using newsprint dialog as a means of soliciting democratic participation. Newsprint dialog is a way to share small group deliberations in a manner that engages all members of a wider community.

The exercise begins with people working in small groups to discuss the same question or decide their response to the same issue. I explain that I want them to record a summary of their discussion on newsprint and that members should make this summary as detailed and specific as possible because everybody else in the room will be reading it carefully after it's posted. When they are ready, groups hang a summary of their deliberations on the wall. I then post a blank sheet of newsprint immediately adjacent to each group's posting.

What would usually happen at this point is that a debriefing of small group postings would proceed, with each group standing by their posting and giving a verbal summary and interpretation of its contents. In my experience this is often antidemocratic. First, as the group reporter is summarizing his group's postings, the rest of the class are watching the teacher's face to see how she responds to the summary. Is she smiling or frowning, nodding enthusiastically or shaking her head sadly from side to side? Does she take notes and ask questions, and if so are these interrogatory or appreciative? Does she make eye contact with the group leader as he's reporting, or does she look at the ground? From all these behaviors students draw meanings as to what a group has done well or badly. The class's attention thus becomes focused on the teacher's evaluative reactions rather than the content of the group's report, thus further entrenching the teacher-student divide.

Second, as members of a group hear their reporter summarizing what the posting means, they are sometimes left silently asking themselves "Was I in the same group he's talking about?" This is because the reporter's version of the group's conversation seems completely unfamiliar and really a statement of where the reporter stands on an issue. Third, the first two or three groups to report do so when energy is highest in the room and therefore benefit unfairly. Groups four, five, and six are left saying "ditto," "as group one also found," or "we found the same thing as group two" as energy slides limply out of the room.

In Newsprint Dialog these difficulties are elided. Once groups have posted their sheets, the teacher tells every student to get a magic marker and to wander around the room at will. Whenever they see something they want to respond to, they write their response directly on the original sheet of newsprint or, if there's not enough space for that, on the blank sheet posted next to it. I tell them to ask questions on the newsprint, to seek clarification for anything that's unclear, to make comments about responses they find helpful or confusing (and to write why this is so), and to comment on contradictions or omissions they observe.

When I do this two things always happen. First, students mill about the room individually reading the postings. Rarely do they stay in their original small group. Second, within about ten seconds total silence descends on the room. And this usually lasts for about ten minutes as people move around, read, and post. The interesting thing about this silence is that I have not said anything about Newsprint Dialog being a silent activity (in the way I do with Chalk Talk). But though silence is never mentioned in my setting up the activity, it always ends up being an integral part of the process.

As with Chalk Talk, the Newsprint Dialog has three democratic merits. First, it leads to much greater participation than would have been the case had we done the small group reports and asked for questions and discussion after each group had reported. In Newsprint Dialog the original postings and the blank sheets next to them quickly fill up. Often one person's response to the original posting becomes the start of a new thread of comments and responses. In about ten minutes the exercise allows a large group to do a pretty thorough debriefing of small group deliberations in a way that involves the majority of participants.

Second, Newsprint Dialog disrupts the usual pecking order of contributors. The verbally articulate person's postings have no more prominence than a posting by someone who has remained silent in class up to that point. Indeed, it may well be a quiet student's question written on one of the sheets that produces the greatest number of postings in response to it. Third, as with Chalk Talk, the exercise uses both silent and visual modalities, thus making it congenial to students whose cultures value silence or students who learn in a visual rather than in an auditory way.

The Three-Person Rule

The three-person rule is a very simple rule I have already mentioned that I use to stop discussions in a large group becoming the preserve of a few articulate members. Learners are told that once someone has spoken in the discussion they are not allowed to contribute again until at least three other people have spoken. The only time this rule can be broken is if someone asks the original speaker to answer a question or invites them to expand on a comment they have already made. I choose three as the number because most people seem to be able to remember the last three people who have spoken in a discussion or meeting.

When I institute this rule I expect things to be awkward until people get used to it. There will be long and uncomfortable silences that would formerly have been filled by the articulate 5 percent of students basically talking to each other. I myself as the teacher also follow the rule and struggle with my desire to chip in when I have just the right response or the perfect example to share. I have to warn students that following this rule will feel strange because of the awkward pauses, but I ask them to remember that for those who like to have time to think and process information before speaking the rule works well.

Structured Silence

If periods of quiet contemplation are an integral part of any group process, then we need to make this silence a regular part of the classroom rhythm. This can be accomplished by introducing another exercise, what I describe as periods of Structured Silence.

Every fifteen to twenty minutes you stop the class and call for a period of intentional silence of maybe two to three minutes. This is a reflective pause when students are asked to think quietly about a question such as "What issue do we most need to address in the next period of our discussion?" or "What has been missed or glossed over in the lecture so far?" You hand out 3x5 cards and students make notes in response to the question. When they've finished, the cards are handed to the front, shuffled, and you (or students you choose randomly) read out several of the cards. This helps structure the next fifteen-minute chunk of class time in a way that's responsive to students' concerns or that builds on their developing understanding. Again, it breaks the habitual reliance on speech and gives equal weight to every reflection. Given the accelerating pace of technological innovation, doing this via a class electronic whiteboard on which students can post anonymously will soon be available in many classrooms.

Nominating Questions

Another way to get students involved in decision making in the classroom is through the Nominating Questions exercise. Often when discussions move from small to large group formats, it's difficult to know which of the issues identified by the smaller groups should be focused on in the whole class conversation. The process of involving students in nominating questions gets students to start making judgments on issues of importance within a subject.

The activity starts with small groups conducting discussions on a topic or issue. They are told that at the end of the small group discussion they must list one or two questions about the issue, topic, or subject that arose during their conversation. When the small group discussion time is up, the groups list the questions each of them generated on the blackboard, or they post them around the room. The whole class is then asked to review and think for a minute or so about all the questions that have been put on the board or flip charts.

The students are then given two to three minutes to vote for no more than two questions they would like to discuss further as a whole class. They do this by all getting up, moving to the blackboard or flip charts, and individually placing checks against two of the questions (out of all those listed) that they would choose to pursue in the whole class discussion. When everyone has had a chance to record their vote, the top two or three questions chosen becomes the ones the whole class focuses on. This is one of the few times when the democracy as majority vote logic is used in my teaching.

Who's the Expert?

The final technique I want to discuss is one I learned from Clover, Jayme, Follen, and Hall's (2010) excellent book on environmental adult education. When they wish to demonstrate that participants at their workshops bring valuable knowledge and expertise, they form people into small groups and ask them to write on newsprint the most pressing questions that have arisen for them during the workshop. These questions are then hung up around the room. People usually expect the facilitator to respond to these questions, but instead participants form into small groups and each group is asked to choose a question they wish to answer.

The groups spend fifteen minutes or so discussing the question and listing the best responses to it that they generate. Each group posts its question and their responses on newsprint, and these are hung up around the room. The whole workshop then reconvenes and each group talks about its responses to the questions they were given and adds any clarifying information. I offer my thoughts on answers to the questions if someone else doesn't provide the response that I'm also thinking about.

In my own case, for example, I regularly run workshops on how to introduce critical thinking to students, clients, patients, colleagues, and community members (Brookfield, 2012). There are always several questions that people raise sooner or later: How do I challenge organizational culture or community norms and keep my job? What do I do when someone absolutely refuses to change their ways? How can I tell a superior that their words are contradicted by their actions? How do I recognize my blind spots? How do I ensure I'm modeling critical thinking? When these questions are posed, my usual response has been to answer them myself under the misguided assumption that no one else in the room has a good answer. Now, as the workshop proceeds, participants add these to a poster that records all the questions that arise during the workshop and towards the end of the event I put people into Who's the Expert? groups. Who's The Expert? underscores the fact that everybody in the room has experience and insight they can draw on to come up with good answers to difficult questions.

Summary

Democracy is messy, complex, and time consuming, and adult teachers who say they wish to work this way have to brace themselves for the fact that students will typically interpret democracy to mean that a majority vote always has the greatest democratic legitimacy. So if you profess to work democratically, you will need to spend some considerable time early on explaining your understanding of how democracy works. Most teachers, however, do have the chance to introduce some elements of democratic decision-making into their classrooms. Even if an outside licensing body has closely prescribed the curriculum and the ways learning outcomes will be assessed, there is still a range of smaller decisions students can make.

For example, students can be given responsibility for deciding classroom policies such as lateness, absence, or the frequency of breaks. They can decide which teaching methods (lectures, discussions, online) should be used in any particular week or for any particular content. They can decide which resources should be required and which should be optional. Through exercises such as Nominating Questions, they can also make content decisions. But wider institutional and societal constraints—all the financial pressures students are under and the multiple work, family, and community roles they juggle—conspire to make students resist the time, effort, and energy democracy requires. In the next chapter I take this theme of resistance in a new direction by exploring how teachers of adults can work with learners who strenuously resist the invitation (or coercion) from teachers to learn about dominant ideological values and the ways these constrain their lives.

6

Teaching About Power

I n their first day account of teaching a course on class, race and gender in a labor studies program in New York, Ramdeholl and Wells (2011) paint a picture that will be familiar to many readers. Ramdeholl—a woman of tri-racial heritage—describes how she is writing on newsprint as the students (mostly White males from a New York–based construction union) file into the room, loudly complaining about having to be in class. She turns round to face them, announces she is the teacher, and a shocked silence descends. As she introduces the syllabus, students start complaining about Barrack Obama's *Dreams From My Father* (2004) being on the reading list. They say they're not reading anything written by a socialist and refuse to buy the book. Ramdeholl insists that reading the text is nonnegotiable as students protest and kick chairs, prompting a teacher who is working next door to come in and check if everything is alright.

Wells, a White man who had worked in the construction industry, describes a muted version of these events on his first day teaching a different section of the same course. His maleness, Whiteness, and construction background mean students respond less vociferously to learning they will be reading Obama's text. There are sighs of annoyance rather than shouts and chairs being kicked. What Wells finds significant is that students resist reading the book because it is written by a politician and, in the students' opinion, all politicians are the same.

This same fatalism is expressed repeatedly throughout the course as students respond to any analysis of entrenched class power by saying something along the lines of "that's how it always has been and always will be." There is a resigned acceptance of class realities that renders any attempt to look at this reality critically or to explore how things could be different as pointless in these students' eyes. Their experience teaches them that structures of power are as entrenched, enduring, and implacable as the Rocky Mountains, so studying this self-evident reality is a complete waste of time. Even with follow-up workshops (Ramdeholl and Wells, 2012), students refuse to move to a critique of structural inequity, just reasserting the ideology of individualism that ultimately people are in control of their own individual histories.

Why Do We Resist Learning About Dominant Power?

There are lots of issues raised in Ramdeholl and Wells' papers. Some have to do with identity politics and the ways students' identities shaped how they viewed the tri-racial woman and White male teacher differently. Others have to do with how people embrace a fatalistic worldview that class division has always been this way and *will* always be this way. Ramdeholl and Wells (2011) try to get the students to consider some tough questions regarding their beliefs about the president being a socialist and about entrenched class power being unchangeable: "Who benefits from presenting these ideas as facts? ... How does it work against you (us) to believe this? Who has something to gain by asking these very questions? Who has something to lose?" (pp. 551–552). For example, Ramdeholl describes her attempts to get students to notice contradictions in their own thinking, as when they declare their neighbors to be lazy freeloaders because they are immigrants, and then talk proudly about their own family histories as children or grandchildren of immigrants.

Teachers who try to push students into considering such questions have to take on a lot of obstacles. There is the fact that the sheer numbers of resistant students far outnumber and can often intimidate the lone teacher. There is the pressure teachers feel to have the course go "well," by which they mean having the students give them good evaluations at the end of the term. In today's era of learning outcomes and teacher accountability, there is the constant awareness that if students' evaluations are only average, teachers could miss promotion, not have their contract renewed, or see the course die because no one will sign up for future sections. Most tellingly, perhaps, there is the weight of years of socialization and its accompanying ideological manipulation that students have behind them. As Grauerholz (2007) points out, getting past students' ideologies is enormously complex.

For example, any teaching that undertakes a critique of a dominant ideology such as capitalism quickly earns you the label of un-American. Coupling support of capitalism with patriotic love of country is a fantastically successful and impressive example of ideological manipulation. It means that discussions of socialism or Marxism are immediately off the table, no-go areas too dangerous to dabble in. In adult education this has begun to change in the last decade (Allman, 2001; Mojab and Gorman, 2001; Holst, 2002; Brookfield and Holst, 2010; Silver and Mojab, 2011; Mojab and Carpenter, 2011; Carpenter, 2012). An interesting and evolving approach to critiquing capitalism is Sandlin's (2004; 2007b) development of critical consumer education in which she explores "culture-jammers" such as the Reverend Billy and the Church of Stop Shopping, who organize anticonsumerist revival meetings in the middle of shopping malls.

When dominant ideology lives unchallenged within students, questioning it seems dangerously antisocial and unpatriotic, or way too risky. If they are recent immigrants who have been the victim of state (Mojab, 2010) or personal (Hyland-Russell and Green, 2011) violence, they are certainly going to be wary of putting themselves in harm's way needlessly by asking critical questions. And challenging dominant power is most definitely doing that. For students to push back against this ideology needs courage. They risk punishment by dominant power, they risk committing cultural suicide and being shunned by their own community for leaving peers behind, and they are sometimes called to question very fundamental aspects of their own identity.

Despite the difficulties outlined above, there is no shortage of advice on the question of how to engage students in an analysis of power. Baptist and Rehman (2011) explore some of the most common classroom approaches: discussion-based and dialogic teaching, collaborative inquiry, the importance of narrative and story, getting students to create collages and other art forms, using popular music, theater, and video, and building a learning community in which people trust it's safe to take risks. They also emphasize the importance of extra-classroom elements such as arranging field experiences that challenge deeply held assumptions. In fact a whole host of community practices and events teach power, such as culture jamming (Scatamburlo-D'Annibale, 2010), invisible theater (Boal, 2000, 2002, 2006), Adbusters (Clover and Shaw, 2010), critical shopping (Jubas, 2012), and the Raging Grannies (Roy, 2002). In these examples, activists stage interventions in public and community spaces such as restaurants, shopping malls, military bases, and street corners to force an awareness of power relationships people take for granted.

What Teaching Practices Explore Power?

The rest of this chapter focuses on classroom-based practices in which someone is clearly in the role of designated teacher. Of course, being the teacher does not always mean standing front and center directing affairs. A teacher is someone who encourages learning and there are a myriad of ways to do that. In my own case I sometimes do look like a fairly traditional teacher, giving minipresentations from the front of the room on things I know something about, particularly if the students ask me to do that. Like Clover, Jayme, Follen, and Hall (2010), I believe that one of a facilitator's tasks is to bring relevant new ideas and supportive theoretical information to a workshop to help participants build a theoretical base.

Sometimes, however, all I do is ask questions, one of the most powerful elements in any teacher's repertoire. At other times I look like a Rogerian-inclined facilitator, serving chiefly as a resource when learners have problems. If circumstances require I am an enforcer, making sure ground rules the group has agreed on are being followed. Maybe I spend a lot of time summarizing and coding different students' responses, playing the role of codifier or meta-analyst. Sometimes teaching about power means forcing the issue and using whatever authority I have to hold students to the fire, knowing this may result in their trying to sabotage or harm me. Sometimes I have to let students squirm as they ponder a difficult idea, process a difficult comment, or struggle with practicing a difficult skill. Often I have to force myself *not* to intervene to end an uncomfortable or dramatic silence.

One thing I think I always am is a pedagogic calibrator, looking to make the course or workshop run as smoothly as a well-oiled engine by making adjustments as I hear changes and new sounds. I want what happens to be as responsive as possible to whatever I find out about how students are experiencing what's going on. This means that sometimes I need to build on serendipitous moments, link them to the focus of the course, and change direction. There's always the risk when you do this of your not making it clear enough to participants why you are taking things in a new direction. When that happens the CIQ responses will refer to the puzzling or distancing aspects of your actions, and that will allow you to clarify your rationale when the class next meets.

A good example of serendipity is provided in Goodman's (2002) description of a peace workshop she was running. During the lunch break one of the students looked out of the window to see some graffiti that said "World Peace Can't Happen," the words surrounded by arrows pointed outward. Goodman felt the energy level palpably drop as the graffiti was brought to the workshop participants' attention. However, she copied the graffiti onto a piece of newsprint, hung it up, and then carried on with the workshop, trusting that something would emerge to challenge this message. After a while a participant suddenly leaped up and added the words "Without You!" to the graffiti, and then another participant added new arrows to the graphic that pointed inward and other arrows that connected the arrows already drawn. In commenting on this experience, Goodman noted "there is a great creative energy to be realized by making use of serendipitous events" (p. 190).

The Power Students Hold

But power is not all in the hands of teachers. Students also exercise power in such situations when they push back and seek to punish teachers for their temerity. As Ramdeholl and Wells illustrate, they will try on all kinds of classroom diversions from direct confrontation (shouting and chair kicking) to a total noncompliance (refusing to respond to questions or participate in discussions). If those don't work, they will complain to your department head or institutional superior in hopes they will try to rein you in. Failing all else, they will wait patiently to punish you on end-of-term evaluations of teaching that threaten your continued employment, promotion, or tenure. In teaching a new course on war, gender and learning, Taber (2011) captures this dimension of student power when she chronicles "the ferociousness of student resistance and the ease with which I can be attacked" (p. 678). She writes of the pressure she felt to get good evaluations from students so that the course would continue and she would be helped in her quest for tenure.

Power is complexified even further when we start to investigate how different students experience power dynamics in the classroom in contrary ways. For example, during a cancer education session she was running, Cuerva (2010) describes how a participant's cell phone rang several times. On their subsequent written reflections, three students recorded how annoying this was as they were trying to learn. At the end of the workshop, however, the student receiving the calls revealed they were from her daughter who had been diagnosed with leukemia and was being admitted into hospital to receive chemotherapy. Cuerva notes "this was a wake up call to dispel judgments and assumptions about the meaning of cell phone rings. Instead of being an annoying interruption it was reframed as a living contribution to the richness of our ongoing, shared story. Life happens" (p. 85).

In classrooms where a minority of students is from a particular racial or class background, attempts by teachers to support such students can backfire, shutting down these students' contributions or even causing them to leave the class entirely. Cale's analysis of his attempt to work critically and democratically in a community college freshman composition class teaching writing through the analysis of race, class, and gender in contemporary America illustrates how, in his terms, resistance becomes reproduction (Cale, 2001). Despite his giving lectures critiquing the concept of meritocracy and outlining capitalism's deliberate creation of an underclass, Cale notes "once I allowed the 'common sense' of the dominant ideology to be voiced, nothing could disarm it" (Cale and Huber, 2001, p. 16).

It did not matter that a disproportionately large amount of time was spent in criticism of this ideology. As long as Cale permitted his White students (the majority in the class) to voice their own opinions regarding racism—opinions based on their own experiences as adults—the focus was continually shifted away from White privilege and toward discussions of reverse discrimination and Black "problems." Cale refreshingly and courageously admits that his efforts to work democratically by respecting all voices and encouraging the equal participation of all learners "actually helped to silence some of my students, to reinforce the dominance of the status quo, and to diminish my own ability to combat racism, sexism, and classism" (Cale and Huber, 2001, p. 17). He concludes that his use of "democratic" discussion achieved little effect other than to provide "opportunities for students to attack and silence oppositional thinkers, including myself" (p. 17).

Setting the Tone

Before trying out any of the exercises or activities described in this chapter, there is a lot you can do to set a tone for learning. First, you can pay attention to the physical space and the cues students pick up when they enter the room. How are the chairs organized—in circles or rows, a rectangle or scattered randomly around the room? I often have recorded music playing and sometimes a music video—Sweet Honey in the Rock's "Ella's Song" is a favorite, Paul Robeson singing the altered lyrics to "Old Man River" another, Billy Bragg's "Help Save the Youth of America" a third.

Then comes the moment of truth when you open your mouth for the first time to welcome participants to the course or workshop. Before you ask anyone to introduce themselves, you must do it yourself. I have two introductions that I use. The first is my autobiography as a learner and how my experiences as a student have shaped who I am as a teacher. Here I talk about being labeled a mediocre student in high school, scraping into the college track, failing part of my high school completion exam, and having all the university places I had offered to me withdrawn. I talk about eventually getting into a technical institute and doing a degree there but performing poorly. I then describe how, when I finally talked my way onto a master's degree, I failed the exam. My point is that all these experiences made me suspicious of standardized evaluations and gave me sympathy and insight into students whom the system labels mediocre. Because I now have a credible reputation as a scholar (my title is Distinguished University Professor for heaven's sake!), I argue that "official" definitions of a person's worth in any sphere are often suspect. I hope that talking about my failing experiences as a learner reduces some of the distance between participants and myself.

Another introduction I use is the one I included at the start of *Teaching for Critical Thinking* (Brookfield, 2012) describing my history of depression. This is a bit more risky, but it's well suited to a course where examining power and ideology are the focus. I describe how I realized that one of the biggest obstacles to my seeking professional help was the way the ideology of patriarchy had lodged itself inside me. Because I had uncritically assimilated the notion that men were logical, rational, and could think their way out of problems, I refused to seek professional help. Going to therapy and using pharmaceuticals were to me signs of weakness. All this was bound up with an ideologically implanted notion of manly strength.

I explain how this refusal to seek help was itself an example of hegemony, of me acting in a way that seemed common sense and desirable but that actually was working against my own best interests. These are all pretty personal disclosures, and I only do it when it's appropriate. But in a session in which I'm trying to get students to see how dominant ideology is embedded in their daily thoughts and actions, I believe it's entirely appropriate to begin with an example of how one of those ideologies wrecked my life for several years. The trick is to make sure students see that you're using a personal story to teach about an important aspect of the material, not to portray yourself as some sort of heroic figure.

As a general rule I always try to introduce a challenging idea with a story of how it has somehow helped illuminate my life. If

I can't think of such an example, I'd find it hard to justify trying to convince anyone else that the idea is important. When I teach about hegemony, I also use the example described at length in *The Power of Critical Theory* (Brookfield, 2004) of how my acceptance of the notion of adult education as a vocation led to me to work all waking hours, visiting community groups or running educational clinics every night of the week. No surprise that I got divorced and that I've had three collapses at work that put me in the emergency room. When I teach about the unbridled consumerism that goes with capitalism, I describe how I gladly take on extra consulting work to pay for the twenty guitars I own. There, I've said it! I own twenty guitars. Who can possible play more than one guitar at a time?

On capitalism I also talk about how the commodification of learning and teaching is lodged inside myself. For example, although I oppose the commodification of learning—the way people's creative engagement with new skills or ideas are turned into a thing that can be measured precisely—I commodify my own practice by believing I've only done a good job if I get a student rating of over 4.5 on a 5-point Likert scale evaluating my teaching. I love it when I get the highest possible performance appraisal rating and fret over judgments that my work is merely "good." I talk about how the language of economic exchange has insidiously worked its way into my conversations, as when I say how important it is to "own" an idea, to get students or colleagues to "buy into" my suggestions for a course, or how I have "invested" in my relationships. I describe how I embody what Fromm (1956) called the social character of capitalism—someone who is punctual, organized, and orderly, who always comes in on time and who exceeds previously declared expectations. When I handed in the draft of this book six months before the projected submission date, I was suitably pumped-up, reveling in my superhuman ability to beat deadlines!

After I have talked about how dominant ideology lives in me, I then try to link this idea to the actual practice of the course or workshop people have signed up for. For example, when I teach graduate courses to educators, counselors, trainers, professional developers, and consultants, I often try to run the class as a professional development experience. But the university and its wider accreditation body requires written evidence that learning has happened. It doesn't matter how diligently people worked in classroom exercises or how much they helped peers to learn during the workshop, the way their learning is assessed is through a paper, an artifact, an object. So when I introduce the requirements for the paper, I tell students this is an excellent example of what critical theory calls objectification and commodification. Learning—the creative flow of collaborative exploration—is required to be converted into a paper that follows APA guidelines and has a minimum word limit if it is to be taken seriously by the institution. I call the paper the "commodified artifact" for the course. This is such a good example, so close to home, that when students e-mail me their papers the message header is often "Here is my Commodified Artifact"!

Finally, I am as explicit as possible in trying to name any positional power or authority I enjoy over students. I tell students I want to be as transparent as possible regarding how I exercise power and that the "elephant" in the adult educational classroom is teacher power. I say I have an agenda I am working from, expectations about what should happen, and, if it's a course students are taking as part of a formal program, that I will be using certain criteria to assess students' work. This may all sound heavy-handed and authoritarian, as my attempt to show them who's the boss. If that's how students perceive me, then that fact is immediately recorded on the first class CIQ responses, and I can come back and address the issue in the second class.

My intent in naming my power is not to intimidate, but to clarify that power is in the room. Part of teaching against power is to be aware of its presence. I try to be respectful and collegial, not to use sarcasm, ridicule or bullying, to use participatory, democratic, and dialogic approaches (see chapters 3 and 5), and to encourage students to take control over learning (see chapter 4). But none of that alters the fact that I have the ability to exercise power, influence and control, and that I can call on the full weight of institutional sanctions if I choose to. It's a major mistake in any organizational setting to be coy about your power. People know it's there and will talk about how you use it when you're out of earshot. Far better, in my view, to acknowledge that reality and to disclose the rationale behind your use of power.

An Icebreaker: Power Calisthenics

A way to begin teaching about power and ideology, and one that takes some of the stultifying seriousness out of the occasion, is to make people do something that is out of the ordinary, preferably something that involves bodily movement and that eschews words. One example of this is Power Calisthenics, an idea I got from Clover, Jayme, Follen, and Hall's (2010) book on environmental adult education. The authors describe their use of Green Activist's Calisthenics, in which participants stand and follow the leader who puts them through exercises such as the Who's in Charge Shrug (relieving tension in the shoulders while shrugging off responsibility), the Side-Stepping the Issue (moving from one foot to the other to avoid dealing with a problem), the Leadership Twist (twisting from one side to the other to hear all viewpoints and criticisms), and the Fundraising Bend (stopping to pick up coins from the street).

I took this idea and adapted it as Power Calisthenics. Here are the moves I propose to learners:-

The Counter-Hegemonic Push-Back Push your arms out repeatedly in front of you in an attempt to push back against the way hegemony has ensnared you.

The Alliance Builder Extend both arms full length to the side than bring them back to your chest in a gesture beckoning others to join you in your change effort.

The Repressive Tolerance Jog Run in place for a few seconds. This illustrates how repressive tolerance tricks you into thinking you are making forward progress when in fact things are staying just the same.

Watch Your Back Put your hands on your hips and twist to your left and right to see who is behind you. This can be to check your allies are still with you and that you are not working alone in taking on power. Or it can be to see who is trying to stab you in the back!

The Manipulation Stoop Put your head in your hands and repeatedly bend over as you realize how you've been manipulated or betrayed by someone in your organization or community you trusted. This was because what they said and what they did were in complete opposition.

The Collective Reach People stand in a circle and hold hands. At the count of three they all raise their hands in the air to symbolize their effort to reach the goals they aspire to. Participants govern how often the whole group does this. When someone shouts out something that the group believes represents a move forward in the quest for a better world, the whole group raises their arms to signal their desire to work for this outcome collectively.

Pretty hokey, eh? Well, not as much as you'd expect. I'm English by birth so grew up very self-conscious about participating in icebreakers or, indeed, about any kind of physical demonstration. I didn't even shake hands with my Dad till late in his life. But there is something playfully enlivening about the physicality of Power Calisthenics. I also encourage people to build Power Calisthenics into the rhythm of learning about how to challenge dominant ideology. So, if someone brings up an example of how they refused to follow a script that dominant ideology had written for them, someone else often jumps up and starts to do the Counter-Hegemonic

Push Back. Or maybe I'll do it myself as the student is speaking. When someone describes how their change efforts were skillfully headed off by leaders in an organization or community, I hope that someone will break into the Repressive Tolerance Jog so I won't be forced to do it myself!

An Alternative Way of Introducing Learners: The Power Bus

In the 1960s The Who sang a song titled "Magic Bus." I like to play this at the beginning of another icebreaker that I also learned from Clover, Jayme, Follen, and Hall (2010), one I call the Power Bus. In their workshops on environmental education, one of the ways the authors find out who is in their workshops is by using the notion of the different experiential buses people have ridden to get to the workshop. They cluster chairs together and put a sign such as health, education, or church on the front chair of the group. When participants enter the room they enter the bus that represents their work experience and tell each other about the activist and professional journeys they took to get to the workshop. Buses then unload and the groups form the whole workshop and talk about the ways their different journeys link to the overall themes of the workshop.

I altered this exercise to represent the experiences of and struggles with power and ideology that brought people to the workshop. One approach is to have buses that correspond to dominant ideologies. Here the signs are Capitalism, White Supremacy, Militarism, Patriarchy, Classism, Heterosexism, and Ableism. As participants enter they sit in the bus that represents the ideology they most struggle against or the one they wish to learn more about. Another way is to label the buses with different kinds of power dynamics. Some of these represent common experiences of feeling abused by the exercise of power, such as Covert Surveillance, When Words Contradict Actions, Caught by Hegemony, and When Deviance

Is Punished. Others represent more positive experiences, such as Empowered to Act, Power Used Transparently, Realizing Collective Power, or Responsible Power. I have found it relatively easy to link experiences from different buses when people talk about the journeys that brought them to this moment in their lives.

Getting Students to Decide on the Use of Power

Gary Cale, professor in the Language, Literature and Arts Department at Jackson Community College (Michigan) has devised an interesting simulation that asks students to decide on how power should be used in an imaginary society. He teaches a course titled Humanities 131: Cultural Connections, a survey course covering Western civilization from the Renaissance until the present. Students take this class mostly to fulfill a general education requirement. They are, by and large, from working-class backgrounds and are working part- and full-time jobs. The class attracts a large number of nursing and allied health students because it fulfills their humanities requirement, and it is capped at thirty members. After reading extracts from Hobbes, Locke, Rousseau, and Jefferson, Professor Cale gives students the following assignment:

Survivor Meets Gilligan's Island Meets Lord of the Flies:

A Social Contract is Born

Based on the excerpts I assigned you to read from Hobbes' *Leviathan,* Locke's *Second Treatise on Government*, Rousseau's *The Social Contract,* lecture notes on absolutism, and Jefferson's *Declaration of Independence*, I want you to devise your own social contract. Your task is to create a new society.

Your contract should be three to four pages in length.

Here's the situation: You are shipwrecked on a small island with a small group of strangers, let's say around 100 people including a dozen or more children. This island is uninhabited and is not paradise; in other words, you will have to work and work hard to survive.

Fishing/crabbing and local fauna will provide you with some of your protein needs, but will not be enough to keep you all fed and healthy. You will need to harvest a variety of indigenous fruits and vegetables as well.

Some of the more intrepid amongst you have been able to salvage some tools and supplies from the ship—an axe, a stray pot or two, a few kitchen utensils, and survival gear in the lifeboats including fishing tackle. A few suitcases washed up on shore later on containing clothes and personal items. However, most survivors escaped with nothing more than the clothes they had on and whatever personal possessions they may have grabbed in the last moments before boarding the lifeboats.

In the devastation of the shipwreck, about 10 percent of you were injured in varying degrees of severity. Many will be able to work again soon, but a number will be unable to work for months. A few will never be able to work again. Neither rescue nor escape is possible. Sorry.

Below are some of the questions you need to consider before developing your contract.

What do you consider to be basic human needs that you want to guarantee? How will you determine what those need are? How will you define the common good? What will you and your fellow survivors be asked to give up and what will you get in return?

How will you divide up or distribute the resources, the goodies, that you harvest, gather, or kill individually? How will you handle the concept of private property? Who will own the "means of production"? How will you reward the labor of individuals?

How will you govern yourselves? Who will make the rules? Why do you think this form of "government" makes the most sense? How will you reach decisions regarding the common good, private property, resource distribution? How does your

underlying political philosophy or view of mankind determine
the kind of institutions you will create?

What will be done about dissent? What laws do you think will
be necessary? What behaviors will you criminalize? Why?

You will need to think about your basic beliefs about the nature of
people (are we nasty brutes or social animals?), about the importance
of individual rights vs. rights of the community, and about the power
of the government system you decide upon.

Many different questions may suggest themselves to you, so feel
free to follow them if they seem more productive, but these should
get you started.

Have fun with assignment, but make sure that your "contract"
is based on the concepts found in Locke, Hobbes, Jefferson, absolutism, or Rousseau. Of course, your ideas may combine elements
from any of the above. Please do not simply say that you would have
exactly the same kind of government or economic system that we
have today without justifying its continued existence. And please do
not simply describe day-to-day activities.

Students bring their written contracts to class meeting and Cale
divides students into groups of three or five survivors. He asks them
to agree on a common social contract, but to validate nonmajority
points of view if there is a huge split in the group. This contract is
turned into a poster highlighting its key points.

Groups then present their ideas to the whole class, and Cale
leads them in a debate about the relative merits of their contracts
and their reasoning. He tries to expose tacit assumptions and contradictions as well as provide contemporary examples and connections to twenty-first century America and past political/social
practices. In essence, the discussion is generally where the real
discoveries occur. Students attempt to defend their notions of

meritocracy, the acceptance or abolition of private property, restrictions on the common good, nascent capitalism, primitive and utopian socialism, and so on. Cale says he usually leaves the discussion exhausted but exhilarated by the frankness of students' views and the engagement they demonstrate.

Using Story and Personal Narrative

Story and personal narrative—I use the terms interchangeably—are powerful tools in teaching against power. This fact is well known in adult education, where story is used to assist in transformative learning (Hoggan, 2009; Nelson, 2009; Tyler, 2009) and activism (Newman 2006). An anthology on *Narrative Perspectives in Adult Education* (Rossiter and Clark, 2010) examines how stories help people make sense of later life (Randall, 2010), how digital storytelling combines image and words (Rossiter and Garcia, 2010), and the way dominant and counternarratives are evident in television (Redmon Wright, 2010). In Europe, biographical and life history perspectives are the terms more commonly used to describe this approach (Merrill, Alheit, Anderson, and West, 2007; Stuart, Lido, and Morgan, 2011).

I myself teach a course annually at the University of St. Thomas with a colleague, Tom Fish, called Leadership Narratives. One of the texts we teach from is a book that Tom worked on with our colleague Sarah Noonan called *Leadership Through Story* (Noonan and Fish, 2007). Although some of the stories in that book are from admired public leaders such as Nelson Mandela or Martin Luther King Jr., many others are from students who have taken the Leadership Narratives course previously. As Sarah and Tom have taught previous iterations of the course, they are always on the alert for good stories that students share. I find that teaching from a book that contains stories collected from former students in the program is a wonderful way to encourage current students to take risks when sharing their own leadership narratives.

Three Pedagogic Uses for Story

But story should not be used just for story's sake. There has to be a thought out rationale why you're emphasizing this approach. In my own teaching I use story for three different purposes depending on the context: to help students learn a difficult idea or practice, to build credibility in the face of resistance, and to vary classroom tempo.

To Help Learn a Difficult Idea or Practice

A good story can help make inaccessible material much more readily understandable to students. For example, I sometimes have to teach a class on critical theory, which, as a body of scholarship, has its own dense and intimidating language (trying saying phenomenological, dialectically, and hegemonic in the same sentence). To illustrate what I think are the crucial ideas sometimes buried behind jargon, I deliberately use stories to convey a point. Or, if students are talking about their own experiences, I try to show how they illustrate certain concepts embedded in the material. I do this deliberately because students tell me they understand the material much better if a story is used to illuminate it. Hoggan's (2009) description of how he used his own story of going into shock (after he was involved in a car crash) to teach his students how to recognize symptoms of shock in patients is a nice example of this.

Of course, not every teaching unit allows for you to draw on personal experience in this way. How can you draw on your experience of being an electron or a Chi-square? But even in information-heavy subjects in which there is little debate about the facts, you can still draw on your personal experiences of how you learned the material you are now teaching, how you realized you'd made a mistake in understanding the material, how you broke through a learning blockage to come to a clear understanding or correct application of the material, and so on. And, of course, given that every subject and discipline has its own "regime of truth," to borrow Foucault's

(1980) term, every scientist, engineer, mathematician, biochemist, or botanist has stories to tell of what happened when they challenged that regime by asking difficult questions, disputing accepted theories and practices, or refusing to do what a teacher or supervisor requested.

To Build Credibility

There have been many times when I've had to face a skeptical audience of students or colleagues. I've had to teach required classes that some students clearly did not want to attend and to run faculty development events where teachers attended only because it was a mandatory development day. Being an academic who's published a lot and who holds the title of Distinguished University Professor works against me in those situations, because I seem so far removed from the students' experiences or appear to have little appreciation of what a "real" teacher does. The preconceptions people have of a Distinguished University Professor actually undermine my authority and set people up to resist or dismiss me.

In each of these situations I find that an early story about how I myself have resisted learning helps establish my experiential bona fides in the students' minds. So I like to talk of my own history of poor performance as a student as a way of demonstrating that my history of learning may have some similarities to their own. When I face a group of hostile teachers, I try to tell a story about a recent event in my own classroom—often one in which I myself tried to deal with resistant, apathetic, or overtly hostile students—to show them that my world is not so dissimilar to theirs. A good story that an audience recognizes can often reduce the distance the audience is trying to create between them and me.

To Vary the Classroom Tempo

My working assumption as a teacher is that every class session should have at least three learning modalities present, three different ways in which students can engage with the material. Story

is a nice addition to my repertoire. Even if I am faced with an audience of several hundred in an auditorium (something that happens
once or twice a month), I feel my lecture, speech, or keynote address needs to include three modalities. So I may (a) periodically
use buzz groups to generate questions, (b) set up a live twitter feed
on a screen next to my Power Point to generate responses, and (c)
tell a story to illustrate how to implement certain practices. When
an appropriate story is brought into my presentation, the whole at-
mosphere changes. People relax because now they feel they're not
doing the "important" stuff of learning facts, skills, or concepts, and
in that moment of relaxation they may actually be more open to
learning. Or, if the energy has dropped because I've been camping
out in the zone of theory or fact for too long, a story can perk people
up and introduce a new energy.

Considerations for Modeling Storytelling About Power

One of the dangers of using storytelling is becoming beguiled by
narrative for narrative's sake. The point of using stories to teach
about power is to help people uncover and challenge dominant ideologies or to understand how power operates, not to provide a pleas-
ant or diverting interlude. For teachers who tell stories as a means
of teaching about power, four considerations need to be borne in
mind. These are that (1) the way the story connects to a learning
point must be made very explicit, (2) the story should be told critically, (3) there should be generalizable elements in the story, and
(4) the story should contain some element of hope. Let me examine how to teach through story in ways that ensure these four things
happen.

Connecting the Story to Learning

If you're going to tell a story that illustrates how power operates, or
one that shows how it can be used to challenge dominant ideology,
the connection should always be clear. Sometimes this can be done
very explicitly as when the teacher as storyteller names the specific

elements of dominant ideology (militarism, capitalism, patriarchy, and so on) addressed in the story. This was the approach I described earlier when linking my refusal to seek treatment for depression to the way patriarchy had a much stronger hold on me than I'd imagined.

An alternative approach is to tell students a story having to do with power dynamics but to leave out any specific reference to power or dominant ideologies. The task for the students is to hear the story and to identify, either individually or in groups, how power is being exercised and which ideologies are in play. One way I like to do this is by putting categories on the board and then asking students to write down moments in the story when they felt a particular event illustrated power or ideology. The categories I list on the board are:

Power—repressive power, emancipatory power, disciplinary power, collective power

Ideology—militarism, capitalism, White supremacy, patriarchy, ableism, heterosexism

Depending on the size of the group, I ask students to come to the board and write directly on there any events in the story that they felt illuminated a certain kind of power or illustrated the presence of a particular ideology.

Here's an example of how this could work. I first used the brief story below—"Experiential Deflowering"—in an edited collection titled *Power in Practice* (Cervero and Wilson, 2001).

Experiential Deflowering

I am seventeen years old in the final year of grammar school in England. A group of my peers and I have been chosen to participate in a week long symposium at Oxford University, designed for high school students who show academic promise and who would therefore be suitable to take the Oxford entrance exam themselves. I am flattered by being chosen to be part of this group and to have the chance to play at being a bona fide intellectual—an Oxford undergraduate wannabe no less.

The first morning of the symposium arrives, and we are told we will spend most of our time in seminar groups. Our opening event is a general address by a well-known Oxford professor of moral philosophy. I understand his greeting of welcome to the symposium but am baffled by pretty much everything else he says. A couple of phrases register—moral imperative, existential dilemma—largely because they are uttered in a tone of portentousness that signifies now we are talking about something *serious* and *important*. I dutifully write them down.

After morning coffee we split into discussion groups. As I take my chair I am gripped by panic. I know I am stupid—a hard worker but someone with no intellectual flair. I knew it was an accident that I was selected to attend this symposium. What can I do to stave off the humiliation that awaits me? I decide to beat the game of intellectual one-upmanship that I know is coming by working the phrase "existential dilemma" into the conversation in the first sixty seconds of the discussion. This I manage somehow to do.

The discussion leader asks me why I think what I've just talked about is an example of an existential dilemma. There's a long silence before I stumble out a pitiful explanation—a stream of consciousness string of the most impressive words I know—which actually is devoid of any meaning. Another silence follows. I know the group are embarrassed at my idiocy and the fact that they have to endure this dolt in their midst. Then and there I resolve to keep my mouth shut for the duration of the week—a resolution I follow to the letter.

This is less a story about a specific ideology, though classism is certainly in there. Part of my impostorship is that I sound like a middle-class Englishman but I was actually born in one of the toughest parts of Liverpool, in Bootle ("Brutal Bootle" as it's not so affectionately known). Liverpool is a proud working-class city and Bootle is an emblematic inner city district in Liverpool. All of my life as an educator, I have been plagued by the sense that I don't have a "real" job because I'm not making anything—a common feeling among working-class academics (Frye et al., 2005). But rather than specific ideologies, I think what "Experiential Deflowering" really addresses is power.

Coding the Story

Here's how I get students to connect the story to learning about power.

1. I hand out the story to them so they have a written record. I give them a couple of minutes to read the story.

2. The students have the chance to ask me questions about the story. These questions must all be requests for information. If they break from that rule and ask me questions about what my interpretation of the story is, I explain I won't answer them but that I'll tell them my interpretation later. Even answering very simple questions like "Why did you call this story experiential deflowering?" can help students with their subsequent analysis.

3. After all the questions have been posed, I then turn it back to the students and ask them to answer two not so simple questions: (1) Whose interests are served in the story? and (2) Whose interests are harmed?

Students then tell me which elements of the story involve different kinds of power. I give them a fourfold classification to help them identify different kinds of power. These four categories are (1) *repressive power*—power used to constrain options, limit freedom, or maintain the status quo, (2) *emancipatory* power—power experienced as motivating or galvanizing and that fuels activism and the desire for change, (3) *disciplinary power*—power that someone in the story exerts on themselves to make sure they stay in line, and, (4) *collective power*—power where the possibility of alliances or movements suggests itself. This obviously works best if you've spent some time discussing what these terms mean and given previous examples of them.

I also ask the students to look for specific examples of *ideological manipulation and control*—instances in which an action or event is framed by someone in authority as being self-evidently a good thing that benefits the majority, when in fact it is harming them.

If the group is large (which for me is around eighty), I ask students to work in small groups of five or six to discuss where they see these different kinds of power in the story or where they identify ideological manipulation. If the group is smaller—say fifteen to twenty—I will often put headings for the four kinds of power, and a fifth heading for ideological manipulation, on the board and ask students to go to the board and write their responses.

I give my own interpretation of the story, which doesn't usually come as much of a surprise since it's embedded in how I've constructed and recounted my narrative. I respond to the students' attempts to identify power and ideology, and talk with them about new interpretations and dimensions that have suggested themselves to me.

In the "Experiential Deflowering" analysis students overwhelmingly identify how I exercise disciplinary power on myself. First, because I've internalized the competitive ethic of capitalism (an example of ideological manipulation students occasionally identify) seen in my desire to get in first in the discussion and say something that sounds intelligent. I'm acting that way, the students tell me, because I assume that's how a smart student acts. Second, students say I'm exercising disciplinary power after my disastrous attempt to sound intelligent by enjoining myself to stay silent and not to open my mouth again. Here the students tell me I am switching from an ideology of *competitiveness* to an ideology of *compliance*, which holds that the best students are those who stay quiet and learn from the acknowledged experts.

I have found that this very short story (only 358 words to be exact) is a wonderful way to teach some basic concepts of critical theory. I can of course try to give crystal clear and accessible explanations of concepts such as disciplinary power and ideological manipulation, but the story concretizes what disciplinary power looks like in a helpful way. In fact it has worked so well that I am now trying to write teaching stories for all the complex concepts in critical theory that students tell me are impossible to understand.

Doing a Critical Analysis of the Story

As mentioned earlier, a story should be more than a compelling narrative that connects to the learning the teacher is trying to encourage. It should also be open to critical analysis. Stories are, after all, personal constructions, framed by our own inclinations and preferences. When I try to get students to analyze a story critically, I focus on them doing one specific thing: on hunting the assumptions that are embedded in the "facts" of the story and in how the story is constructed and told. Here's how hunting assumptions looks using the "Experiential Deflowering" story as an example.

Hunting Assumptions

In small groups, discuss the kinds of assumptions embedded in the "Experiential Deflowering" story. Look for:

Causal Assumptions — These are assumptions we make about cause and effect. For example, "If I increase my caffeine intake I will be able to stay awake longer and get more good work done."

Prescriptive Assumptions — These are assumptions we make about how we ought to or should think or act. For example, "A good student always submits her work on time."

Paradigmatic Assumptions — These are the more deeply embedded assumptions that we take for granted. They seem so obviously common sense statements of reality that we don't recognize them as assumptions when they are pointed out to us. For example, "Adult students are self-directed."

Assumptions of Power — These are specific assumptions we make about how power operates. For example, "Rotating the chair at meetings prevents any individual voice from dominating" or "Working in teams builds trust and group cohesion."

Hegemonic Assumptions — These are assumptions we believe are widely shared and ones we embrace enthusiastically without realizing they are harming us. For example, "A good teacher of adults is available to students 24/7."

Applying the Hunting Assumptions categories to the "Experiential Deflowering" story, students have proposed the following assumptions they believe are embedded in the way I tell the story.

Causal Assumptions

My selection to attend the Oxford week is due to some kind of administrative error.

If something is spoken in a certain way it must be important.

If I sound smart people will think I'm smart.

If I stay silent after a mistake people will eventually forget my error.

My comment has caused people to think I'm an idiot

Prescriptive Assumptions

A good student speaks well and uses academic terms appropriately.

A good student never says anything wrong.

Paradigmatic Assumptions

I have made a dramatic mistake.

Everyone is watching me.

The keynote speaker is more intelligent than I.

I am stupid but have hidden it up till now.

Assumptions of Power

The discussion group is a contest at which I need to shine.

It's important for me to impress people and be taken seriously.

I will impress people by speaking in an "intellectual" way.

The discussion leader's question is designed to humiliate me.

The silence following his question to me is designed to humiliate me.

My poor response to the question has caused the group to lose respect for me and has resulted in my being marginalized.

Hegemonic Assumptions

To be taken seriously I need to speak intellectually.

If I go to Oxford University I will demonstrate my superiority.

An Oxford education is the ultimate experience I should strive for.

As I hope is clear, a 358-word story can lead to a lot of useful analysis. If there is sufficient energy in the group and I feel the story still has some traction, I may do one more thing—ask students to pose alternative interpretations of the story. These are versions of the same events covered in the story that do not have the interpretation I placed on them. Alert readers will recognize that this is another implementation of the basic protocol I illustrated in chapter

2 with the Scenario Analysis and the Critical Conversation Protocol exercises. Here are two alternative interpretations students have proposed, for "Experiential Deflowering," one more charitable than the other.

> "Everything is about you—Stephen—in this story. You seem to think people are watching you carefully waiting for you to slip up and make a fool of yourself. This seems pretty paranoid, not to say self-centered. You're not the center of the universe. It could be that no one really noticed what you did, and that if they did, they didn't dwell on it. The way you tell this story it's as if all your actions have some great significance. Get over yourself."

> "The whole way you've told this story is very down on yourself. You say your being selected was a mistake, you call yourself stupid and an idiot, and you say you've caused yourself humiliation. You seem to interpret everything that happened in a way that hurts you. I didn't realize your self-esteem was so poor! Maybe the other students liked that you spoke first and broke the ice. Maybe they admired you for doing your best to respond to the discussion leader's question. Maybe they actually didn't think your first or second comments were that off the mark. I mean no one, not the teacher or the students, said anything bad about you in the story. And there seems to be no hostility that anyone displayed to you. So how come you're being so negative?"

Identifying Generalizable Elements in the Story

In some important ways every story is unique, experienced by particular people in a particular space and time. But every story also has generalizable elements embedded within it. Sometimes these are similarities that readers see between the story and their own experiences. Here the analysis often stays at the level of being glad that someone else has experienced the same kinds of things that you have. Sometimes listeners take a leap across contexts and draw lessons, tips, or insights from the story that they transfer to their own situations. Here something in the original story prompts a new idea about how to respond creatively to an analogous situation.

One of the few things I can rely on when I teach about power is that pretty much every adult I work with has felt they've been on the wrong end of power exercised either brutally (with the intent of excluding, marginalizing, humiliating, or punishing someone) or stupidly (with little forethought to how that exercise of power is perceived and what its consequences will be). There is also a chance (though definitely not a certainty) that people will have some experience of seeing power used well. Sometimes that's because an individual or group with positional authority or community credibility uses that authority to support learning and growth in others, or to encourage them to form empowering alliances with like-minded others. Sometimes it's because a collective realizes the power it holds is greater compared to when individuals act alone. The leaders that Stephen Preskill and I profiled in *Learning as a Way of Leading* (Preskill and Brookfield, 2008) all exercised power in this supportive way.

To get students to search for generalizable elements in a story I use a specific technique, the Power Trajectory. Here I try to get students to understand the line or arc of the story, the direction in which the narrative goes, and in particular the changes in direction that occur as power is used or experienced in different ways. The instructions for this exercise are below.

The Power Trajectory

As you read the story, try and identify the narrative trajectory the story contains about the use of power. What was the first exercise of power? When did characters in the story first become aware of power? What was the first moment of pushing back against power? When was power combined in a collective effort? How did different power dynamics in the story change or develop with events? What were the main turning points in how power was used or experienced? Where did power end up?

Spend five minutes making notes on your own about (a) the initial trigger event in the story where power was clearly present, (b) the key moments when power is exercised, either to repress or galvanize, (c) the major turning points in the way power is either used or experienced, and (d) how power is portrayed at the story's end compared to its portrayal at the opening.

1. Form a group with three or four others and share your power trajectories. Spend fifteen minutes composing a group trajectory that tries to represent in a graphic manner some of the common themes you noted in each other's trajectories. You can use any graphic or visual you want to represent your trajectory. When you're done, post your trajectory where the whole class can see it.

2. Wander around the room and view the other trajectories groups have posted. As you do this, be thinking about situations in your own life when you have seen power exercised or displayed that fit or come close to some of the trajectories posted.

3. We will reconvene as a whole class to deal with any questions, comments, or observations people wish to make about any of the trajectories. I will try to draw on my own experience to show how the different trajectories are similar to experiences of power in my own life.

4. The homework assignment this week is for you to write a story (500–750 words maximum) drawing on your experience in any situation that illustrates aspects of the power trajectories you saw posted on the walls in class. Feel free to take photos of the postings on your cell phone to help you with this. I will also post them on Blackboard.

When we resume class the next week, I ask different students to read their stories out loud. After each one is read, I ask for others to comment on the story. I ask that comments be given either in the form of recognition or the form of advice. Recognition comments are those comments students offer about the way they've experienced a similar power dynamic in their own life, how they've experienced emotions similar to those conveyed in the story, how they recognize some of the turning points or critical incidents, or how they've questioned some of the same assumptions questioned in the story. Advice comments are ones students offer where they tell the storyteller what elements of her actions and reasoning they agree with, and what actions they would advise against or do differently. As they give their advice comments, they are enjoined to disclose how the advice they offer springs from their own personal experiences.

The Story Should Contain Some Element of Hope

In teaching about power one of the things you always risk is inducing radical pessimism. By that I mean that students are radicalized in that they become aware of how dominant ideology lives within them and underscores so many daily organizational and community practices. But the awareness of how ideology is so effortlessly manipulated and how power is so entrenched in history, culture, the state, and civil society, brings with it a resigned shrug, a feeling that the forces ranged against change are so huge and immovable that there is no point in trying to push back.

If a story that helps you to become more aware of how power and ideology operate leads only to a resigned acceptance of there being no prospect for change, then it's almost better that it not be told. So, even as we tell stories of defeat, despair, and demoralization, what we should take from them at the very least are lessons of how to avoid these things happening so disastrously in the future. When I ask students to analyze stories that seem only to illustrate the malevolent domination of power exercised to constrain and re-press, I introduce two quotes from Foucault that I feel are pertinent: "There are no relations of power without resistances; the latter are all the more real and effective because they are formed right at the point where relations are exercised" (Foucault, 1980, p. 142) and "There is no relationship of power without the means of escape or possible flight [because] every power relationship implies . . . a strategy of struggle" (Foucault, 1982, p. 225). I then ask them to conduct the Trawling for Hope exercise.

Trawling for Hope

Trawling for Hope asks students to focus on hopeful aspects of a story. As they read a story I ask them to think of how they could intervene in the story to influence its narrative trajectory so that even if the outcome was not a success, less damage was done than was contained in the original narrative. This is a variant of Boal's (2000) Forum Theater described in the next chapter, where the scene is stopped and audience members are invited to come into the scene and take it in a different direction.

Trawling for Hope can be done as a small group exercise in class, or as an individual analysis, perhaps a homework assignment. Students are directed to ask the same questions in both applications:

Trawling for Hope Instructions

You are reading a story of struggle and disappointment that illustrates how easy it is for dominant ideology to exert power to constrain people's choices, limit their thinking, and stop them pushing for change. As you read this narrative, please look for hopeful elements in the narrative by asking yourself at least three of the following questions:

Putting myself in the shoes of one of the characters in the story, how could I act differently to take the story in a different and more hopeful direction?

If I could speak to the central characters in the story, what would I tell them about how they could have acted to change the story's outcome?

What lessons do I take from this story that will help me avoid a similar situation in the future?

What did the lead character do in the story that I could build on in my own practice?

How did the lead characters push back against power and ideology?

What opportunities to push back against power and ideology did the lead characters miss?

How could the story be rewritten to lead to a powerful and more hopeful end?

What Trawling for Hope does is ask students to change the story they read or listen to so that it becomes an example of what Bell (2010) calls an emerging or transforming story. It has some similarity to the counterstorytelling approach of critical race theory, except that it is either wholly fictional or a mix of fiction and "fact" as the student draws on her own experiences to construct a counternarrative.

Summary

In this chapter I have explored some typical ways to set a tone to teach about power and described some specific exercises I use that focus chiefly on personal narratives. In the next chapter I want to broaden my analysis of teaching about power to include creative, artistic, and musical approaches in this work. But before you decide to skip that chapter because you don't think of yourself as an actor, creative artist, or musician, let me emphasize that the possession of artistic talent is completely irrelevant to whether or not these might be useful for you. I can't draw, am inhibited by acting or role-playing, and am unable to read music. But I have found all the approaches I outline in the next chapter to be adaptable to my own classrooms and workshops.

7

Teaching Using the Creative Arts

I choose the title of this chapter with some trepidation. That's because the word *arts* is such a big word. As Hoggan, Simpson, and Stuckey (2009) note, "Art carries with it some important baggage that can be limiting for adults" (p. 1). That's certainly the case for me. I have memories of being laughed at in art class, of having my stick figures providing a source of fun for other students (I am no L. S. Lowry). I remember my Dad telling me my people looked like sad cows! Combine this with the idea floating in my brain that artists are profoundly creative people engaged in producing something *significant* and you have a double whammy—a one-two punch that stops me dead in my tracks. If I'm in a workshop and the facilitator tells me I'm going to create a drawing or graphic representation of my ideas, I'm struck with panic and usually retreat to hiding in the shadows of any small group I can find!

What is even worse for me is being told that I'm going to have to use my body as a site for learning. I live so much in my head that, were I to be informed that I would be using some of the embodied reflection approaches described by Pyrch (2012) or Ryan (2012), I would probably feign a fainting fit and be taken to the emergency room! Ryan (2012) urges moving away from written and discussion-based forms of reflection so prevalent in higher education to incorporate "dance, expressive or calculated movement, mime or acting" (p. 219). Intellectually I understand that "the body as a site of knowledge can enact a system of meaningful movements to communicate ideas about the world, yet it can also be a locus of self-discovery and reflection" (p. 218). Just don't ask me to do anything kinesthetic!

Yet, as a member of a punk rockabilly band (The 99ers) I know exactly what Lester Bangs meant when he wrote of a show by The Clash "for once if only then in your life, you were blasted outside of yourself and the monotony which defines most life anywhere at any time, when you supped on lightning and nothing else in the realms of the living or dead mattered at all" (2004, p. 90). If punk rock is considered art, then absolutely it has a galvanizing effect on me in a way that, say, reading Marx doesn't. So if the definition of art is broadened to include rock and roll, TV, film, and cyberspace, then I relax. It's the high culture connotations of art, the notion that art is Mozart or the Kronos Quartet, Van Gogh or Chagall, that's intimidating.

The Aesthetic Dimension

Despite these connotations, teachers have long recognized the arts as an unusually rich source of ideas and practices for those concerned to uncover, illustrate, and teach about power. Much of this goes back to the critical theorist Herbert Marcuse (Reitz, 2000; Miles, 2012) who explored the notion that the aesthetic dimension of life contained spontaneous, nonrational, and emotional elements of our being that were potentially radical. If these could be released, they were a powerful challenge to the way ideological manipulation kept our thought within rational tramlines, what Marcuse called "one-dimensional thought" (Marcuse, 1964). Such thought privileged technical rationality that focused on solving problems that interfered with the smooth functioning of capitalism, and it labeled Utopian thinking that dealt with big ideas such as justice, freedom, or compassion as immature, not properly adult.

To Marcuse (1978), "art subverts the dominant consciousness, the ordinary experience" (p. ix) through introducing into life a dimension that does not conform to the prevailing one-dimensional logic. Hence, "the political potential of art lies only in its own aesthetic dimension" (p. xii). What art offers us is a chance of breaking with the familiar, of inducing in us an awareness of other ways of being in the world. Art "opens the established reality to another dimension; that of possible liberation" (1972, p. 87). If radical political practice is focused on creating "a world different from and contrary to the established universe of discourse and behavior" (1969, p. 73), then working to create a free society therefore "involves a break with the familiar, the routine ways of seeing, hearing, feeling, understanding things so that the organism may become receptive to the potential forms of a non aggressive, non exploitative world" (1969, p. 6).

Marcuse can get wordy, but I read him as advocating a very understandable view; namely, that when you engage with art—either as a creator or active spectator—you are living in the world in a different way. You are temporarily estranged from your typical experience of work, chores, obligation, and routine, and lifted into a different way of being. This is what Lawrence (2012b) describes as getting out of our heads. I once heard English philosopher Marghanita Laski on a radio talk show speaking about the notion of everyday ecstasy—the way listening to music for a few minutes, smelling or tasting a new food, or letting your eyes linger on something you thought to be beautiful, took you into a different and heightened sensuous way of being for a brief time each day (Laski, 1980). I think what Laski was talking about was essentially the same as Marcuse's idea that an aesthetic experience challenges the normal ways of thinking and feeling in everyday life.

The political significance of this kind of engagement with art is that it helps us break with the quotidian, the ordinary, and gives us new forms of visual and spoken language that opens us to new ways of sensing and feeling. In Marcuse's view learning these different forms of communication and perception is the inevitable precursor to social action.

Adult education that focuses on developing artistic sensibility is, in its way, as full of revolutionary potential as Freireian culture circles, participatory research, or education for party activism. Lewis (2012) explores how Freire and French philosopher Jacques Ranciere both explore aesthetic experiences as opportunities to disrupt conventional notions of who can speak and think. The politicizing function of aesthetics is why Marcuse felt that the development of the aesthetic dimension of life was as much a part of political struggle as the democratizing of decision making, rejection of consumer culture, or the abolition of the exchange economy. A liberated society presupposes a type of person with a different sensitivity "guided by the imagination, mediating between the rational faculties and the sensuous needs" (Marcuse 1969, p. 30).

Marcuse is one of the few critical theorists who racialized his analysis to include artistic expression that did not mirror Eurocentric, "high" culture. For him the Black Power movement was a "subversive universe of discourse" (1969, p. 35). In the language of Black militants, particularly their claiming of soul—"in its essence lily-white ever since Plato" (p. 36)—and their declaration that "Black is beautiful," Marcuse detected "the ingression of the aesthetic into the political" (p. 36). Black Power represented "a systematic linguistic rebellion, which smashes the ideological context in which the words are employed and defined, and places them in the opposite context—negation of the established one. Thus, the blacks 'take over' some of the most sublime and sublimated concepts of Western civilization, desublimate them and redefine them" (p. 35). To emerging African American scholars of the time, such as Lucius T. Outlaw Jr. (1996, p. xxvii), Marcuse's work was an entry point into critical theory that connected it to Black nationalist critiques of White supremacy.

Marcuse's argument was that any kind of art, even nonpolitical art like a Shakespeare play at Stratford-on-Avon or The New York

Ballet at Lincoln Center, was inherently revolutionary. It did not have to be explicitly political to lift you out of everyday experience. When it comes to teaching about power, however, I am also interested in art that is intentionally political. Many musicians, film makers, visual artists, writers, and sculptors deliberately include political images and messages as a way of teaching about the history of political struggle or illuminating aspects of that struggle that are not well known. From Paul Robeson to Chuck D, Sweet Honey in the Rock to Sister Souljah, Patricio Guzmán to Ken Loach, Woody Guthrie to Billy Bragg, Bob Marley to Joe Strummer, artists have created art with explicit political intent. This is work that teaches us about struggle: the history of struggle (Patricio Guzmán's film *The Battle of Chile* or Ken Loach's *Land and Freedom*), the costs of struggle (Billie Holliday's "Strange Fruit," or Chris Menges' *A World Apart*), the centrality of art to the struggle (*Amandla* or "We Shall Overcome"), alternative epistemologies and ontologies (Woody Guthrie's "Ship in the Sky," Mercedes Sosa's "Cambia, Todo Cambia" [Change, Everything Changes], Gil Scott Heron's "The Revolution Will Not Be Televised") and the way art builds peoples' pride.

A fine example of art with activist intent is provided in Grace, Hill, and Wells' (2009) account of what happened when attendees at the Lesbian, Gay, Bisexual, Transgender, Queer, and Allies (LGBTQ&A) preconference of the 2005 Adult Education Research Conference (AERC) produced an art installation called the Triangle Project. When the preconference ended and the main conference began, this installation was placed in the public refreshments area near the book display table. On the morning of the second day, staff of the Continuing Education Center of the University of Georgia (where the conference was being held) received complaints from parents of children attending a reading enrichment class in a room across from the art installation. The center staff then placed the installation behind a crimson curtain.

On returning from a mid-morning session to find the installation newly concealed, Grace angrily announced to the assembled participants (I was one) what had happened, denounced the attempt to block out the LGBTQ&A presence, and invited participants to post their reactions to the concealment directly onto the crimson curtains that were now opened to reveal the installation behind. As the authors document, "in that moment the art installation started to become the site of dialogue and interaction that we had hoped it would be at the conference . . . supporters posted heartfelt comments that began a process of healing and recovery from one more rightist assault" (Grace, Hill, and Wells, 2009, p. 72).

Beginning with Intuition

For those intimidated by the term *art*, a useful way to begin an artistic engagement is to focus instead on intuition. Intuition is not a dirty word for most people, and it's something that everybody acknowledges has played a role in their life. But intuition, like art, is extrarational, existing outside the world of careful calculation. Harteis and Gruber (2008) identify three common kinds of intuition that adult teachers exhibit: acting without thinking (as when no conscious rational analysis precedes action, you "just do it"), sudden inspiration (as when a new idea or practice "just comes" to you), and gut feeling (as knowing that something "just feels right" or "just feels wrong" without you knowing why). Lawrence (2008, 2009, 2012a) broadens the analysis of intuition in adult education to consider approaches such as dream analysis and intuitive painting as two methods that place intuition at the heart of creative work. Being somewhat anal compulsive, I don't feel confident or skilled enough to try either. But I do use two intuitive workshop exercises to teach about power as described below.

Intuitive Critical Incidents

This exercise begins with participants spending five to ten minutes thinking about a time when they dealt with power in an intuitive rather than a rational way. Building on Harteis and Gruber (2008) above, I ask them to focus on two types of intuition about power—resistance intuition and empowering intuition—and to identify moments when one (or both) was present.

Resistance Intuition: This would be a time when you had no clear way to deal with power that was being used to constrain or limit you, but, out of sheer frustration, you found yourself doing something that took you by total surprise. For example, when faced with a group of students who refused to say anything, I found myself telling them (almost without realizing what I was doing) that it was fine for them not to talk and that I wouldn't interpret their silence as sabotage or disinterest, but just as their way of learning. Almost immediately this got them talking and at the break several people told me they spoke up when usually they never said anything.

Empowering Intuition: This would be a time when on the spur of the moment you did something with no rational planning that served to galvanize learners into action. For example, I remember the first time I talked about the racist attitudes I had internalized over the years in front of a group of students. This happened in response to a question that came out of the blue one day in class about how to define racism. In trying to explain this was a matter of certain ideologies being embedded in organizational cultures and practices, I found myself talking about the ways I immediately granted extensions to Black students while quizzing White students at some length about why they wanted to hand in a paper late. The discussion immediately became energized as some students contested my example and we were able to delve much more deeply into this topic than was usually the case.

After their individual thinking time is complete, people form small groups of about five members to share their incidents. I ask each group to choose one or two of the most dramatic or unexpected intuitive events to report back to the whole class. I also ask them to report any insights about the nature of power uncovered at their tables. For example, in my first incident above, what the resistance people seemed to feel about speaking up was grounded in a fear of surveillance, of saying something stupid in front of the whole class. In the second incident above, it was my taking the risk to model a personal disclosure of my own learned racism that raised the energy in the room.

Word or Image Association

A second exercise to use intuition is to adapt the word or image association technique so beloved of media depictions of psychiatry. In these depictions the patient lies on the couch as the psychiatrist shows a picture or says a word, and the patient says the first thing that comes into their head. In comedy sketches the patient usually gives a sexual connotation to every the word or image suggested to them, no matter how humdrum these may be.

Word association is very simple to do. You give the class a word such as *power, resistance, action, strength,* or *solidarity* and ask them to shout out whatever image or words come into their heads. You can also do this visually by shouting out a word then giving people one minute to draw what this word conveys to them. This visual response can be as simple as choosing to put a color or combination of colors that represents the word on a piece of newsprint. Or you can ask students to draw a mathematical or any kind of shape to symbolize the word. After the minute is up, everyone holds up their visual for others to see.

Image association requires a little more preparation, as you have to find the images that you will show to students. With advances in technology, however, on any given day you can find images online from any number of daily papers across the globe that somehow pertain to power. These can be from sporting events, street scenes, commercials, or press conferences with "official" spokespersons or community activists. Now that personal photo archives can easily be accessed online, you can also use your own photographic images for this exercise.

Image association works much like word association. You show an image and then ask students to tell you what thoughts, ideas, or experiences connected to power the image suggests for them. The more complex the image, the more interesting are the responses. For example, a picture in which multiple racial groups and both genders are represented tends to provoke more varied interpretations than one with only men or women from a single racial group. This is particularly the case if the class is made up of students with different racial backgrounds.

Another variant of image association is to give a concept (oppression, empowerment, or exclusion, for example) and then allow students to search online in real time to find an image that they feel conveys some aspect of that word. I like doing this because it means that those students who are online anyway (doing e-mail, checking e-Bay listings, ordering shoes, or posting on Facebook) can now legitimately use their online presence in class. This also allows students to bring into the classroom their knowledge of sports, music, celebrity lives, or YouTube videos that have gone viral. You can put students into groups, ask them to share their online images with each other, and then choose one to share with the rest of the class. During this sharing students describe exactly what it is about the image that in their view conveys power.

Collage

If you use the word *art*, people often immediately assume they are going to have to draw something and are beset by fear and embarrassment regarding their lack of talent. But tell people they are going to be working on a collage and all that goes away. With collage you work from ready-made images in magazines, newspapers, flyers, your own photographs, or downloaded from online, or you glue small objects onto a poster. You don't need to be an artist to make a collage or to be good at graphic design or draftsmanship; all you need are magazines, glue, and a pair of scissors.

Yet, as Simpson's (2009) account of her participation at a workshop for cancer patients illustrates, the freedom collage affords can be galvanizing and meaningful. She describes how, when participants were working on collages "the workshop was alive with color, cutting, and pasting, tears, laughter, a buzz of emotion, depth of understanding, optimism, and hope. THIS creative energy was exactly what I wanted to surround myself with. And this particular art form was clearly accessible to everyone in the room regardless of age, life place, previous creative experience, or artistic skill" (pp. 78–79). Cranton offers a similar verdict (2009) on using the method with vocational trades instructors at a Canadian community college. Teaching a unit on learning styles, she asked these instructors to create collages to illustrate the different learning styles they felt they exhibited. She recounts how "both the process of finding or creating images and the creation of the collage itself led to a deeper examination of learning style, and the ensuing discussion in the whole group led us to question the premise of the concept of learning styles and challenge the idea of creating teaching methods to support each learning style" (p. 186).

One of the most powerful uses of collage is Grace and Wells' (2007) description of their work with sexual minority youth. To illustrate the way people's identity became separated from their external presentation of self, participants worked with old school lockers to create an in/out representation of how they felt about themselves as compared to the way they were seen by the world. On the outside of the lockers were stereotypical depictions of lesbian, gay, bisexual, and transgendered people, representing how participants felt they were viewed by teachers, parents, classmates, and communities. The inside of the lockers contained images, collages, and dioramas that depicted the inner selves they kept hidden from families, friends, and teachers. One participant combined shards of broken glass and fragments of a smashed mirror with disembodied and scratched-out photographs, with the phrase "running scared" written amidst pairs of eyes watching the viewer.

Found Poetry as Collage

If drawing is intimidating then writing a poem is, for many, the most pretentious task they could be given. Poetry is considered effete, only for the sensitive, definitely not for the sort of down-to earth-practitioners that adult educators often consider themselves to be. Yet, as mentioned in the next chapter's discussion of soul work, poetry can open up responses that would never ordinarily be called forth. A poem is a sort of emotional Rorschach test. A poem's words, pauses, and flow can produce widely varying reactions in its hearers. An unexpected contribution from a group member that is prompted by a poem can move a group into a richly serendipitous conversation. But for people to be open to using poetry, it is sometimes necessary to be creative in demystifying the associations of pretentiousness and portentousness that poetry contains for many adults.

One way to do this is to turn poetry into a kind of collage through the medium of "found poetry" (Love, 2012). Found poetry is "a qualitative reporting medium that weaves selected words and phrases from participants' research reports into poetry" (p. 41). This is the literary equivalent of a collage; the words of the poem already exist in research reports, but decisions regarding which words and phrases to select and where to place line breaks are left to the poet. Love (2012) describes a Montana experiment for clergy and congregational leaders in which teleconferences were used to build trustful, intense conversations. In reporting the results of this initiative, a series of found poems ("Failure of Logistics," "Out of the Blizzard," "Loving the Questions," "In Need of Circles," and "Over Many Miles That Separate" were some of the poems' titles) were created from responses participants submitted to the evaluators of the project.

Teachers that have used activities or exercises that involved posting students' work on newsprint around the classroom wall can adapt this technique at the end of this activity. Instead of asking for summary comments or final reflections, you can ask students to create found poems summarizing their understandings of the material. Alternatively, questions can be posed in the form of found poems. A few minutes spent writing and then posting found poems based on the newsprint posters around the room is often a welcome alternative to the kind of low energy discussion that often ends an activity. It honors the work students have already conducted and also provides an avenue for sharing reactions that allows introverts to have as much classroom space as extroverted speakers. Found poems can thus interrupt habitual classroom power dynamics in a creative and energizing way.

Cultural Collage

As outlined by Davis (2009), a cultural collage is an introduction of self to others. Preparers use "photos, food wrappers, crafts, maps and other visual aids" to create a collage that tells the rest of a class or workshop who they are. These collages are posted around the room and people can wander around them at any point of the workshop to look at them in more detail. An extension of this I have played with is to ask each learner to take one piece of their collage and to affix it to blank newsprint to make a community cultural collage that represents the different identities and histories in the room.

Quilts of Power

The creation of a community collage—or quilt—described above can also be adapted to focus specifically on power. Here the participants are given a theme such as "Fighting Back" or "Pushed Around" and they generate a community quilt on that theme in three steps. First, each person constructs her own individual collage to illustrate how she experiences the power dynamic the group is focusing on. These are then posted around the room as a gallery for people to view.

After a suitable time has elapsed, people are invited to suggest pieces of different collages (not their own) that they feel would be good elements in a group collage. They get out of their seat and wander over to the collage concerned, explain why they like that particular part of the collage, and ask for permission to cut it out so it can be part of a community quilt of power. If the collage producer agrees, then the piece is cut out and laid on a blank sheet of newsprint at the front of the room.

When enough bits of different collages have been chosen and placed on the blank quilt, the group then constructs the community quilt collectively. People might propose to group three or four different collage pieces together to make a subtheme of a particular power dynamic being explored. Someone else might choose two radically different collage pieces and suggest they be placed at each end of the newsprint because they represent two ends of a continuum of experiences. They then invite others to place different collage bits at various points along this continuum. After a suitable time a community collage emerges, and participants take cell phone photos of it to take home and study. If this is done in a course in a formal adult education institution, learners write an interpretation of the final collage that explains how they believe it illustrates the particular power dynamic named.

Drawing and Collaging Discussion

Drawing and Collaging Discussion is an exercise Steve Preskill and I have done in workshops we run on our book *Discussion as a Way of Teaching* (2005). Here groups of six or seven students are formed and given a topic to discuss, usually having to do with the different ways power is experienced in discussion groups. Examples of such questions might be "How does power manifest itself in discussion?" "What is a powerful discussion?" or "What makes discussion groups counterfeit democracies?"

Students are supplied with large newsprint to draw on, plenty of colored markers, pens, rulers, scissors, and tape to help them create fairly traditional two-dimensional drawings. They also receive magazine photographs, cloth scraps, and other textured materials for creating a mixed-media collage. The process begins with students individually creating a collage on a sheet of newsprint that represents their response to the discussion question.

The small group members then come together, and each person explains their drawing or collage to the other group members. The group then takes elements of the individually prepared drawings and collages to prepare a group poster that represents the conversation that ensued as the individual drawings and collages were discussed. Each person's work is somehow included on the final poster.

As the group is constructing the final poster, one member volunteers to take notes of what the group is trying to communicate so s/he can interpret the drawing to the large group and respond to any questions they have. This person is called, obviously enough, the Designated Interpreter. When all of the groups have completed their task, each group displays their work somewhere in the room for all to observe at their leisure. A blank sheet of paper is posted next to each drawing or collage.

All the participants then wander around the room, and, on the blank pieces of paper next to the group collages, they add their individual responses to the pictures or collages. They make comments, ask questions, provide reactions, and suggest ways for the meanings of the collage to be extended or linked to new themes. They can use words to give their responses or stick with using drawings. The exercise ends when participants gather as a whole class for the chance to talk about each of the postings and the reactions posted to it. The designated interpreter is the person who usually ends up responding the most to questions about the postings, but any member of the group is free to jump in.

Metaphorical and Analogical Collages

Ever since the popular success of Lakoff and Johnson's *Metaphors We Live By* (2003), the pedagogic use of metaphors has received attention from adult educators (Goss 2001; Parvaresh, 2008; Pierson, 2008). In science teaching, the use of analogy is widespread (Heywood and Parker, 2010). So many people think and communicate metaphorically, using a metaphor as a shorthand summary of a lot of complex ideas. In her workshops on creating a culture of peace, Goodman (2002) writes of how the metaphor of the earthworm as peace promoter works well across different contexts and how it's sometimes taken in directions she didn't anticipate (as when a teacher using her peace culture kit found students using the earthworm metaphor to describe the Underground Railroad during the American Civil War).

Analogically, people often explain a complex and unfamiliar idea by comparing it to a well-known process. I myself often compare teaching to water-based themes such as surfing or white water rafting. I talk of experimenting with a new teaching approach as being like a surfer riding a new wave or a rafter maneuvering a new set of rapids—dangerous, unpredictable, and exciting. I also talk about how every teacher wipes out or capsizes as things get out of control and don't pan out as planned.

Power is often spoken of in metaphorical or analogical terms. We talk of surges of power, using electrical metaphors, or like Foucault (1980), of power as an electric current moving around a room. I like to refer to times when government and media combine to use power to force change (as in the "Shock and Awe" campaign when the United States invaded Iraq) as a tsunami washing away all resistance as it crashes down. However, others might use the tsunami metaphor to describe the way power slowly builds to ignite a broad-based social movement that is unstoppable.

Metaphors and analogies can be combined with collage very effectively in the study of power. This process begins with students being asked to complete a sentence in a metaphorical or analogical way. Such sentences could be:

"Empowerment is like . . ."

"Hegemony feels like . . ."

"Racism is a . . ."

"Confronting power is a . . ."

"Resistance is . . ."

"Militarism is present when . . ."

Students come up with individual responses such as empowerment is like "an express train," "being able to breathe again," "a dam breaking," or "a flower blooming." They then form small groups to share these metaphors and analogies, and the group chooses one to depict in a collage. So, a group constructing a metaphorical or analogical collage on empowerment might choose to depict a dam breaking and symbols of oppressive power (dollar bills, a gun, a lectern, a TV station's antennae or a receiving dish) being borne away in the flood.

Incorporating Theater

If being told you're going to do an artistic activity fills you with dread, imagine how terrifying it must be to be informed you're going to be involved in some kind of theater! For that reason I don't usually frame theatrical activities that way. Instead, I prefer to tell students we're going to do a role-play, or that we're going to try and understand something using movement rather than words, or even that we're going to play a game. As Boal's *Games for Actors and Non-Actors* (2002) outlines, you don't need to be an actor to play a game that has theatrical elements embedded in it. Charades, for example, involves a great deal of acting and representation, some of it needing you to bend and manipulate your body in weird and wonderful ways. But no one would think you need an Actor's Equity card to play charades.

Sometimes I incorporate theater by borrowing something I've seen in a theatrical production and then bringing that theatrical element into my teaching without naming it for students. For example, in my faltering teenage attempts to follow Shakespeare's plays (I was required to study these continuously throughout high school), it helped me enormously if, whenever I was watching a theatrical performance of *Hamlet*, *Richard III*, or *Othello*, the actors wore strikingly different costumes. I could follow the action and understand the narrative arc or plot much more clearly if I could identify certain characters by their costume and know that a particular and distinct costume represented someone who played a particular role in the play's narrative. I took this element of costuming and have adapted it to situations when I'm trying to teach about different perspectives, theories, or frameworks that students find it hard to distinguish between.

An example of this is something as simple as having two baseball caps in different colors, or representing two different football teams, and telling students that when you're wearing one cap you're speaking from one theoretical perspective but that when you change caps that signals you're now speaking from another perspective. To illustrate the difference between two theoretically dense and difficult perspectives—say Frankfurt School critical theory and French poststructuralism—I use two different caps. When I have a Bayern Munich cap on I'm speaking as a Frankfurt school theorist, and when I'm wearing a Paris St. Germain cap I'm speaking as a French poststructuralist. I view this as a theatrically derived technique because it goes back to my high school struggles to follow Shakespearian narratives.

When it come to teaching about power and ideology, theater is especially useful in conveying dramatically how power constrains and limits people, and also how it galvanizes action (Butterwick, 2012; Butterwick and Lawrence, 2012). Bringing the body into learning is for many a powerful experience (Snowber, 2012). Getting the body up out of a chair to illuminate or express an idea is usually remembered much more clearly than an explanation from an instructor, no matter how lucid. But the degree to which participants are pushed is a matter of judgment. At its extremes, the use of theater is disturbing and upsetting.

A good example of the dangerous and discomforting nature of theater is Butterwick and Selman's (2003) account of a series of workshops among feminist groups in Vancouver. The project titled *Transforming Dangerous Spaces* was intended to explore conflicts and tensions common to feminist coalitions. Butterwick recalls a scene where a Subha (a pseudonym)—a woman of color—played a White woman and asked Butterwick to play a woman of color. Butterwick was somewhat intimidated by this prospect but agreed to go along with the exercise. Subha then stood on a chair and asked Butterwick to sit in front of her on the same chair. Subha talked loudly and forcefully while pressing her hands down on Butterwick's head, forcing her to bend to her knees. Butterwick eventually found herself folded in half struggling to breathe.

Butterwick recalls the debriefing of the scene: "I spoke of how powerful the scene was—of my deeper and embodied appreciation of White privilege and racial domination. I also expressed my fears of playing a woman of color, of stereotyping and essentializing. Sheila (the facilitator) asked why I had agreed to play the character. In my response, I said that I had deferred to the request—sensing the scene would be risky but important. Sheila challenged me, noting that deference can be a form of racism" (Butterwick and Selman, 2003, p. 14).

Scenes like the one above are indeed dangerous educational spaces to create, and they need skilled facilitators and willing participants to engage in them. In the *Dangerous Spaces* project the participants were experienced and committed feminist activists. As such, there was a readiness to take much greater risks than would be the case in, say, an adult literacy class or a college preparation for adults program. As Butterwick and Selman (2003) note, "a power and danger of drama process is that it can trigger participants in unexpected directions, and they can find themselves exploring, experiencing, and processing emotions, memories, and other aspects of themselves that were previously unknown or private. The results can surprise, shock, and reveal the unexpected" (p. 14).

Because teaching about power involves moments of surprise and shock, and because it is often experienced emotionally in the way the examples above were, many adult educators who identify as critical teachers use some variant of Augusto Boal's theater of the oppressed (Boal, 2000, 2002, 2006). Boal's work has been widely used around the globe, and not just with adults. A recent volume (Duffy and Vettraino, 2010) provides accounts of theater of the oppressed being adopted in early childhood classrooms, elementary education, high schools, in Israeli-Palestinian encounters, and with incarcerated youth. In India, Ganguly (2010) estimates that Boal's methods have been used extensively for the past thirty years to reach over a quarter of a million villages in West Bengal alone.

Forum Theater

Three kinds of theater are typically derived from Boal's work. Forum Theater is probably the most widely used. In Forum Theater a community watches a scripted scene in which a typical kind of oppression is acted out. So, for example, a group of adult illiterates watch a job interview in which the applicant tried desperately to hide his inability to read or fill in a required form. The "Joker" (a key actor in Forum Theater) then asks the audience to suggest different ways the actor experiencing oppression could have responded to the situation. As alternatives are suggested, the Joker entices audience members to come in and play the scene using the different alternatives they've suggested. Different audience members suggest different ways of confronting the oppression, and after each replaying of the scene everybody discusses what just happened and what might be changed.

Forum theater can be used in multiple settings where people feel they are being pushed around. A good example of its adaptability is Tania Giordani and Mike Brayndick's Forum Theater piece titled "The End Game at Jansen School." Dr. Giordani is a parent of school-age children in Chicago. In 2010 she conducted interviews with parents and students faced with a round of public school closings and then developed a Forum Theater script designed to animate discussion about ways local communities could mobilize to fight these. The script has been performed in multiple settings: at a Midwest Title 1 conference with parents from Milwaukee, Detroit, and Chicago, at Francis W. Parker School in Chicago, and sometimes with students as young as fourth grade being involved.

This last iteration was particularly powerful, according to Giordani: "Students thanked me at the end for including them in the conversation about what was happening at their own school. That was pretty powerful because as parents we tend to want to protect our children from what is going on, especially as we fight with hope against the school closures. Through the plays and discussion, we (parents) are realizing, we should invite our children to join the conversation and fight. The dialogues after the performances are so intense and engaging, we are always going over our 2 hour time." (Giordani, 2012, personal communication).

The idea for Forum Theater is that it is a rehearsal for life. It provides a relatively safe space for people to try out different approaches to confronting power and pushing back against it. Of course it's not totally safe because people take a risk to get up and try out their suggested alternatives. For people unused to performing, theater can be intimidating. But it is safe in that there are no political consequences to their improvisations.

Image Theater

Image Theater is the use of the body to create images of oppression. It is meant to be physically as well as intellectually liberating. Contorting the body into shapes that represent how oppression feels, or arranging several bodies that interact in a sculpture or tableau to represent interpersonal dimensions of oppression, is something that does not come easily to academic classrooms. So a crucial element in the use of Image Theater is teachers' readiness to risk looking weird or foolish by being willing to contort their own bodies. As explained by Williams (2010), "the body is liberated from unconscious movement, routine movement resulting from socioeconomic exploitation, and from the reduction of the body into an automaton" (p. 272).

In her adaptation of Image Theater, Lawrence (Butterwick and Lawrence, 2009) describes how a gay male participant created a sculptured image of how he had experienced oppression using his and other learners' bodies. He placed his body in the middle of the sculpture holding his head to ward off blows in a schoolyard bullying and placed a circle of people gathered round him pointing, jeering, and raining blows on him. The audience did not know his beating was because he was gay, since no talking is allowed during this kind of sculpting.

After the sculpture was "unfrozen," those playing the oppressors and the gay participant playing the oppressed talked about how they had experienced the situation. The oppressed revealed his gay identity as the cause of the beating, and those playing oppressors spoke about their discomfort in that role. The discussion was then broadened to include learners not in the sculpture who had been observing it. The exercise ended with people suggesting alternative ways of staging a sculpture. In one, a person playing the role of the gay student held his head high with a confident expression on his face as those playing oppressors turned away from him. In another, he was leaning forward with a finger pointing out addressing the oppressors who were listening attentively. A third scenario had two former oppressors recast as allies to the gay student with the three of them challenging the other oppressors.

Invisible Theater and Culture Jamming

The practice of Invisible Theater is less easily adapted for classroom use since its logic is that it takes place in community settings and in everyday situations. In this instance, the actors rehearse a script that portrays the oppressive dimensions of a common situation. This "play" is then enacted in a real situation with onlookers and participants unaware that this is a rehearsed play. Members of the community concerned are sometimes involved as "co-conspirators" to bring the existence of power dynamics out as explicitly as possible.

Boal's Invisible Theater has similarities to the kinds of "Culture Jamming" explored in Sandlin and McLaren's (2010) collection on critical pedagogies of consumption. Culture Jamming occurs when activists and educators insert themselves into real-life cultural events and try to disrupt the expectations and behaviors of those involved. In Sandlin's (2007a) words, it has a "pedagogical hinge in the ways it creates possibilities for change in audience members" (p. 77). One of the most infamous examples is the 2004 fake press announcement from the Yes Men—a group of activist artists posing as Dow Chemicals spokespersons—that claimed Dow accepted full responsibility for the Bhopal catastrophe and would spend $12 billion on medical care for the victims. The Yes Men described this event as "identity correction" (The Yes Men, 2006), what Darts and Tavin (2010) define as "a culture jamming tactic in which members impersonate corporate or governmental officials in an effort to reveal the true ideology of a given organization" (p. 238).

One of the most dramatic, energizing, and humorous jamming disruptions is the Reverend Billy's Church of the Stop Shopping. Reverend Billy (Bill Talen) stages "retail interventions" in shopping malls and retail stores in the form of church services accompanied with the Stop Shopping Gospel Choir. His troupe performs collective exorcisms, hears public confessions of congregation members' shopping addictions, and honors new saints. He also authors guides to retail interventions such as the "Starbucks Invasion Kit."

In her description of Reverend Billy's work, Sandlin (2007b) describes his intervention at a Disney store in which members of his "church" carried crosses with Mickey and Minnie Mouse crucified on them. Sandlin quotes Billy as saying, "the Disney Company is the high church of retail. And that's why we put Mickey Mouse on the cross. We're taking two great organized religions

[Christianity and what he calls the "Church of Consumerism"] and grinding them together and trying to confuse people so they can think in a new way" (Sandlin, 2007b, p. 543). In Sandlin's (2007b) view, "the cultural resistance that occurs as an educational strategy within Reverend Billy's movement by its very nature addresses power and seeks change" (p. 544).

Reverend Billy clearly uses humor as a tool of power analysis, something that is relatively rare in accounts of teaching about power. Yet culture jamming, street theater, and groups like the Raging Grannies all have the absurd as a central element in their work. From the situationist movement to postmodernism the ludic, spontaneously playful elements of resistance are often acknowledged. Roy's (2002) account of the interventions and demonstrations of the Raging Grannies (a group of women peace activists originally based in British Columbia) reports "more than one said that they had fun and if it was not fun they did not do it" (p. 266). Clover et al.'s (2010) compendium of environmental adult education approaches makes the same point. They argue "as adults learn, as they open up the vistas of their value systems, cognitive frames and affective potential to an unknown, they often need humor to get them across the borders. Humor not only lightens and creates a more relaxed environment, it also enlightens" (p. 41).

I am not one of those who feels teaching always has to be fun or entertaining. But I do believe in the power of creative engagement. One of the reasons why the films of Michael Moore or the TV shows hosted by John Stewart and Stephen Colbert reach far more than *The Nation* or *Socialist Worker* is because of their use of comedy to mock the rationalizations those in power give for their actions. In my own teaching, I try to puncture my own mistaken estimate of how significant my work is by joking about it. When the normal classroom routine is broken by something like collage or theater, a sense of playful unpredictability often emerges that lifts the energy in the room. As Roy (2002) comments, "having fun may be more important to resistance than traditional analysis has allowed" (p. 266).

Games and Simulations

One teaching approach that is usually reported by adult students to be more fun than traditional lecture or seminar-based approaches is that of games and simulations. After all, when a game is introduced in class we usually talk about "playing" it. When it comes to teaching about power, one of the best sources of ideas for games and simulations is the field of teaching sociology. Since part of sociology deals with power dynamics, social control, and structured inequity, there are many games that teach about the arbitrary use of authority to keep systems intact and practices unchallenged. Some of these, such as StarPower and Power of Leadership are long established and widely used (Dundes and Harlow, 2004). In both these games players are led to believe that the chance to perform well is largely a matter of chance and skill, when in fact the games have been rigged (something that is not made clear at the outset). There are many other context-specific games that can be found in the literature of teaching sociology such as Choices and Chances (Simpson and Elias, 2011), Sociopoly (Jessup, 2001), That's Not Fair (Coghlan and Huggins, 2004), Bittersweet Candy (Harlow, 2009), and Vanishing Dollar (Harlow, 2009).

Daily Power Simulations

One of my intentions as a teacher is to move away from abstract analyses of power and to show how it is experienced as the sometimes deliberate, sometimes arbitrary, exercise of authority over those who have little chance to push back. To move in that direction I use brief simulations called Daily Power.

Being Ignored

In the first Daily Power exercise, Being Ignored, I ask for a volunteer to lie in the doorway of the classroom for the duration of our break. The rest of the students are told to have no interaction with that volunteer, not to look at the student, speak to them, or make any acknowledgment that someone is there. Students have to step over that person to get to the bathrooms and coffee machines, and again when they return to class. The student who's volunteered is not allowed to get up and go to the bathroom or to enjoy coffee; he or she has to stay lying in the doorway for the whole break time. Then, when students reenter the classroom they again have to step over the student volunteer.

Now everyone knows this is a very brief artificial simulation, and so it can hardly replicate what it feels like to be marginalized on a daily basis over a lifetime. But when we resume class and move into a discussion, I begin by asking the student volunteer to talk about how it felt to be stepped over and ignored. As he or she talks about her feelings and emotions, I ask others in the class to try and remember situations in their lives when they have felt the same emotions and feelings the volunteer expresses. Then the conversation broadens out to include considerations of times when people felt ignored, smothered, looked down on, and immobile. Beginning such a conversation with this exercise seems to get us into deeper analytical waters much more quickly than if I had just asked the students to talk about times when they experienced those feelings. I can build on personal stories and link them to structural dimensions of oppression.

Microaggressions

The second Daily Power exercise, Microaggressions, focuses on microaggressions, the daily examples of racism, sexism, homophobia, and other forms of exclusions that are embedded in tone of voice, body language, and gestures, as well as direct speech. The nature of microaggressions is that their perpetrators strenuously deny their existence and that when they are committed the receiver is often left wondering "did that really happen?" When they bring the microaggression to the notice of colleagues from the dominant group, they are often told not to be so sensitive, that they are seeing evil intent when none existed, and that if anything did happen it was no more than a slip of the tongue or an accidental behavioral tic.

Because microaggressions are habitual everyday actions, part of an unremarked on set of routine behaviors and practices, they are unintentional in the sense that no overt act of exclusion or diminishment is deliberately planned. Games and simulations usually require a degree of intentionality, so it's hard to replicate what a real microaggression looks like. But I do try to do this in the following way. I begin by asking for five volunteers to play the role of school board members discussing a proposal to remove a unit on ethnic studies" from the standard curriculum taught in city high schools. This is based on an actual event, the 2012 removal of Mexican American studies from the Tucson Unified High School District's curriculum.

Ethnic Studies

The five volunteers are told they are holding a school board meeting to respond to a call to ban ethnic studies classes, and that the meeting is held in public but with no public interruptions allowed. The rest of the class watching the simulation of the meeting are rather like members of the public who show up to observe school board meetings in real life. I tell students that the school board is comprised of only White males, but that volunteers for the simulation do not have to have that identity. Volunteers are told to commit as many microaggressions as they can think up during the meeting time (usually around ten minutes). The students watching the meeting make a note of gestures, grimaces, body language, tones of voice, and actual comments that represent microaggressions. They also try to clarify the belief or assumption that lies behind the specific aggression.

When the ten-minute "meeting" is done, the class resumes and we debrief the microaggressions. The students who have been the observers report out the different aggressions they've noticed and then lay out the belief or assumption the particular aggression exemplifies. Sometimes the microaggressions that are reported out are denied by the players in the simulation, a nice enactment of the nature of such aggressions! It's also noticeable that when women or people of color volunteer to play the all White, all male school board they come up with wonderfully subtle examples of aggressions. The White male volunteers, on the other hand, often commit aggressions that are more heavy-handed, such as racist or sexist jokes in bad taste.

Now this is not a very accurate simulation of microaggressions for two reasons. First, the aggressions are not directly committed against women or people of color who are in the room as it's happening. Second, the volunteers have a mindful awareness of the need to commit microaggressions that is not present when such aggressions are committed in real life. After all, their very nature is that they are implicit, tacit, not intentionally designed to exclude. However, this simulation does show the self-confirming nature of ideology, the way it's reinforced in same race, same gender, situations without that dynamic ever being acknowledged by those involved.

The Marcuse Academy

I use this simulation to teach about microaggressions, but also about the critical theorist Herbert Marcuse's notion of repressive tolerance (Marcuse 1965). Repressive tolerance argues that organizations and institutions effectively head off challenges to their authority by appearing to cede ground and acknowledge the challenge while actually nullifying its threat. For example, curricula are opened up to different, racially based forms of knowledge (Africentric, Tribal, or Indigenous) that are added to a Eurocentric body of ideas, what Johnson-Bailey (2002) calls the "add and stir" approach to multiculturalism.

As long as the Eurocentric mainstream perspective is retained in the curriculum, Marcuse would argue, the same dynamic always manifests itself. The other "new" perspectives are always unconsciously positioned in relation to this mainstream. The Eurocentric perspective in effect is the sun the other perspectives revolve around. Students regard these alternatives as exotic intellectual destinations and visit them as tourists, rather than revising them as a legitimate alternative mainstream. This is because students' ideological formation outside the classroom is so strong it will always marginalize the way these other perspectives are viewed within the classroom.

For Marcuse, the only solution to this is to outlaw the mainstream perspective from the curriculum all together. This idea earned him death threats during his life and is still the source of great anger on the right (see the Haters Page on the website maintained by his grandson: http://www.marcuse.org/herbert/booksabout/haters/haters.htm). Below is the simulation I designed to teach about Marcuse's idea of repressive tolerance as well as about microaggressions:

Marcuse Academy—"The Way Forward"

Marcuse Academy is a charter elementary school in its second year of operation on the east side of St. Paul. The school was situated in a multiracial, less affluent neighborhood to increase the likelihood of fulfilling its mission of combining a rigorous academic preparation for junior high, high school, and college with promoting cultural competence for a multiracial world.

During the first year of operation, staff and teachers have been getting used to the building, learning about charter school operations, and making sure the first intake of students is settled in well. There has also been an attempt to build links to community organizations and to let local parents know of the school's existence.

One trend the staff and teachers have noted in the first year intake is an overrepresentation of children from the more affluent, and mostly White, west side of St. Paul. At the school forums held during the first year, the parents who have attended are overwhelmingly White, middle-class, college-educated, and liberally inclined. Attrition has been minimal during this first year, and there have been several successful fundraising efforts already conducted. The superintendent of schools has cited Marcuse Academy as an example of how to set up a successful charter school.

To make sure the mission of blending academic rigor with multi-cultural competence is accomplished, a curriculum task force is created of parents and teachers. They will propose recommendations for a plan—"The Way Forward"—being developed for the school's next five years.

The task force members are . . .

Shirley—the principal who is in her first principalship. She is proud of what she has accomplished during the first year, feels she has earned the superintendent's trust, and is aware that this work could be the stepping stone to a superintendent's post in the future. Shirley is African American, in her late thirties, and considers herself an excellent administrator. She is enrolled in the University of St. Thomas doctoral program in educational leadership.

Paul—is a parent who holds a PhD in sociology. He sent his only son to the school because he is committed to the ideal of a rainbow school that looks like the rest of America. He has connections to both Move On and to Occupy Minneapolis and considers himself left of center politically. Paul is White Euro-American, in his thirties, and a community college professor. He is of Scandinavian descent and proud of the social welfare heritage he feels himself a part of. He wants his son to go to an elite, progressive school like Macalester College, his alma mater.

Brian—is another parent who is a lawyer. He sent his younger daughter to the school after his disappointing experience sending his elder child to a local neighborhood school. He feels the neighborhood school is staffed by uninspiring, unmotivated teachers who have low expectations of their pupils. Marcuse Academy, on the other hand, seems to take pride in holding students to high academic standards. Brian is African American and in his early forties. He hopes for an Ivy League education for his son and is proud of President Obama.

Lily (her American name)—is a parent in her mid-twenties with a son and daughter at the school. Lily is Hmong and lives in the neighborhood. Her parents don't speak English, and she has grown up as the cultural broker between her extended family and many educational, social, and health agencies. She has a high school diploma and a strong desire to create a good life for her children, including a college education. She works in a low-paying service job but already puts a small amount away each month to pay for college for her kids.

Dave—is a parent of two daughters at the school. He is a lifelong east side resident and has seen the neighborhood be in constant flux with successive waves of new immigrant groups arriving since his childhood. Dave is White Euro-American, though he would not describe himself as anything but American. Dave was a high school dropout but earned a GED and wants a better life for his kids. He works as a union carpenter and believes the president is a socialist. Dave is in his late forties and this is his second marriage. He has Rush Limbaugh on his headphones when working.

H.J.—is a Korean teacher at the school in her early twenties. She is on an annually renewable visa, and did her undergraduate work in education at the University of Minnesota. She is anxious to stay in the United States and is applying for a green card. The Confucian tradition of teachers as experts and students as receivers of expert knowledge lives strongly within her, even though she went through a very student-centered BA program. She is traditional in her approach to teaching and proud of the performance of her pupils during the first year of the school.

Linda—is an experienced teacher with many years in the public school system. She has joined Marcuse Academy to give herself a "lift." After feeling she was getting into a rut, she wants to work with a vibrant new school that is already getting a good reputation in the area. Linda is Latina, a second- generation Mexican American. In her fifties, she is the eldest member of the task force and is regarded as a source of veteran wisdom by teachers and parents. At school forums her comments are always listened to carefully and taken seriously.

The First Task Force Meeting

Shirley opens the meeting as principal. She begins by inviting one of the parents to be the task force chair and convener. She wants to get "buy in" from others on the team and feels that having a parent lead this task force will do that and also give it greater legitimacy in the community.

Paul immediately volunteers for the position and, with no one else stepping up, is quickly installed as the chair. He then asks for agenda items for that evening from committee members.

Linda says she has been thinking about the textbooks that are used to teach English, maths, science, and social studies in the school. She says they reflect a Euro-American perspective and should be replaced with texts that are culturally grounded. She says it's important that children see images of themselves in the materials they study and introduces the notion of self-ethnic reflectors. From now on, she proposes, the school should only use texts written from a non-European background. Examples she gives off the top of her head are a Hmong approach to science education, an Africentric approach to teaching language, a Latino/a approach to social studies, a Native American approach to drama, and so on.

The meeting continues . . .

I hold this simulation as a variant of a Fishbowl exercise in which the rest of the class observes the seven students participating in the task force meeting. Students who are not participating in the simulation look for actions and comments that represent repressive tolerance in action, as well as the presence of racial microaggressions. After ten minutes or so of the simulation, I end it and we debrief what happened. First, I ask the observers to point out examples of how they thought repressive tolerance manifested itself and to identify the racial, class, and gender microaggressions they noticed. Then, I ask the participants who played the seven roles to talk about how that felt, the microaggressions they committed that the observers didn't notice, and any new understanding of how repressive tolerance works that they gained in the exercise.

Summary

This chapter has tried to explore creative and often playful approaches to teaching about power. It has argued for exercises and techniques that depart from the more traditional academic presentation and discussion of knowledge, arguing that such approaches are likely to connect with and engage students. But I don't mean to suggest that these so-called "irrational" or "playful" approaches should comprise the whole curriculum. There are times when students need to struggle with understanding new ideas or learning new skills. Sometimes we need to get out a dictionary and read a paragraph several times before we start to glean some level of understanding from it. And perfecting the practical application of a new skill often requires repetition and practice, until the skill is lodged in one's muscle memory. I know this only too well as a guitar player who is sometimes required to play solos as well as chords! In the next and final chapter I move away from the focus on activities to explore how we might negotiate the emotional ups and downs of teaching about power.

8

Negotiating the Emotions
of Powerful Teaching

The first seven chapters of this book have been chiefly concerned with describing tools, techniques, and exercises. This seems entirely appropriate for a book titled *Powerful Techniques for Teaching Adults*. In this final chapter I want to move in a different direction and turn my attention to the experiential canvas on which these techniques are drawn, to the emotional backdrop that frames the teaching scripts and instructional practices we enact. Although teaching is suffused with emotion and feeling, you wouldn't know it from reviewing the kinds of protocols typically used to evaluate teachers' effectiveness. These are pretty bloodless, focusing on pedagogic mechanics such as how well the class was paced or if sufficient time for questions was allowed. All these are obviously important questions to ask, but they focus on the outside of teaching as against our inner lives. And it's our inner worlds that frame so many external actions and decisions.

Focusing on the outside of teaching is hardly a surprise. After all, it's much easier to focus on external practices such as how clearly teachers explain the material, how they use technology, or whether they employ a mix of instructional approaches. Because of the subjectivity of how emotions are felt in the body, capturing inner turmoil or elation, angst or joy, anticipation or dread, is something that eludes rubrics designed to measure teaching effectiveness. Adult teachers may practice their craft somewhere between dissonance and grace, as Davison and Burge (2010) suggest, but to use such language to describe the daily reality of one's practice is seen as unreliably "soft" in the discourse of teacher accountability. Imagine trying to get students to rate a teacher's attainment of grace!

Yet any teacher who is awake in her practice knows the extent and permanence of emotion in her work. Dirkx's anthology *Adult Learning and the Emotional Self* (2008) looks at emotions in basic education classrooms, online learning, adult higher education, workplace training, multiculturalism and diversity courses, nonformal education, and the arts. Across these settings, Dirkx argues, adult teaching is rooted in the multiple and complex relationships established between teachers and students. For this reason, it is inherently emotional. Judgments of an effective or wasted class, a successfully or poorly applied technique, or a good or bad discussion are usually emotionally determined. Peak experiences are considered so primarily because of the joy they produce and only secondarily because a lesson has proceeded as planned. Bad days are recalled because they produce depression and despair in us, not because students don't seem to be engaged.

The emotional nature of teaching is evident when we try to explain how we arrived at judgments regarding our teaching effectiveness. Typically, we express these in external, behavioral terms by saying an effective class was one in which students showed through the quality of questions they asked just how well they understood the material. Or, we say a discussion was awful because two or three students monopolized the conversation punctuated by long periods of embarrassed silence. But it is our emotional responses that signal the significance of these external indicators. We feel pleasure and excitement when students ask a stream of thoughtful, smart, provocative questions. We feel panicky, demoralized, and exhausted when our efforts to generate student participation are met with silence. Were these things to occur with no strong or searing emotional response on our part we would not remember them. They become significant primarily because of the emotions that attend their emergence. In the experiential topography of a teacher's life, the emotional apexes and nadirs are far more prominent, and shape our actions far more significantly, than those days when things tick over nicely.

Emotion and Power

This books focuses on how power dynamics are a central feature in adult classrooms and on ways to teach about power, and both these areas of practice are infused with emotions. Bierema (2008) observes, "power is malleable, linked to feelings of fear, humiliation, pride and achievement" (p. 59) and "emotion can be manipulated to preserve power relations" (p. 59). An example of this is the segregation of women in service industries to perform emotionally draining tasks. For example, customer service holds that the customer is always right, and female workers are expected to accommodate outbursts of rudeness, anger, and sexism directed at them by consumers while remaining compliant.

In the helping or human service professions (for example, nursing, social work, counseling), the mostly female labor force is expected to engage in emotional labor—work that produces or manages emotions in others, where the private emotions of worker and clients serve corporate and organizational ends. Malcolm's (2012) analysis of being a qualitative researcher who used empathy and warmth to get her subjects to open up describes this as "deep acting" (p. 260). In describing how she acted out being emotionally connected to and supportive of one of her subjects, a woman named Patricia, Malcolm notes how "although I was deeply in the role of empathic 'friend,' I was not Patricia's friend" (p. 263). The performative aspects of her role as researcher (acting as friend, being a deep listener, empathetically and supportively responding to tales of distress and pain) were enacted to induce her respondents to talk about their deeper thoughts. Malcolm feels she was complicit in manufacturing emotions to serve the ends of the project she was hired to complete: "I used a range of emotions to respond empathically when an interviewee recounted something funny, or explained a bad experience" (p. 260).

Teachers who wish to teach about power and to challenge dominant ideology live with the daily reality of emotion. Any kind of teaching about racism "is particularly bound to emotional responses because of the level of risk and openness being asked of workshop participants" (Somers, 2011, p. 655). Students resist this by maintaining a commitment to color blindness (Bonilla-Silva, 2009), by expressing "race fatigue," or by engaging in a self-absorbed confession of guilt and shame "without moving on and seeing how White privilege affects the larger world" (Baumgartner and Johnson-Bailey, 2008, p. 50). In critical classrooms, members of the dominant culture may feel attacked, consumed by a "fear of being labeled, of being embarrassed, of hurting someone else" (Callahan, 2004). However, if a self-absorbed focus on guilt and shame leads into considering ways of reducing racism and equalizing power, then feelings of hope and possibility are often generated.

Although accounts of critical teaching are usually quick to mention the predictable backlash of student anger and hostility, we need to remember too that "emotions can also be a tool to break the cycle of reproducing structures of domination" (Callahan, 2004, p. 76). Emotions are central to empowerment, to feeling an enhanced sense of personal confidence, because one has accomplished a difficult task. When a group realizes its collective power, there is a joyful recognition of future possibilities. The kinds of intuitive, narrative, and artistic approaches explored in chapter 7 can bind students together in a sense of shared outrage that propels them to explore how they can act in the world. When students are so annoyed and frustrated with a teacher that they refuse to comply with her directions and proceed to challenge her authority, this is upsetting for the teacher but empowering for students. This dynamic can be extremely complex. After all, a blunt refusal by students to confront racism that a teacher insists needs to be addressed is empowering for students, if we judge being empowered by whether or not you'll realize your agenda. But from my own perspective on the effective use of power, I would not call this an empowered classroom.

An excellent example of empowerment leading to unexpected and unwanted consequences is provided in Hunt's (2006) description of a 2004 class project in which one group of students decided to investigate the claims of the Swift Boat Veterans regarding John Kerry's unsuitability to be president. This group, formed by Republicans to challenge Kerry's war record, put out a series of commercials questioning Kerry's description of his Vietnam War service. The assignment to investigate these claims was meant to teach students skills of information retrieval and analysis, by them applying critical analysis to make informed judgments about the accuracy of media and online sources. The teacher's role in this project was simply to offer advice and suggestions on locating and assessing resources. Hunt writes, "our primary goal was not to ensure that students came to believe what we thought was 'the truth' about the Swift Boat Veterans" (p. 61) but to let students "have the freedom to conduct the investigation in the way they thought best" (p. 61).

Despite all attempts to suggest ways students might investigate the Swift Boat Veterans' claims, Hunt and his colleagues "watched the train rumbling down the tracks" (p. 61) to the conclusion that Kerry was not fit to be a candidate for the presidency. Like Cale's (2001) earlier analysis of how his attempts to teach against dominant cultural values only served to confirm the strength of these values to students, Hunt documents his unease at students' misconceptions. Yet his public and private commitment to not intervening and not influencing students to provide findings that they thought would please professors, meant he held back from directly telling students they were wrong. To him, "a misconception about a historical event and a document buying into a propaganda campaign, was far less important than the long-term lessons about autonomy, independent learning, and public responsibility that the students had the opportunity to learn by being given their head" (p. 62).

Were the students in Hunt's class empowered by being free of teacher intervention? A humanistic perspective would certainly maintain that once Hunt told the students they were responsible for their own conclusions, it would then have been inconsistent for him to intervene when he saw the "wrong" direction students were taking. From a critical theory perspective, however, you could argue that the students were actually disempowered by the project. They had accepted dominant ideology and false propaganda, yet now believed they were properly critical and had learned ways of detecting such falsity. The big question, of course, is who decides empowerment has taken place? Is this purely a subjective judgment by the students, so that if they feel empowered they actually are empowered? Or is it a teacher's judgment? If the latter, then the teacher would decide students had been empowered when they started to push back against ideological manipulation and political propaganda.

Answering this question takes us straight to the discussion of how an adult teacher should use her positional authority and her power as a content expert in ways that are ethical and responsible. Because my students are adults I usually feel fine intervening to point out the shortcomings of an approach they suggest. I think it is possible to register your disagreement and alarm at the direction a project is taking, yet still remain committed to letting students have the final say. If, in my opinion, students were ignoring or misapplying criteria for assessing accuracy, I would have to bring that to their attention. Students could choose to ignore my advice, in which case I would question them very closely in their final presentation. They may, of course, still reach what I believe to be an erroneous and misinformed conclusion. But they would not be able to get there without responding to my questions and objections. Of course, having chosen to ignore my advice they would feel wonderfully empowered when they presented a project that went directly against my wishes!

So in situations like the one described above, how are we to decide what constitutes a responsible use of teacher power? In chapter 1 I proposed that teacher power should be transparent, that it should be used for the good of students' learning, that it should be open and responsive to critique, and that it should be exercised carefully, not arbitrarily. Each of these proposed guidelines is subjective, slippery, and contradictory (welcome to teaching!). After all, what if being transparent about your agenda to make students think more critically means they avoid your classes or become blocked by anxiety at the prospect that awaits them? What if something that you feel is in the students' best interests (such as teaching about the persistence of racism) is something they oppose? What if, in seeking critique from students, they ask you to stop doing something you are committed to? And what if you are preparing students to work in settings in which confrontation, hostility, and bigotry are commonplace? To teach in ways that avoid such emotionally charged dynamics doesn't really prepare students to deal with them outside the classroom.

Unanswerable questions like these are endemic to any kind of teaching that takes power seriously. They perplex us and can leave us feeling demoralized and hopeless. It seems that no matter where we turn, we are caught in a morally compromising maze that stymies us from working in a manner consistent with the spirit of adult education. This can be emotionally draining to the point that we may decide the struggle is not worth it. Knowing that by teaching about power dynamics and ideologies you are intentionally going to create anger or anxiety in students hardly fires you up with dynamic enthusiasm. I admire Somers's (2011) argument that when teaching people about racism we need to extend compassion to all learners including "involuntary learners, those who are angry and speak with 'venom'" (p. 657). But I have to admit I find this exhausting. To hear a cloistered egomaniac hold forth to the class on the way affirmative action is undemocratic and has restricted his freedom to prosper requires more compassion that I can ever muster.

Surviving the Emotional Demands of Powerful Teaching

I believe that as important as it is to be skilled in using different teaching approaches that connect well to students' experiences and help them learn new skills, dispositions, and information, equally important for powerful teaching is the ability to negotiate the topography of one's emotional landscape. Anyone who tries to get students to exercise power in class, or introduces them to ideas they believe are subversive, unpatriotic or needlessly partisan, has to expect their life to be something of an emotional roller coaster. You know that a normal day will most likely include anger, fear, hostility, and contempt—and that's just from your colleagues! All jokes aside, when your main agenda is to teach about and against power, you sometimes feel as if your models are Canute or Sisyphus. No one can persist for very long at an activity they feel is enervating and pointless.

If this is true, then it's shocking how any sustained attention to emotional survival is absent from the curriculum of professional preparation in adult education. A typical diploma or master's degree in adult education will include courses on adult learning, program planning, history and philosophy of adult education, adult development, and teaching adults. There is usually nothing in the formal curriculum that prepares adult teachers for the emotionally draining aspects of their work. Instead, we have to learn through experience, through trial and error, through introspection or talking to colleagues, through calling on faith, and through revisiting the well of whatever experience or authority was the crucible for our own commitment. This is what Dirkx (2012) calls the soul work adult teachers need to do to survive. In soul work we "attend to and work imaginatively with the emotions and feelings associated with our teaching, and the images that come to animate these emotions and feelings" (Dirkx, 2004, p. 31). Dirkx advocates journaling to capture emotional experiences as fully as possible and to attend in a nonjudgmental way to the feelings we have as we recreate the experience.

Another way to attend to soul work is through intense and open conversation with peers. In a study of "soul-role dialogues" (Michalec and Brower, 2012, p. 15) at the University of Denver, monthly conversations based on Parker Palmer's Circle of Trust idea (Chadsey and Jackson, 2012) used poetry and journal excerpts "to encourage personal understanding of the soul-role conflict at work" (Michalec and Brower, 2012, p. 17). In this conflict "the institutional pressures they faced drove a wedge between their soul and role" (Michalec and Brower, 2012, p. 22). Poetry in particular was found to be very productive in opening people up to consider questions of soul. It functioned as a sort of Rorschach test, provoking uniquely emotional responses in different members of the conversation groups.

In an ideal world, we would be granted time and space by our employers to write journals and create poems of our emotional journeys that we could share with peers engaged in the same process. But teachers who push back against power are often lone voices in their programs or working ridiculous hours for poorly funded community organizations. What if you're essentially the only person in your department who teaches from the particular convictions you hold? What if the pressures of teaching load, publishing, and service mean it's easier to go along with the crowd and teach in ways that please students? What if you don't have a partner, friend, or mentor who can read your journal and help talk you down from bad experiences?

What I would like to do in the next section is sketch out a preliminary curriculum for emotional survival that is framed around what seem to me to be the most important learning tasks or projects we need to conduct in order to stay sane and committed to the kind of powerful teaching outlined in this book. I will do this while trying to keep in mind the typical working conditions of activist-inclined teachers—underpaid, overworked, with few institutional resources, and surrounded by uncomprehending or suspicious colleagues.

Recognizing What's Emotionally Important

In her analysis of how Canadian diversity and antiracist adult educators handle the emotional challenges of their work, Somers (2011) builds on the notion of the identity needs of radical teachers. One of the most significant elements of a teacher's identity is recognition of the effects her work is having on and in the world. This is not recognition as in teacher of the year awards or community honors; instead, Somers argues, we need to recognize signs and cues that our work is making some kind of difference. Teachers who try to get students to push back against dominant ideology sometimes forget just how fundamental the need to be recognized for their work is to their identity.

As an identity need, recognition is inherently external. Certainly, we can recognize a good day's work and congratulate ourselves on a difficult classroom situation that was negotiated well or an exercise that got people challenging power almost without their realizing this was happening. But this kind of internal, self-generated recognition is a finite resource. If all you can draw on in the face of difficulty, resistance, and hostility is your self-belief that you are doing the best you can do, this will sustain you only for so long.

Somers argues that if we are to continue to work in emotionally draining territory we need some kind of external recognition. This can come from multiple sources: our own students, our teaching colleagues, the broader professional reference group we interact with at conferences, e-mail inquiries about our work, and interested noneducators' comments (partners, family, friends, lovers). This recognition can be explicit, as when students give us good evaluations or colleagues compliment us on our practice. It can be implicit, as when the energy seems to lift in a classroom or the discussion seems to "take off," because of some intervention you made. Less prominently it can be structural, as in being given a certain rank or title, or awarded a salary increase for your work.

When I talk to my teaching peers, I don't usually hear anything about this notion of recognition. We take a martyr's pride in soldiering on courageously in the face of obstacles that would crush lesser mortals. In our own estimation, we are fired by conviction and cause, not by needing anything as crass as recognition. "The work is its own reward" is the cry. In fact, a lack of positive recognition is sometimes worn as a badge of honor. I have often said that I measure myself by my enemies and that if my enemies are people who I feel are egomaniacal, manipulative, and, let's be blunt, not very smart, then I'm in good shape. If we are asked to serve in any mainstream capacity, we believe we risk being co-opted into the mainstream, rendered ineffective by the power we are trying to challenge.

But when I think about the kind of thing that keeps me going in difficult situations, the emotional fuel I need to power my engine of action, I have to admit that it involves a good measure of recognition. The greatest emotional high in my work is when a student says that something I did or said really helped them in some way. I long ago realized that part of my identity was somehow bound up with the sense that I was being useful to people. This need undergirds central elements of my practice, particularly the Critical Incident Questionnaire (CIQ). By using the CIQ to find out how students experience learning week in, week out, I am able to constantly craft and shape my teaching to take account of what will best help students learn. I am, in other words, trying to be as helpful as possible. I don't think I'm atypical in this regard. When I talk to adult educators at conferences around the world, it seems that many of us come into this work to be of service to people whom the educational system has previously dismissed as mediocre and talentless.

Now the only way I know if a project central to my identity (being helpful) is being realized is through some kind of external recognition. I need students and colleagues to tell me I am doing something useful for them, helping them in some way. This does not have to happen every class or every week. But to run a professional development institute, teach a new chord sequence, or oversee a course or program, I need an occasional acknowledgment that something I'm doing is helpful. If that's not there in some minimal measure, then I become demoralized, eager to get things over as quickly as possible.

How to Gain Recognition of Our Work

The idea that recognition might be an unacknowledged identity need for many adult teachers immediately suggests four specific practices. The first is the need to undertake some kind of running classroom assessment of what and how students are learning. This does not need to be time-consuming. I typically allow the last five minutes of the last class or training session of the week for participants to fill out the CIQ, and then five minutes to report the results out at the beginning of the first class the following week. In the literature on classroom assessment and student engagement (Barkley, 2010), there are multiple suggestions for ways of getting a quick "read" of the emotional rhythms of a class. Interestingly, when I'm working with a group that feels apathetic or hostile, the CIQ often informs me that my judgment of the group's reactions is overly pessimistic. I am often surprised to read comments from students about engaging moments and helpful actions that take me by surprise and keep my despair in check.

Second, if recognizing how our work is having some kind of effect is important for our identity, then we need to try and find ways to connect with other adult teachers engaged in similarly purposeful work. In my book *Becoming a Critically Reflective Teacher* (Brookfield 1995), I explored in some detail how conversations with colleagues could throw new light on our practice and help us become aware of our assumptions. One benefit I did not explore in that text was how such conversations could be an important source of recognition. For example, when I talk to a colleague about a problem I'm facing that I assume no one else is bothered by, and I find my colleague is also dealing with the same issue, then I realize I'm participating in a common experience that is familiar to teachers across the field. So one way of ensuring recognition would be to find ways of creating conversation groups with colleagues throughout the year.

Unfortunately the number of organizations who create time and space for teachers and trainers to talk to and learn from each other is, in my experience, pitifully small.

One exception to this is Luther Seminary in St. Paul, Minnesota, which hosts a teacher conversation group once a month for all untenured faculty. No tenured member is allowed in the room (unless invited) so people can share their frustrations and anxieties relatively openly. I have been employed as the external consultant for this group, so, once a month for the past several years, I sit in on these conversations. I so enjoy doing this that in 2008 Mary Hess (the convener of the first group I worked with) and I edited a book written solely by group members titled *Teaching Reflectively in Theological Contexts* (Hess and Brookfield, 2008). One function of this group is to allow people to share their ongoing problems and frustrations, which in turn bring recognition that what we thought were contradictions unique to our classrooms, are, in fact, shared.

The explosion of online communication has, I believe, also helped in meeting the need for recognition. Blogs, wikis, online clearinghouses, and chat rooms allow people to share methods, exercises, techniques, and reflections. On my own home page (www.stephenbrookfield.com) I make available all my classroom exercises for free download. I urge people to steal from it whatever seems useful and, in so doing, I realize I'm meeting my identity need for recognition. If you're an adult teacher working within professional development and you have a problem you're trying to deal with, or a response to a problem you're ready to share, just go on the Professional and Organization Development Network in Higher Education (POD) list serve and type in your problem or question to produce a stream of thoughtful responses and suggestions (http://www.podnetwork.org/listserv.htm). You quickly recognize that there are multiple colleagues across the network dealing with exactly the same dilemma that you thought was so unique.

Finally, receiving recognition is one of the ancillary benefits of team teaching. When conceived and practiced properly—with every member of the team simultaneously present for all planning meetings, classes, and debriefings—team teaching works to provide teachers with a built in source of recognition. One of the responsibilities of team members is to serve as supportively critical mirrors to each other, reflecting back images of the class that might not have been recognized by one of the team. Many times during team teaching I have thought a segment I was leading was not going well, but my teaching colleague has pointed out to me things I had missed or has provided a different, more nuanced interpretation of events. Or, even if things went as badly as I'd feared, my colleague will sympathize and talk about similar situations she has had to endure. In many ways the recognition of a commonly experienced failure is just as significant as an acknowledgment of an individual success.

Monitoring Your Anticipatory Anxiety

As someone who suffers from chronic anxiety and clinical depression, I know well the phenomenon of anticipatory anxiety, the feeling that the task that lies before you (for example, getting uninterested or hostile students to become aware of ideological manipulation) is so challenging and complex that you have no chance of success. Anticipatory anxiety is self-engineered, but it is usually not a wholly unrealistic fantasy, being rooted, at least to some degree, in past experience. A troubling situation in which something has gone awry and left us feeling embarrassed, confused, humiliated, and in psychic or physical danger comes to dominate the way we frame our approach to similar situations that await us in the future. The anxiety-provoking feature of the past event then defines future ones for us. A self-fulfilling dynamic emerges in which anxiety that a future event will be disastrous is so strong that it ensures the disaster we'd feared actually occurs.

Anticipatory anxiety is a visceral, bodily state that manifests itself in palpitations, nausea, fainting, and an overwhelming feeling of impending doom, even death. In extreme situations, I have passed out three times because of this. There was no immediate physical threat posed to me, just a scenario I had created from selected elements of my past experiences that loomed ahead of me guaranteeing disaster. Because it's nonrational, talking your way out of anticipatory anxiety often has limited success. Yet, to teachers, trained as we are to respect the power of analysis and reason, trying to talk ourselves down is usually our remedy of choice.

What works better, in my experience, are bodily and breathing exercises that have nothing to do with rational thought, in conjunction with appropriate, mood-controlling prescription drugs, and experience. Talking is important, but this kind of anxiety is hard to control through rational thought. I speak here not as anyone with any clinical or therapeutic training, but as a sufferer. When confronting anticipatory anxiety, I do use cognitive behavioral therapy scripts that try to provide a realistic alternative explanation of what might happen. But the anxiety is so strong that I think of my scripts as a single flickering candle trying to stay lit as a tornado approaches. I really am only able to use them to any effect when my mood has already been stabilized by medication.

One mild form of anticipatory anxiety around teaching power is the phenomenon of impostorship, the sense that you are a permanent rookie or novice who doesn't really deserve to be doing the work you do because you have no real idea exactly what it is you're supposed to be doing! If you suffer from impostorship, you have a mild level of anticipatory anxiety constantly present as you teach. The fear you live with is that one day you will do or say something so obviously incompetent that the false face of being in command that you have created will shatter and people will see you as you really are—hopelessly unfit to do the job you have.

Impostorship is triggered by very predictable events. Receiving negative evaluations is one of the most common. Even if 98 per cent of student evaluations sing your praises, the 2 percent that criticize you will be the ones that register with you. You will dismiss the 98 per cent as not being smart enough to realize you've hoodwinked them into thinking you know something. But the 2 percent of negative comments will be ones you'll attribute to the smartest students in the group. In your mind their negative comments mean they are operating at a higher level of critical discrimination than the majority of their peers. You attribute superior intelligence to them because they've caught you out in the lie of your impostorship.

In the preceding section I extolled the virtues of team teaching, but I have to admit that a major trigger to my own impostorship is knowing that there will be a colleague in the room watching what I do. "I can fool my students into thinking I know something" is the script in my head, "but how on earth can I keep up that pretense in front of someone who really knows the subject?" That's why I find peer evaluations of my teaching so anxiety provoking, and why I am usually much more nervous giving an academic presentation at a conference than teaching my own students.

Whenever I take a group into contentious areas having to do with understanding power, I feel like a total impostor. After discussions have become highly contentious (as they almost always do), I am left with the feeling that if I'd actually known what I was doing I could have piloted us to a safe haven of peaceful, intersubjective understanding. When students cry, shout out in anger, and accuse me or their peers of racism, I always leave the room wishing I could roll back the tape, put in a fresh spool (an old analogy, but hang in there with me), shout "action!" and press the record button for a second take.

Over time experience does help put impostorship in perspective. The more you encounter complex situations where no clear, calm resolutions or responses emerge, the more you understand that the reasons these responses never suggest themselves is because they don't actually exist. That helps you to be a little more forgiving to yourself when you leave a group feeling totally bewildered. This is where I think experienced teachers have a singular role to play. Their longevity means they have probably lived through the same dilemmas and contradictions numerous times. If such staff can talk publicly about their own anxiety and impostorship, this helps to normalize these same feelings for new or junior teachers. As someone with the exalted title of Distinguished University Professor, I feel I need to take the lead with new teachers at my institution to talk about my own impostorship, anxiety, and continued bewilderment at how to teach well.

Cultivating Empathic Detachment

Empathic detachment contains two dimensions. The first is the ability to understand why learners are reacting with hostility to learning and not to take onto yourself the responsibility of thinking you are always the cause of this reaction. In simple terms, it's not taking things personally. This happens when you understand that the reason people are so angry is because of the threatening nature of the learning tasks. Asking people to question dominant values and behaviors they have always taken for granted, or getting them to realize that many problems don't have a right or wrong answer (only degrees of contextually appropriate responses), are learning tasks fraught with peril. Once you understand this you realize that it really doesn't matter how subtle or diplomatic you are when introducing a provocative idea about the workings of power (such as hegemony), students will experience this as a classroom explosion designed to destroy the flimsy shelters of their assumptive frameworks.

The other dimension of empathic detachment has to do with the tricky problem of deciding when a teacher should refrain from helping a student struggle with a difficult learning episode, thereby allowing the student to chart her own way through the struggle. By the teacher not intervening, the student eventually realizes they managed to learn a new skill on their own. This then allows them to transfer aspects of that experience (which approaches worked best, which resources were most useful, how to deal with momentarily flagging motivation, and so on) to future learning projects. For a teacher like myself who is psychologically programmed to be helpful, and for whom the idea of being recognized as helpful is an important identity need, cultivating this kind of detachment is hard. Plenty of students have come up to me over the years to thank me for explaining complex ideas clearly, helping them develop as writers and thinkers, or giving them useful practical tools. But offhand I can't think of a single student who has come up to me and thanked me for letting them flounder or for the way I deliberately prolonged their uncertainty until the moment of comprehension dawned.

Cultivating empathic detachment, like managing impostorship, comes from three sources. First is the importance of your personal experience. After multiple attempts experimenting with different approaches to head off students' resistance, it gradually dawns on you that the resistance will be there no matter what you do. From that point of awareness, it's a short step to understanding that not only does it not matter what approach you take, the fact that you are the teacher is also irrelevant. It's the nature of the learning that's causing the resistance, not your actions. This helps you stop taking resistance personally.

Second, hearing from peers and colleagues about their own struggles with this kind of teaching helps you realize that you are not unique in your frustrations. As with impostorship, if experienced and credible teachers are willing to talk publicly about their difficulties and to document what they consider to be failures and missteps, it normalizes and legitimizes your own problems. This is why a study such as Gary Cale's "When Resistance Becomes Reproduction" (Cale, 2001) is so helpful. Cale is singularly courageous in laying bare how his sincerest efforts to radicalize his community college students backfired horribly and ended up entrenching their conservatism. Yet, in reading it, you learn that Cale is a committed and thoughtful teacher trying to engage students in challenging learning.

Cale's work is an example of educational research that is generally frowned upon as unrigorous and subjective, a scholarly personal narrative (SPN). Championed by Robert Nash (Nash, 2004; Nash and Bradley, 2011) an SPN is a story written by the central character in the narrative who interweaves into her personal account references to relevant scholarly literature and self-critique. It is hard to pull off, needing a high level of self-awareness and an ability to write fluently, but when it works, as in Cale's case, it is a wonderfully helpful resource. You enter the narrative as a sympathetic observer and see your own disappointments and confusion reflected in the SPN's narrative. This is powerfully reassuring to anyone trying to keep students' resistance in perspective. SPNs are starting to appear (Taylor, 2009; Swanson Brookes, 2011), and they seem to me to be particularly suited to efforts to document how we struggle through our efforts to help students learn about power.

Reading more traditional formal scholarly research on adult development (see for example, Moshman, 2003; Skinner and Pitzer, 2012) is a third way you can keep students' anger and hostility in perspective and come to understand it as an essential dynamic of challenging learning, not as a sign of your inability to engage learners. The move from dualistic to multiplistic reasoning, and the development of postformal modes of thought such as informal logic and dialectical thinking, may sound too esoteric and rarified to be of much interest to a harried and exhausted teacher, but these concepts all explain why so many adults resist the trajectory outlined in transformative learning theory (Mezirow and Taylor, 2009; Taylor and Cranton, 2012). Changing meaning schemes and perspectives you have lived by for decades is exhausting work filled with danger. It's not surprising that any adult teacher who either nudges or confronts students in this direction is going to encounter substantial resistance.

Managing Epistemological Confusion

In *Becoming a Critically Reflective Teacher* (Brookfield, 1995), I wrote about epistemologically challenged colleagues who mistakenly believed that every problem had an answer and that this answer could be discovered if you just looked long and hard enough. I called this erroneous perception *Deep Space Nine—The Answer Must Be Out There Somewhere*, after the 1990s *Star Trek* spinoff TV series. At the time I argued that complex problems rarely had solutions, only partial responses that were more or less contextually appropriate. Twenty years have passed since I wrote those words, and my conviction that the toughest teaching problems don't have solutions has only deepened.

The road to understanding the false promise of *Deep Space Nine* is a highly emotional one marked by hope, excitement, frustration, despair, and demoralization. As new books are published, new web pages are created, new workshops are offered, and new self-help programs are advertised that promise to tell us how we can solve problems of student disinterest and disengagement, we experience hope and excitement. Finally, we think, someone has spent time figuring out what we can't understand and has a program for us to follow that will fix things in our world. So we buy the book, subscribe to the web page, or attend the workshop to learn about the solutions offered.

Then comes the hard part. Back home on our own territory we try to make the generalized strategies and techniques we've learned fit the particularities of our own classrooms, subjects, and students. Invariably we run into problems, kinks, and contradictions that the book, workshop, or website doesn't deal with. We keep trying to make the exercise or method fit our world, but, like Play Dough that has been left out and become calcified, it refuses to conform to the contours of our experience. Annoyed, we try to slot the calcified Play Dough into spaces where it doesn't fit, and we watch as it crumbles under the pressure we're exerting.

Now comes the despair. We've studied the book, diligently followed the workshop instructions, and still nothing changes! Will this feeling of being stymied never go away? Why does nothing ever seem to work? Are we condemned to feel permanently defeated? When a promise to solve your problems is perceived as hollow, it's depressing and demoralizing. We resolve never again to be conned into thinking that some "expert" can help us; until, of course, the next seductively written flyer crosses our desk or slides past our spam filter to end in our e-mail inbox.

I feel a little strange writing the words above because I try to publish books, some of which (like this one) are full of suggested strategies, techniques, exercise, and methods. I run a home page where I offer all kinds of what I hope will be helpful material for free. And I'm often asked to travel outside Minneapolis-St. Paul to deliver workshops on teaching, critical thinking, and discussion methods. So aren't I making myself obsolete by casting doubt on the value of my books, home page, and workshops?

Perhaps so. But my intent in throwing copious amounts of mud on the wall of possible practices is to provide starting points that will help teachers develop approaches that fit their situation. Whenever I do a workshop I urge people to steal from my home page and to change, add to, delete from, and generally do violence to anything that seems useful but that needs to be altered to make sense in their own classrooms. Part of managing the frustration pro-duced by epistemological confusion is to understand that a truly responsive teacher is always the expert on her own classroom and students. When you have to choose between sticking to the "right" way of implementing a method, and deciding to rip it apart and re-build it in a way that makes sense only to you, always go with the latter option.

If the peddlers of "best practices" such as myself are honest we have to admit that we know nothing about the particularities of the worlds that our readers, workshop attendees, or website plunderers inhabit. And because of that fact, we have to acknowledge that our models, lists, and tips have limited utility. The more open we are about admitting the constrictions and foolishness of having to apply our tools in exactly the way we prescribe, the less epistemological confusion we'd be responsible for.

By the way, I don't believe that materials containing examples of exercises and techniques are misguided. As I say, I write them myself and, as a working teacher, I love to read them when others write them. There is nothing more pleasing for me than discovering a technique online or in a book and seeing how it could be adapted into one of my own courses. I love to steal (though I always at-tribute), adapt, and experiment with a good practice someone else has generated. My point is simply that an exercise generated by an-other educator will usually need to be altered in some way, and we should not feel we are dong violence to the integrity of the exercise when we do that.

Keeping Going—Nourishing Your Soul

An important element of soul work is making sure that you re-member those teaching episodes when something good happened. I remember in the first few years of my adult educational career receiving a letter of thanks from a student, complimenting me on how much she had learned in class and how skillfully I had run the discussions. At the time I was dealing with the growing suspicion (and later reality) that I was going to lose my job. I was feeling very unappreciated and thinking I'd made a big mistake choosing to work in a sector (adult education) that was the last to be funded and first to be cut. So when this letter arrived in my mailbox out of the blue, it gave me a big jolt of confidence. I kept it, read it regularly, and though it didn't stop my program ultimately being closed down, it did help me remember that sometimes my work meant something.

Since that time I have kept a nourishment file, either as a paper file labeled "nourishment" in my filing cabinet, or as an e-mail folder named "appreciations." Opening that electronic file as I write this paragraph, I see it goes back to the last century (1999). Every time I get an e-mail that says something positive about my work, I reply to it and then place it in my appreciations folder. I also have hard copies of letters of appreciation I've received over the years that in my opinion went beyond a ritualistic acknowledgment thanking me for visiting a campus, community, or organization. Basically, anytime someone provides me with a communication—paper or electronic—that I've done something that someone likes, I archive it.

Now you could, understandably, conclude a couple of things from this practice. One is that I'm an egomaniac who loves to take out his notes of appreciation late at night and pore over them, much as a miser pores over his money. Or, you could decide that my ego is so frail and I am plagued by such insecurities, that I only exist in other people's positive estimations of me, that unless I'm receiving praise I turn into a ghostly, ethereal mist. Both, of course, are at least partly true. I love to receive recognition and I constantly feel like an impostor. But the real reason I keep my nourishment file and my appreciations folder is to counterbalance the emotional dives I take on bad days of teaching.

I feel my failures deeply. My memory archives them, even though I tell myself to forget them. When I feel a situation is spiraling out of my control, when I am embarrassed by my actions, or humiliated by my obvious incompetence, this hits me very hard. These events etch themselves into my consciousness so that years later, the memory of them floods back easily and causes me to walk around an empty room hitting my forehead and repeating "Stupid! Stupid! Stupid!" to myself. In my thirties two important professional events happened to me—I was awarded tenure and full professorship at an Ivy League university, and I was fired from a community education program in England. Guess which I experienced more emotionally? The first event was validating, but emotionally it had nothing like the devastating impact of feeling I was being discarded as an unnecessary mistake.

Somehow the successes are never experienced in such an emotionally intense way as the failures. When a class or workshop goes well, I go home in a good mood, feeling I've earned my money. On those days my working-class notion that I'm not doing a "real" job since I'm not producing anything concrete recedes a little. But pleasure at work well done is, emotionally speaking, just that—pleasure. It's a warm glow of satisfaction, a feeling that I'm good at what I do. This glow is lovely and suffuses my mood. But it is nothing like as intense as the emotional tornado that hits and leaves me reeling in its wake when I feel I've been idiotic, stupid, incompetent in class. Just look at the emotional power of those words—idiotic, stupid, incompetent—and compare them to the blander language I use to describe good days—pleasure, warm glow, satisfaction. It's clear that the significant moments in my teaching that I remember most easily are ones that cause me emotional distress.

It's on those bad days that the nourishment file or appreciations folder does its best work. To stop myself hitting the rock bottom of self-loathing despair, I go to these two resources and read through them. This doesn't stop the tsunami of negative emotions washing over me, but it does help me remember other times when things went very differently. A basic tenet of cognitive behavioral therapy that I've learned from being counseled for my depression is the need to construct alternative scripts of your experience that challenge the ones you're ensnared by. So, reading the file and folder of good things sometimes allows me to challenge the script of "you're a total impostor, an incompetent who's learned nothing from forty-five years of teaching" to one of "you have good days and bad days and there are probably more students who remember you for good days than for bad ones."

Incidentally, the nourishment file and appreciations folder have political benefits, aside from the emotional one. Essentially, the data they contain stands as a public record of the good things you've done. So when a colleague or student complains either that you're not doing your job properly or that you're not doing it at all, you have information to counter this accusation. After losing a job fairly early on in my career (horrible at the time but valuable in that it taught me a lesson regarding the limits of organizational loyalty), I realized how important it was to keep any and all information regarding the ways students and colleagues viewed my work positively. When political enemies have tried to undermine my credibility by whispering behind my back, I have what I hope is viewed as hard evidence that I am doing good things.

Summary

So now we're at the end of this exploration of powerful teaching techniques. Although I have always been interested in power dynamics and teaching about power, this is the first time I have made the pedagogy of power the central theme of a complete book. As I was writing it, I was very aware of the power I was exercising. First of all, as a well-published author, I know I have the power of the gatekeeper. After all, not everyone gets to write a book for a major publishing company that will be read by at least some professionals in their field. I try to use that power for good by supporting authors and projects that otherwise might not get published, and by focusing on questions and ideas that I feel are being ignored. In this book

I tried to cast my net wide as wide as possible as I looked for authors and sources to include.

I also had authorial power. I could choose the words, select only examples that confirmed my points, and slide in emotive language when I wanted to underscore something that was important to me. If something challenged my argument, I could just ignore it and then plead ignorance of it after reviews of the book brought it to my attention. I had the power of an uninterrupted voice. No one could stop me if I was on a roll by raising an inconvenient question or just asking me "What's that sentence mean?" Part of my authorial power was that I had much greater discretion in how I wrote than if I were a junior assistant professor knowing reappointment and tenure were just around the corner. I often feel I only started to hit my stride as a writer after I had been awarded tenure at Columbia.

Again, I've tried to use this authorial power for good. Because I've sold a lot of books for my publishers, I feel I've proved my point that writing in a personal, self-disclosing style is appreciated by readers. Good sales equal good profits and to be in the black is always helpful for a writer. And because six of my books have won scholarly awards, I don't feel the need to pepper every chapter with multiple academic citations or to use a lot of impressive sounding jargon. I feel I've earned the right to be regarded as a legitimate adult education scholar and that, in turn, gives me the right to abandon trying to impress people with my vocabulary and to adopt a less formal, anecdotal style. I believe that in a field of applied practice such as education, and particularly in a field broadly concerned with giving people a second chance like adult education, we need literature that speaks in a direct and accessible way to people. So I spent part of my authorial capital in trying to promote a more colloquial, conversational form of writing.

Part of having authorial power is, I hope, using that power to help readers. Certainly, as this final chapter has made clear, I have a strong identity need to be seen as being helpful to people. To that end I've tried to give as many specific examples of practice and suggest as many concrete activities and exercises as I felt readers could handle. I wanted this book to occupy a space somewhere between a workbook that contained lists of tools and techniques, and a personal reflection on power in the adult classroom. My hope is that having read it you will come away with four things:

- A greater awareness of the constant presence and workings of power in your classrooms

- Some tools that will help you teach in ways that nurture learners' sense of themselves as powerful creators of knowledge and agents of action

- Some techniques you can use to help students learn about the ways dominant ideology constrains their lives and to push back against this

- A better understanding of how you can use your power as a teacher in a responsible manner

And should you want to challenge, contradict, extend, or clarify anything I've written in this book I look forward to you contacting me via my home page: http://www.stephenbrookfield.com

References

Adams, K. L. "The Critical Incident Questionnaire: A Critical Reflective Teaching Tool." In *Exchanges: The Online Journal of Teaching and Learning in the CSU*, 2001. Retrieved from http://www.exchangesjournal.org/classroom/ciq_pg1.html

Albert, M. *Parecon: Life After Capitalism*. London: Verso, 2004.

Albert, M. *Realizing Hope: Life Beyond Capitalism*. New York: ZED, 2006.

Alfred, M. V. "Epistemology, Learning, and Self-Development Among Immigrant Women of Color: The Case of British Caribbean Women in the United States." In R. O. Smith, J. M. Dirkx, P. L. Eddy, P. L. Farrell, and M. Polzin (Eds.), *Proceedings of the 42nd Annual Adult Education Research Conference*. East Lansing, MI: Department of Higher and Adult Education, Michigan State University, 2001, pp. 1–6.

Allman, P. *Critical Education Against Global Capitalism: Karl Marx and Revolutionary Critical Education*. Westport, CT: Bergin & Garvey, 2001.

Ampadu, L. M. "Gumbo Ya Ya: Tapping Cultural Stories to Teach Composition." *Composition Studies*, 2004, *32*(1), pp. 73–88.

Andruske, C. L. "Self-directed Learning as a Political Act: Learning Projects of Women on Welfare." In T. J. Sork, V. L. Chapman, and R. St. Clair (Eds.), *Proceedings of the 41st Annual Adult Education Research Conference*. Vancouver: Center for Adult Education, University of British Columbia, 2000, pp. 11–15.

Archibald, T., and Wilson, A. "Rethinking Empowerment: Theories of Power and the Potential for Emancipatory Praxis." In S. Carpenter, S. Dossa, and B. J. Osborne (Eds.), *Proceedings of the 52nd Annual Adult Education Research Conference*. Toronto: Department of Adult Education, University of Toronto, 2011, pp. 22–28.

Areglado, R. J., Bradley, R. C., and Lane, P. S. *Learning for Life: Creating Classrooms for Self-Directed Learning.* Thousand Oaks, CA: Corwin Press, 1996.

Ayers, W., Kumashiro, K., Meiners, E., Quinn, T., and Stovall, D. *Teaching Toward Democracy: Educators as Agents of Change.* Boulder, CO: Paradigm, 2010.

Bagnall, R. G. *Discovering Radical Contingency: Building a Postmodern Agenda in Adult Education.* New York: Peter Lang, 1999.

Bangs, L. "The Clash" In A. D'Ambrosio (Ed.), *Let Fury Have the Hour: The Punk Rock Politics of Jose Strummer.* New York: Nation Books, 2004, pp. 69–118.

Baptist, W., and Rehman, J. *Pedagogy of the Poor: Building the Movement to End Poverty.* New York: Teachers College Press, 2011.

Baptiste, I. "Beyond Reason and Personal Integrity: Toward a Pedagogy of Coercive Restraint" *Canadian Journal for the Study of Adult Education,* 2000, *14*(1), 27–50.

Baptiste, I. "Exploring the Limits of Democratic Participation: Prudent and Decisive Use of Authority in Adult Education." In D. Nitri (Ed.), *Models for Adult and Lifelong Learning, Vol. 3: Politicization and Democratization of Adult Education* (pp. 1–34). Detroit: Office of Adult and Lifelong Learning Research, Wayne State University, 2001.

Baptiste, I. and Brookfield, S.D. "'Your So-Called Democracy is Hypocritical Because You Can Always Fail Us': Learning and Living Democratic Contradictions in Graduate Adult Education" In P. Armstrong (Ed.), *Crossing Borders, Breaking Boundaries: Research in the Education of Adults.* London: University of London, 1997.

Baumgartner, L. M., and Johnson-Bailey, J. "Fostering Awareness of Diversity and Multiculturalism in Adult and Higher Education" In J. M. Dirkx (Ed.), *Adult Learning and the Emotional Self.* New Directions for Adult and Continuing Education, No. 120. San Francisco: Jossey-Bass, 2008, pp. 45–53.

Bell, L. A. *Storytelling for Social Justice: Connecting Narrative and the Arts in Antiracist Teaching.* New York: Routledge, 2010.

Bembenutty, H. "Self-Regulation of Learning in Postsecondary Education." In H. Bembenutty (Ed.), *Self-Regulated Learning.* New Directions for Teaching and Learning, No. 126. San Francisco: Jossey-Bass, 2011.

Bierema, L. "Adult Learning in the Workplace: Emotion Work or Emotion Learning?" In J. M. Dirkx, (Ed.), *Adult Learning and the Emotional Self.* New Directions for Adult and Continuing Education, No. 120. San Francisco: Jossey-Bass, 2008, pp. 55–64.

Biswalo, P. "The Role of Adult Education in the Integration of Inmates into Society after a Jail Term: Practical Experiences from Swaziland." *International Journal of Lifelong Education*, 2011, 30(1), pp. 71–81.

Black, L.W. "Blog, Chat, Edit, Text, or Tweet? Using Online Tools to Advance Adult Civic Engagement" In, L. Munoz and H. S Wrigley (Eds.). *Adult Civic Engagement in Adult Learning*. New Directions for Adult and Continuing Education, No. 135, Fall, 2012, pp. 71–80.

Boal, A. *Theater of the Oppressed*. London: Pluto (3rd ed.), 2000.

Boal, A. *Games for Actors and Non-Actors*. New York: Routledge, 2002 (2nd ed.).

Boal, A. *The Aesthetics of the Oppressed*. New York: Routledge, 2006.

Bonilla-Silva, E. *Racism Without Racists: Color-Blind Racism and the Persistence of Racial Inequality in America*. Lanham, MD: Rowman and Littlefield, 2009.

Boucouvalas, M., and Lawrence, R. L. "Adult Learning." In C. E. Kasworm, A. D. Rose, and J. M. Ross-Gordon (Eds.), *Handbook of Adult and Continuing Education*. Thousand Oaks, CA: Sage, 2010, pp. 35–48.

Bronte de Avila, E., Caron T., Flanagan, P., Frer, D., Heaney, T., Hyland, N., Kerstein S. "Learning Democracy/Democratizing Learning: Participatory Graduate Education." In P. Campbell and B. Burnaby (Eds.), *Participatory Practices in Adult Education*. Toronto: Lawrence Erlbaum Associates, 2000, pp. 221–236.

Brookfield, S. D. (Ed.). *Learning Democracy: Eduard Lindeman on Adult Education and Social Change*. New York: Routledge, 1988.

Brookfield, S. D. *Becoming a Critically Reflective Teacher*. San Francisco: Jossey-Bass, 1995.

Brookfield, S. D. "Self-Directed Learning as a Political Idea." In G. A. Straka (Ed.), *Conceptions of Self-Directed Learning: Theoretical and Conceptual Considerations*. Berlin/New York: Waxmann, 2000, pp. 9–22.

Brookfield, S. D. *The Power of Critical Theory: Liberating Adult Learning and Teaching*. San Francisco: Jossey-Bass, 2004.

Brookfield, S. D. *The Skillful Teacher: On Technique, Trust and Responsiveness in the Classroom*. San Francisco: Jossey-Bass, 2006 (2nd ed.).

Brookfield, S. D. "Ideological Formation and Oppositional Possibilities of Self-Directed Learning." In J. L. Kincheloe and R. A. Horn (Eds.), *The Praeger Handbook of Education and Psychology: An Encyclopedia*. Westport, CT: Greenwood Press, 2007, pp. 331–340.

Brookfield, S. D. "Learning Democratic Reason: The Adult Education Project of Jurgen Habermas." In M. Murphy and T. Fleming (Eds.), *Habermas, Critical Theory and Education*. New York: Routledge, 2010.

Brookfield, S. D. "When the Black Dog Barks: Adult Learning In and On Clinical Depression." In T. Rocco (Ed.), *Challenging Ableism*,

Understanding Disability: Including Adults with Disabilities in Workplaces and Learning Spaces. San Francisco: Jossey-Bass, 2011, pp. 35–42.

Brookfield, S. D. *Teaching for Critical Thinking: Tools and Techniques to Help Students Question their Assumptions.* San Francisco: Jossey-Bass, 2012.

Brookfield, S. D., and Holst, J. D. *Radicalizing Adult Learning: Adult Education for a Just World.* San Francisco: Jossey-Bass, 2010.

Brookfield, S. D., and Preskill, S. J. *Discussion as a Way of Teaching: Tools and Techniques for Democratic Classrooms.* San Francisco: Jossey-Bass, 2005 (2nd ed.).

Butterwick, S. "The Politics of Listening: The Power of Theatre to Create Dialogic Spaces." In L. Manicom and S. Walters (Eds.), *Feminist Popular Education in Transnational Debates.* New York: Palgrave, 2012.

Butterwick, S., and Lawrence, R. "Creating Alternative Realities: Arts-based Approaches to Transformative Learning." In J. Mezirow and E. Taylor (Eds.), *Transformative Learning in Practice: Insights from Community, Workplace, and Higher Education.* San Francisco: Jossey-Bass, 2009, pp. 35–45.

Butterwick, S., and Lawrence, R. L. "Embodied Knowledge and Decolonization: Walking with Theater's Powerful and Risky Pedagogy." In R. L. Lawrence (Ed.), *Bodies of Knowledge: Embodied Learning in Adult Education.* New Directions for Adult and Continuing Education, No. 134. San Francisco: Jossey-Bass, 2012, pp. 5–14.

Butterwick, S., and Selman, J. "Deep Listening in a Feminist Popular Theater Project: Upsetting the Position of Audience in Participatory Education." *Adult Education Quarterly*, 2003, 54(1), pp. 7–22.

Cale, G. "When Resistance Becomes Reproduction: A Critical Action Research Study." In *Proceedings of the 42nd Adult Education Research Conference* East Lansing: Department of Adult Education, Michigan State University, 2001.

Cale, G., and Huber, S. "Teaching the Oppressor to be Silent: Conflicts in the 'Democratic' Classroom." In *The Changing Face of Adult Learning: Proceedings of the 21st Annual Alliance/ACE Conference.* Austin Texas: 2001.

Callahan, J. L. "Breaking the Cult of Rationality: Mindful Awareness of Emotion in the Critical Theory Classroom." In R. St. Clair and J. Sandlin (Eds.), *Promoting Critical Practice in Adult Education.* New Directions for Adult and Continuing Education, Number 102: San Francisco: Jossey-Bass, 2004, pp. 75–83.

Carmichael, P., The Independent Learning Centre in the Secondary School Context: How Deep Is the Learning?" *International Journal of Self-Directed Learning* 2007, *4*(2), pp. 69–80.

Carpenter, S. "Centering Marxist-Feminist Theory in Adult Learning." *Adult Education Quarterly*, 2012, *62*(1), pp. 19–35.

Cervero, R. M., and Wilson, A. L. (Eds.). *Power in Practice: Adult Education and the Struggle for Knowledge and Power in Society.* San Francisco: Jossey-Bass, 2001.

Chadsey, T., and Jackson, M. "Principles and Practices of the Circle of Trust Approach." In M. Golden (Ed.), *Teaching and Learning From the Inside Out: Revitalizing Ourselves and Our Institutions.* New Directions for Teaching and Learning, No. 130. San Francisco: Jossey-Bass, 2012, pp. 3–14.

Chase, S. E. *Ambiguous Empowerment: The Work Narratives of Women School Superintendents.* Amherst, MA: University of Massachusetts Press, 1995.

Clover, D. E. "From Sea to Cyberspace: Women's Leadership and Learning Around Information and Communication Technologies in Coastal Newfoundland." *International Journal of Lifelong Education,* 2007, *26*(1), pp. 75–88.

Clover, D.E., Jayme, B., Follen, S., and Hall, B. *The Nature of Transformation: Environmental Adult Education.* Victoria, BC: Educational Psychology and Leadership Studies, University of Victoria, 2010 (3rd ed.).

Clover, D. E., and Shaw, K. "Re-Imagining Consumption: Political and Creative Practices of Arts-based Environmental Adult Education." In J. A. Sandlin and P. McLaren (Eds.), *Critical Pedagogies of Consumption: Living and Learning in the Shadow of the 'Shopocalypse'* New York: Routledge, 2010, pp. 203–213.

Coghlan, C. L., and Huggins, D. W. "'That's Not Fair!': A Simulation Exercise in Social Stratification and Structural Inequality." *Teaching Sociology* 2004, *32*(2), pp. 177–187.

Collins, J. B., and Pratt, D. D. "The Teaching Perspectives Inventory at 10 years and 100,000 Respondents: Reliability and Validity of a Teacher Self-Report Inventory." *Adult Education Quarterly,* 2011, *61*(4), pp. 358–375.

Colin S.A.J. III, and Heaney, T. "Negotiating the Democratic Classroom." In C. Hansman and P. Sissel (Eds.), *Understanding and Negotiating the Political Landscape of Adult Education.* New Directions for Adult and Continuing Education, No. 91. San Francisco: Jossey-Bass, 2001, pp. 29–38.

Cranton, P. *Becoming an Authentic Teacher in Higher Education.* Malabar, FL: Krieger, 2001.

Cuerva, M. "A Living Spiral of Understanding: Community-based Adult Education." In C. L. Lund and S.A.J. Colin III (Eds.), *White Privilege and Racism: Perceptions and Actions.* New Directions for Adult and Continuing Education, No. 125. San Francisco: Jossey-Bass, 2010, pp. 79–90.

Darts, D., and Tavin, K. "Global Capitalism and Strategic Visual Pedagogy." In J. A. Sandlin and P. McLaren (Eds.), *Critical Pedagogies of Consumption: Living and Learning in the Shadow of the 'Shopocalypse'* New York: Routledge, 2010, pp. 237–248.

Davis, A. "Socially Constructing a Transformed Self-View and Worldview." In B. Fisher-Yoshida, K.D. Geller, and S.A. Schapiro (Eds.), *Innovations in Transformative Learning Theory.* New York: Peter Lang, 2009, pp. 133–154.

Davis, C. A., Bailey, C., Nypaver, M., Rees, T., and Brockett, R. "Learning Projects of Graduate Students: An Update of Tough's Study." *International Journal of Self-Directed Learning.* 2010, 7(1), pp. 14–28.

Davison, P., and Burge, E. J. "Between Dissonance and Grace: The Experience of Post-Secondary Leaders." *International Journal of Lifelong Education,* 2010, 29(1), pp. 111–131.

Dirkx, J. M. "Authenticity and Imagination" In P. Cranton (Ed.), *Authenticity in Teaching.* New Directions for Adult and Continuing Education, No. 111. San Francisco: Jossey-Bass, 2004, pp. 27–39.

Dirkx, J. M. (Ed.). *Adult Learning and the Emotional Self.* New Directions for Adult and Continuing Education, No. 120. San Francisco: Jossey-Bass, 2008.

Dirkx, J. M. "Nurturing Soul Work: A Jungian Approach to Transformative Learning." In E. W. Taylor and P. Cranton (Eds.), *The Handbook of Transformative Learning: Theory, Research, and Practice.* San Francisco: Jossey-Bass, 2012, pp. 116–130.

Du Bois, W.E.B. *Dusk of Dawn: An Essay Toward An Autobiography of a Race Concept.* New York: Schocken Books, 1971.

Duffy, P., and Vettraino, E. (Eds.), *Youth and Theater of the Oppressed.* New York: Palgrave Macmillan, 2010.

Dundes, L., and Harlow, R. "Illustrating the Nature of Social Inequality with the Simulation Star Power." *Teaching Sociology,* 2004, 33(1), pp. 32–43.

Ebert, O., Burford, M. L., and Brian, D.J.G. "Highlander: Education For Change." *Journal of Transformative Education,* 2004, 1(4), pp. 321–340.

Ehrenreich, B. *Fear of Falling: The Inner Life of the Middle Class.* New York: Harper Collins, 1990.

English, L. M., and Mayo, P. *Learning with Adults: A Critical Pedagogical Introduction*. Boston: Sense Publishers, 2012.

Fenwick, T. "The Audacity of Hope: Towards Poorer Pedagogies." *Studies in the Education of Adults*, 2006, 38(1), pp. 9–24.

Finkel, D. L. *Teaching with Your Mouth Shut*. Portsmouth, NH: Boynton/Cook, 2000.

Foucault, M. *Power/Knowledge: Selected Interviews and Other Writings, 1972–1977*. New York: Pantheon Books, 1980.

Foucault, M. "The Subject and Power." In H. L. Dreyfus and P. Rabinow (Eds.), *Michel Foucault: Beyond Structuralism and Hermeneutics*. Chicago: University of Chicago Press, 1982.

Frego, K. "Authenticity and Relationships with Students." In P. Cranton (Ed.), *Authenticity in Teaching*. New Directions for Adult and Continuing Education, No. 111. San Francisco: Jossey-Bass, 2006, pp. 41–49.

Freire, P. *Pedagogy of the Oppressed*. New York: Continuum, 1970.

Freire, P. *Pedagogy of Commitment*. Boulder, CO: Paradigm, 2011.

Fromm, E. *The Sane Society*. London: Routledge, Kegan and Paul, 1956.

Frye, S. B., Curran, R., Pierce, C. A., Young, E., and Ziegler, M. "Crashing the Party: A Working Class Perspective on the Ivory Tower." In R. J. Hill and R. Kiely (Eds.), *Proceedings of the 46th Annual Adult Education Research Conference*. Athens, GA: Department of Adult Education, University of Georgia, 2005, pp. 147–152.

Furness, Z. (Ed.). *Punkademics: The Basement Show in the Ivory Tower*. Brooklyn, NY: Minor Compositions, 2012.

Gabrielle, D. M., Guglielmino, L.M., and Guglielmino, P. J. "Developing Self-Directed Learning Readiness of Future Leaders in a Military College Through Instructional Innovation." *International Journal of Self-Directed Learning*, 2006, 3(1), pp. 24–35.

Ganguly, S. *Jana Sanskriti: Forum Theater and Democracy in India*. New York: Routledge, 2010.

Gelpi, E. *A Future for Lifelong Education: Volume 1, Lifelong Education Principles, Policies and Practices*. Manchester: Manchester Monographs 13, Dept. of Adult and Higher Education, University of Manchester, 1979.

Glowacki-Dudka, M., and Barnett, N. "Connecting Critical Reflection and Group Development in Online Adult Education Classrooms." *International Journal of Teaching and Learning in Higher Education* 2007, 19(1), 43–52.

Goodman, A. "Transformative Learning and Cultures of Peace." In E. V. O'Sullivan, A. Morrell, and M. A. O'Connor (Eds.), *Expanding the*

Boundaries of Transformative Learning. New York: Palgrave, 2002, pp. 185–198.

Goss, D. "Chasing the Rabbit: Metaphors Used by Adult Learners to Describe their Learning Journeys" *Adult Learning,* 2001, *12*(2), pp. 8–9.

Grace, A. P, Hill, R. J., and Wells, K. "Art as Anti-Oppression Adult Education: Creating a Pedagogy of Presence and Place." In R. J. Hill and A. P. Grace (Eds.), *Adult and Higher Education in Queer Contexts: Power, Politics and Pedagogy.* Chicago: Discovery Association Publishing House, 2010, pp. 69–86.

Grace, A. P., and Rocco, T. S. (Eds.), *Challenging the Professionalization of Adult Education: John Ohliger and Contradictions in Modern Practice.* San Francisco: Jossey-Bass, 2009.

Grace, A. P., and Wells, K. "Using Freirean Pedagogy of Just Ire to Inform Critical Social Learning in Arts-Informed Community Education for Sexual Minorities." *Adult Education Quarterly,* 2007, *57*(2), 95–114.

Gramsci, A. *Selections from the Prison Notebooks* (Q. Hoare and G. N. Smith, Eds.). London: Lawrence and Wishart, 1971.

Grauerholz, E. "Getting Past Ideology for Effective Teaching." *Sociological Viewpoints,* 2007, No. 15, pp. 15–28.

Guglielmino, L. M., Asper, D., Findley, B., Lunceford, C., McVey, R. S., Payne, S., Penney, G., and Phares, L. "Common Barriers, Interrupters and Restarters in the Learning Projects of Highly Self-Directed Adult Learners." *International Journal of Lifelong Education,* 2005, *2*(1), pp. 71–93.

Guglielmino, L. M., and Hillard, L. C. "Self-Directed Learning of Exemplary Principals." *International Journal of Lifelong Education,* 2007, *4*(2), pp. 19–37.

Guy, T. C. *Prophecy from The Periphery: Alain Locke's Philosophy of Cultural Pluralism and the American Association in Adult Education.* Unpublished Doctoral Dissertation. DeKalb, IL: Northern Illinois University, 1993.

Guy, T. C., and Brookfield, S. D. "W.E.B. Du Bois' Basic American Negro Creed and the Associates in Negro Folk Education: A Case Study of Repressive Tolerance in the Censorship of Radical Black Discourse on Adult Education." *Adult Education Quarterly,* 2009, *60*(1), pp. 65–76.

Habermas, J. *Communication and the Evolution of Society.* Boston: Beacon Press, 1979.

Habermas, J. *Between Facts and Norms: Contributions to a Discourse Theory of Democracy.* Cambridge, MA: MIT Press, 1996.

Halx, M. D. "Re-conceptualizing College and University Teaching Through the Lens of Adult Education: Regarding Undergraduates as Adults." *Teaching in Higher Education*, 2012, *15*(5), pp. 519–530.

Hansman, C. A., and Mott, V. W. "Adult Learners." In C. E. Kasworm, A. D. Rose, and J. M. Ross-Gordon (Eds.), *Handbook of Adult and Continuing Education*. Thousand Oaks, CA: Sage, 2010, pp. 13–24.

Harlow, R. "Innovations in Teaching Race and Class Inequality: Bittersweet Candy and the Vanishing Dollar." *Teaching Sociology* 2009, *37*(2), pp. 194–204.

Harteis, C., and Gruber, H. "How Important is Intuition for Teaching Expertise in the Field of Adult Education?" *Studies in the Education of Adults*, 2008, *40*(1), pp. 96–108.

Hess, M., and Brookfield, S. D. (Eds.), *Teaching Reflectively in Theological Contexts: Promises and Contradictions*. Malabar, FL: Krieger, 2008.

Heywood, D., and Parker, J. *The Pedagogy of Physical Science*. New York: Springer, 2010.

Hiemstra, R. "Is the Internet Changing Self-Directed Learning? Rural Users Provide Some Answers." *International Journal of Self-Directed Learning*, 2006, *3*(2), pp. 45–60.

Hill, R. J., and Grace, A. P. (Eds.). *Adult and Higher Education in Queer Contexts: Power, Politics and Pedagogy*. Chicago: Discovery Association Publishing House, 2010.

Hoagland, S. L. "Oaths." In J.A. Sandlin, B. D. Schultz, and J. Burdick (Eds.), *Handbook of Public Pedagogy: Education and Learning Beyond Schooling*. New York: Routledge, 2011, pp. 93–102.

Hoban, G., and Hoban, S. "Self-Esteem, Self-Efficacy, and Self-Directed Learning: Separate, but Interrelated." *International Journal of Self-Directed Learning*, 2004, *1*(2), pp. 7–25.

Hoggan, C. "The Power of Creative Story: Metaphors, Literature, and Creative Writing." In C. Hoggan, S. Simpson, and H. Stuckey (Eds.), *Creative Expression in Transformative Learning: Tools and Techniques for Educators of Adults*. Malabar, FL: Krieger, 2009, pp. 51–74.

Hoggan, C., Simpson, S., and Stuckey, H. (Eds.), *Creative Expression in Transformative Learning: Tools and Techniques for Educators of Adults*. Malabar, FL: Krieger, 2009.

Holst, J. D. *Social Movements, Civil Society, and Radical Adult Education*. Westport, CT: Praeger, 2002.

hooks, b. *Talking Back: Thinking Feminist, Thinking Black*. Boston: South End Press, 1989.

hooks, b. *Teaching to Transgress: Education as the Practice of Freedom*. New York: Routledge, 1994.

Horton, M. *The Long Haul: An Autobiography*. New York: Doubleday, 1990.

Horton, M. *The Myles Horton Reader: Education for Social Change*. (D. Jacobs, Ed.). Knoxville: University of Tennessee Press, 2003.

Huffington Post "Young People More Likely to Favor Socialism than Capitalism: Pew." Retrieved from: http://www.huffingtonpost.com/2011/12/29/young-people-socialism_n_1175218.html.

Hunt, R. "Institutional Constraints on Authenticity in Teaching." In P. Cranton (Ed.), *Authenticity in Teaching*. New Directions for Adult and Continuing Education, No. 111. San Francisco: Jossey-Bass, 2006, pp. 51–61.

Hyland-Russell, T., and Green, J. "Marginalized Non-Traditional Adult Learners: Beyond Economics." *Canadian Journal for the Study of Adult Education*, 2011, 24(1), pp. 61–79.

Illich, I. *Deschooling Society*. London, UK: Marion Boyars Publishing, 2000.

Jessup, M. "Sociopoly: Life on the Boardwalk." *Teaching Sociology* 2001, 29(2), pp. 102–9.

Johnson-Bailey, J. "Race Matters." In J. M. Ross-Gordon (Ed.), *Contemporary Viewpoints on Teaching Adults Effectively*. New Directions for Adult and Continuing Education, No. 93. San Francisco: Jossey-Bass, 2002.

Jubas, K. "Critically Minded Shopping s a Process of Adult Learning and Civic Engagement" In L. Munoz and H. S Wrigley (Eds.). *Adult Civic Engagement in Adult Learning*. New Directions for Adult and Continuing Education, No. 135, Fall, 2012, pp. 61–70.

Jun, J., and Park, J.H. "Power Relations within Online Discussion Contexts: Based on International Students' Perspectives and Their Participation in the Learning Context." In D. Flowers, M. Lee, A. Jalipa, E. Lopez, A. Schelstrate, and V. Sheared (Eds.), *Proceedings of the 44th Annual Adult Education Research Conference*. San Francisco: Center for Adult Education, San Francisco State University, 2003, pp. 193–198.

Keefer, J. "The Critical Incident Questionnaire: From Research to Practice and Back Again." In *Proceedings of the 2009 Adult Education Research Conference*. Chicago: Dept. of Adult and Continuing Education, National Louis University, 2009, pp. 177–182.

Kenkmann, A. "Power and Authenticity: Moving from the Classroom to the Museum." *Adult Education Quarterly*, 2011, 61(3), pp. 279–295.

Kilgore, D. "Towards a Postmodern Pedagogy." In R. St. Clair, and J. Sandlin (Eds.), *Promoting Critical Practice in Adult Education*. New Directions for Adult and Continuing Education, Number 102: San Francisco: Jossey-Bass, 2004, pp. 45–53.

Lakoff, G., and Johnson, M. *Metaphors We Live By*. Chicago: University of Chicago Press, 2003 (2nd ed.).

Laski, M. *Everyday Ecstasy: Some Observations on the Possible Social Effects of Major and Minor Ecstatic Experiences in Our Daily Secular Lives*. London: Thames and Hudson, 1980.

Lawrence, R. L. "Powerful Feelings: Exploring the Affective Domain of Informal and Arts-Based Learning." In J. M. Dirkx (Ed.), *Adult Learning and the Emotional Self*. New Directions for Adult and Continuing Education, No. 120. San Francisco: Jossey-Bass, 2008, pp. 65–77.

Lawrence, R. L. "The Other Side of the Mirror: Intuitive Knowing, Visual Imagery, and Transformative Learning." In C. Hoggan, S. Simpson, and H. Stuckey (Eds.), *Creative Expression in Transformative Learning: Tools and Techniques for Educators of Adults*. Malabar, FL: Krieger, 2009, pp. 129–144.

Lawrence, R. L. "Intuitive Knowing and Embedded Consciousness." In R. L. Lawrence (Ed.), *Bodies of Knowledge: Embodied Learning in Adult Education*. New Directions for Adult and Continuing Education, No. 134. San Francisco: Jossey-Bass, 2012a, pp. 5–14.

Lawrence, R. L. "Transformative Learning Through Artistic Impression: Getting Out of Our Heads." In E. W. Taylor and P. Cranton (Eds.), *The Handbook of Transformative Learning: Theory, Research, and Practice*. San Francisco: Jossey-Bass, 2012b, pp. 425–437.

Lee, H. J. "Thrust into Leaning and Thinking Critically: East Asian Doctoral Students' Experience, Meaning, and Process of Engaging in Critical Reflection at U.S. Universities." *Proceedings of the Transnational Migration and Adult Education Conference: Global Issues and Debates*. Toronto: Dept. of Adult Education, Ontario Institute for Studies in Adult Education, 2011.

Lewis, T. E. *The Aesthetics of Education: Theatre, Curiosity and Politics in the Work of Jacques Ranciere and Paulo Freire*. New York: Continuum, 2012.

Liddell, T. N. "Self-Directed Learning of Women Executives of Philanthropic Organizations." *International Journal of Self-Directed Learning*, 2008, 5(1), pp. 15–29.

Lindeman, E.C.L. "The Place of Discussion in the Learning Process" (1935). In S. D. Brookfield (Ed.), *Learning Democracy: Eduard Lindeman on Adult Education and Social Change*. Beckenham, Kent, UK: Croom Helm, 1987.

Love, C. T. "Dialing into a Circle of Trust: A 'Medium' Tech Experiment and Poetic Evaluation." In M. Golden (Ed.), *Teaching and Learning From the Inside Out: Revitalizing Ourselves and Our Institutions*. New Directions for

Teaching and Learning, No. 130, San Francisco: Jossey-Bass, 2012, pp. 37–52.

Love, D. "Lifelong Learning: Characteristics, Skills, and Activities for a Business College Curriculum." *Journal of Education for Business*, 2011, 86(3), pp. 155–162.

Malcolm, I. "'It's For Us to Change That': Emotional Labor in Researching Adults' Learning: Between Feminist Criticality and Complicity in Temporary, Gendered Employment." *Adult Education Quarterly*, 2012, 62(3), pp. 252–271.

Marcuse, H. *One Dimensional Man.* Boston: Beacon, 1964.

Marcuse, H. "Repressive Tolerance." In R. P. Wolff, B. Moore, and H. Marcuse. *A Critique of Pure Tolerance.* Boston: Beacon Press, 1965.

Marcuse, H. *An Essay on Liberation.* Boston: Beacon Press, 1969.

Marcuse, H. *Counterrevolution and Revolt.* Boston: Beacon Press, 1972.

Marcuse, H. *The Aesthetic Dimension: Toward a Critique of Marxist Aesthetics.* Boston: Beacon Press, 1978.

McCauley, V., and McClelland, G. 'Further Studies in Self-Directed Learning in Physics at the University of Limerick, Ireland." *International Journal of Self-Directed Learning* 2004, 1(2), pp. 26–37.

McCormack, J. "Critical Pedagogy, Experiential Learning and Active Citizenship: a Freirean Perspective on Tenant Involvement in Housing Stock Transfers." *International Journal of Lifelong Education*, 2008, 27(1), pp. 3–18.

McDermott, C. "Teaching to Be Radical: The Women Activist Educators of Highlander." In L. Servage and T. Fenwick (Eds.), *Learning in Community: Proceedings of the 48th Annual Adult Education Research Conference.* Halifax, Nova Scotia: Department of Adult Education, Mount Saint Vincent University, 2007, pp. 403–408.

Merrill, B., Alheit, P., Anderson, S. A., and West, L. *Using Biographical and Life History Approaches in the Study of Adult and Lifelong Learning: European Perspectives.* Berne, Switzerland: Peter Lang, 2007.

Mezirow, J. *Transformative Dimensions of Adult Learning.* San Francisco: Jossey-Bass, 1991.

Mezirow, J., and Taylor E. (Eds.). *Transformative Learning in Practice: Insights from Community, Workplace, and Higher Education.* San Francisco: Jossey-Bass, 2009.

Michalec, P., and Brower, G. "Soul and Role: Dialogues in Higher Education: Healing the Divided Self." In M. Golden (Ed.), *Teaching and Learning From the Inside Out: Revitalizing Ourselves and Our Institutions.* New

Directions for Teaching and Learning, No. 130, San Francisco: Jossey-Bass, 2012, pp. 15–25.

Miles, M. *Herbert Marcuse: An Aesthetics of Liberation*. London: Pluto Press, 2012.

Mill, J. S. *The Philosophy of J. S. Mill*. (M. Cohen, Ed.). New York: Random House, 1961.

Mok, M. C., Leung, O. S., and Shan, P. W. "A Comparative Study of the Self-Directed Learning of Primary Students in Hong Kong and Macau." *International Journal of Self-Directed Learning*, 2005, 2(2), 39–54.

Mojab, S. (Ed.). *Women, War, Violence and Learning*. New York: Routledge, 2010.

Mojab, S., and Carpenter, S. (Eds.). *Educating from Marx: Race, Gender and Learning*. New York: Palgrave Macmillan, 2011.

Mojab, S., and Gorman, R. "The Struggle Over Lifelong Learning: A Marxist-Feminist Analysis." In R. O. Smith, J. M. Dirkx, P. L. Eddy, P. L. Farrell, and M. Polzin (Eds.), *Proceedings of the 42nd Annual Adult Education Research Conference*. East Lansing, MI: Department of Adult Education, Michigan State University, 2001.

Moore, T., Houde, J., Hoggan, C., and Wagner, J. "Re-viewing Adult Learning: A Collaborative Self-Directed Learning Model for Adult Educators." In R. J. Hill and R. Kiely (Eds.), *Proceedings of the 46th Annual Adult Education Research Conference*. Athens, GA: Department of Adult Education, University of Georgia, 2005.

Moshman, D. "Developmental Change in Adulthood." In J. Demick and C. Andreoletti (Eds.), *Handbook of Adult Development*. New York: Springer, 2003, pp. 43–61.

Nash, R. J. *Liberating Scholarly Writing: The Power of Personal Narrative*. New York: Teachers College Press, 2004.

Nash, R. J., and Bradley, D. L. *Me-Search and Re-Search: A Guide for Writing Scholarly Personal Narrative Manuscripts*. Charlotte, NC: Information Age Publishing, 2011.

Nelson, A. "Storytelling and Transformational Learning." In B. Fisher-Yoshida, K. D. Geller, and S. A. Schapiro (Eds.), *Innovations in Transformative Learning Theory*. New York: Peter Lang, 2009, pp. 207–222.

Newman, M. *Teaching Defiance: Stories and Strategies for Activist Educators*. San Francisco: Jossey-Bass, 2006.

Noonan, S. (with Fish, T.). *Leadership Through Story: Diverse Voices in Dialogue*. Lanham, MD: Rowman and Littlefield Education, 2007.

Obama, B. H. *Dreams From My Father: A Story of Race and Inheritance.* New York: Broadway, 2004.

Outlaw, L. T., Jr. *On Race and Philosophy.* New York: Routledge, 1996.

Park, E., Candler, C., and Durso, S.C. "Medical Students' Perceptions of Selected Instructional Methods." *International Journal of Self-Directed Learning* 2006, 2(2), pp. 55–65.

Park, E., Christmas, C., Schmaltz, H., and Durso, S.C. "The Perceived Change of Diverse Clinician-Educators Through an Intensive Course on Teaching Geriatrics." *International Journal of Self-Directed Learning* 2005, 3(1), pp. 36–51.

Parvaresh, V. "Metaphorical Conceptualizations of an Adult EFL Learner: Where Old Concepts Are Impregnable." *Novitas-Royal: Research on Youth and Language,* 2008, 2(2), pp. 154–161.

Paterson, R.W.K. "The Concept of Discussion: A Philosophical Approach." *Studies in Adult Education,* 2(1), 1970, pp. 28–50.

Peters, J. M., and Grey, A. "A Solitary Act One Cannot Do Alone: The Self-Directed, Collaborative Learner." *International Journal of Self-Directed Learning,* 2005, 2(2), pp. 12–23.

Peterson, E. A., and Brookfield, S. D. "Race and Racism: A Critical Dialogue." In L. Servage and T. Fenwick (Eds.), *Proceedings of the 48th Adult Education Research Conference,* Halifax, Nova Scotia: Department of Adult Education, Mount Saint Vincent University, 2007, pp. 481–486.

Pettit, J. M. "Power Relationships in Two Web-Based Courses." In J. M. Petit and R. P. Francis (Eds.), *Proceedings of the 43rd Annual Adult Education Research Conference.* Raleigh, NC: Department of Adult and Community College Education, North Carolina State University, 2002, pp. 312–326.

Phares, L. T., and Guglielmino, L. M. "The Role of Self-Directed Learning in the Work of Community Leaders." *International Journal of Self-Directed Learning,* 2010, 7(2), pp. 35–53.

Phelan, L. "Interrogating Students' Perceptions of their Online Learning Experiences with Brookfield's Critical Incident Questionnaire." *Distance Education,* 2012, 33(1).

Pierson, C. "Reflections on Educational Metaphors for Teaching English as a Second Language to Adult Learners." *PAACE Journal of Lifelong Education,* 2008, Vol. 17, pp. 51–61.

Ponton, M., Derrick, G., Confessore, G., and Rhea, N. "The Role of Self-Efficacy in Autonomous Learning." *International Journal of Self-Directed Learning,* 2005a, 2(2), pp. 81–90.

Ponton, M. K., Derrick, G. J., Hall, M. J., Rhea, N., and Carr, P. "The Relationship Between Self-Efficacy and Autonomous Learning: The Development of New Instrumentation." *International Journal of Self-Directed Learning*, 2005b, *2*(1), pp. 50–61.

Popper, K. R. *The Logic of Scientific Discovery*. New York: Routledge, 2002 (2nd ed.). Originally published 1959.

Pratt, D. D., and Associates. *Five Perspectives on Teaching in Adult and Higher Education*. Malabar, FL: Krieger, 1998.

Pratt, D. D. "Good Teaching: One Size Fits All?" In J. M. Ross-Gordon (Ed.), *Contemporary Viewpoints on Teaching Adults Effectively*. New Directions for Adult and Continuing Education, No. 93: San Francisco: Jossey-Bass, 2002.

Preskill, S. J., and Brookfield, S. D. *Learning as a Way of Leading: Lessons from the Struggle for Social Justice*. San Francisco: Jossey-Bass, 2008.

Pyrch, T. *Breaking Free: A Facilitator's Guide to Action Research Practice*. http://www.lulu.com, 2012.

Rager, K. B. "The Organizing Circumstance Revisited: Opportunities and Challenges Posed by the Influence of the Internet." *International Journal of Self-Directed Learning* 2006, *3*(1), pp. 52–60.

Ramdeholl, D. *Adult Literacy in a New Era: Oral Histories from The Open Book*. St. Paul, MN: Paradigm, 2010.

Ramdeholl, D., Giordani, T., Heaney, and Yanow, W. "Race, Power, and Democracy in the Graduate Classroom." In D. Ramdeholl, T. Giordani, T. Heaney, and W. Yanow (Eds.), *The Struggle for Democracy in Adult Education*. New Directions for Adult and Continuing Education, No. 128. San Francisco: Jossey-Bass, 2010.

Ramdeholl, D., and Wells, R. "From Resistance to Solidarity: Teaching Race, Class and Gender to Working Adults." In S. Carpenter, S. Dossa, and B. J. Osborne (Eds.), *Proceedings of the 52nd Annual Adult Education Research Conference*. Toronto: Department of Adult Education, University of Toronto, 2011, pp. 550–555.

Ramdeholl, D., and Wells, R. "The World As it Could Be: Class, Race and Gender for and with Working Class Students." In J. Ruban and D. Ramdeholl (Eds.), *Proceedings of the 53rd Annual Adult Education Research Conference*. Saratoga Springs, NY: Department of Adult Education, Empire State College, 2012, pp. 251–257.

Randall, W. "Storywork: Autobiographical Learning in Later Life." In M. Rossiter and M. C. Clark (Eds.), *Narrative Perspectives in Adult Education*.

New Directions for Adult and Continuing Education, No. 126. San Francisco: Jossey-Bass, 2010, pp. 25–36.

Redmon Wright, R. "Narratives from Popular Culture: Critical Implications for Adult Education." In M. Rossiter and M. C. Clark (Eds.), *Narrative Perspectives in Adult Education*. New Directions for Adult and Continuing Education, No. 126. San Francisco: Jossey-Bass, 2010, pp. 49–62.

Reitz, C. *Art, Alienation and the Humanities: A Critical Engagement with Herbert Marcuse*. Albany: State University of New York Press, 2000.

Rogoff, B., and Lave, J. *Everyday Cognition: Its Development in Social Context*. Cambridge, MA: Harvard University Press, 1999.

Rossiter, M., and Clark, M. C. (Eds.). *Narrative Perspectives in Adult Education*. New Directions for Adult and Continuing Education, No. 126. San Francisco: Jossey-Bass, 2010.

Rossiter, M., and Garcia, P. A. "Digital Storytelling: A New Player on the Narrative Field." In M. Rossiter and M. C. Clark (Eds.), *Narrative Perspectives in Adult Education*. New Directions for Adult and Continuing Education, No. 126. San Francisco: Jossey-Bass, 2010, pp. 37–48.

Roy, C. "The Transformative Power of Creative Dissent: The Raging Grannies Legacy." In E. V. O'Sullivan, A. Morrell and M. A. O'Connor (Eds.), *Expanding the Boundaries of Transformative Learning*. New York: Palgrave, 2002, pp. 257–272.

Ryan, M. "Conceptualising and Teaching Discursive and Performative Reflection in Higher Education." *Studies in Continuing Education*, 2012, 34(2), pp. 207–223.

St. Clair, R. "Success Stories: Aspirational Myth in the Education of Adults." *International Journal of Lifelong Education*, 2004, 23(1), pp. 81–94.

Sandlin J. A. "Consumerism, Consumption, and a Critical Consumer Education for Adults." In R. St. Clair and J. Sandlin (Eds.), *Promoting Critical Practice in Adult Education*. New Directions for Adult and Continuing Education, Number 102: San Francisco: Jossey-Bass, 2004, pp. 25–34.

Sandlin J. A. "Popular Culture, Cultural Resistance, and Anti-Consumption Activism: An Exploration of Culture Jamming as Critical Adult Education." In E. J. Tisdell and P. M. Thompson (Eds.), *Popular Culture and Entertainment Media in Adult Education*. New Directions for Adult and Continuing Education, No. 126. San Francisco: Jossey-Bass, 2007a, pp. 73–82.

Sandlin J. A. "Living and Learning in the Shadow of the Shopocalypse: Reverend Billy's Anti-Consumption Pedagogy-of-the-Unknown as

Critical Adult Education." In L. Servage and T. Fenwick (Eds.), *Proceedings of the 48th Adult Education Research Conference*, Halifax, Nova Scotia: Department of Adult Education, Mount Saint Vincent University, 2007b, pp. 541–546.

Sandlin J. A., and McLaren, P. (Eds.). *Critical Pedagogies of Consumption: Living and Learning in the Shadow of the 'Shopocalypse.'* New York: Routledge, 2010.

Scatamburlo-D'Annibale, V. "Beyond the Culture Jam." In J. A. Sandlin and P. McLaren (Eds.), *Critical Pedagogies of Consumption: Living and Learning in the Shadow of the 'Shopocalypse.'* New York: Routledge, 2010, pp. 224–236.

Sheared V., Johnson-Bailey, J., Colin S.A.J. III, Peterson, E., and Brookfield, S. D. (Eds.). *The Handbook of Race and Adult Education: A Resource for Dialogue on Racism.* San Francisco: Jossey-Bass, 2010.

Shor, I. *When Students Have Power: Negotiating Authority in a Critical Pedagogy.* Chicago: University of Chicago Press, 1996.

Silver, T., and Mojab, S. "The Rise and Fall of Socialist Adult Education in North America: Theorizing from the Literature." In S. Carpenter, S. Dossa, and B. J. Osborne (Eds.), *Proceedings of the 52nd Annual Adult Education Research Conference.* Toronto: Department of Adult Education, University of Toronto, 2011, pp. 631–637.

Simpson, J. M., and Elias, V. L. "Choices and Chances: The Sociology Role-Playing Game—The Sociological Imagination in Practice." *Teaching Sociology*, 2011, 39(1), pp. 42–56.

Simpson, S. "Raising Awareness of Transformation: Collage, Creative Expression, and Transformation." In C. Hoggan, S. Simpson, and H. Stuckey (Eds.), *Creative Expression in Transformative Learning: Tools and Techniques for Educators of Adults.* Malabar, FL: Krieger, 2009, pp. 75–101.

Slate. http://www.slate.com/id/2302617/pagenum/2 (Retrieved, August 17th, 2011)

Smith, H. "The Foxfire Approach to Student and Community Interaction." In L. Shumow (Ed.), *Promising Practices for Family and Community Involvement during High School.* Charlotte, NC: Information Age Publishing, 2009.

Smith, T. V., and Lindeman, E. C. *The Democratic Way of Life.* New York: New American Library, 1951.

Snowber, C. "Dance as a Way of Knowing." In R. L. Lawrence (Ed.), *Bodies of Knowledge: Embodied Learning in Adult Education.* New Directions for Adult and Continuing Education, No. 134. San Francisco: Jossey-Bass, 2012, pp. 53–60.

Somers, K. "How Canadian Diversity and Anti-Oppression Educators Handle the Emotional Challenges of Their Practice." In S. Carpenter, S. Dossa, and B. J. Osborne (Eds.), *Proceedings of the 52nd Annual Adult Education Research Conference.* Toronto: Department of Adult Education, University of Toronto, 2011, pp. 654–660.

Stuart, M., Lido, C., and Morgan, J. "Personal Stories: How Students' Social and Cultural Life Histories Interact with the Field of Higher Education." *International Journal of Lifelong Education, 2011, 30*(4), pp. 489–508.

Sue, D. W., Capodilupo, C. M., Torino, G. C., Bucceri, J. M., Holder, A.M.B., Nadal, K. L., and Esquilin M. "Racial Microaggressions in Everyday Life: Implications for Clinical Practice." *American Psychologist,* 2007, *62*(4), pp. 271–286.

Sun, Q. "Confucian Educational Philosophy and Its Implication for Lifelong Learning and Lifelong Education." *International Journal of Lifelong Education,* 2008, *27*(5), pp. 559–578.

Sunstein C. *The Second Bill of Rights: FDR's Unfinished Revolution and Why We Need It More Than Ever.* New York: Perseus Books, 2006.

Swanson Brookes, T. "Lessons Learned: A Crisis Responder's Journey Supporting Friends in Crisis." Unpublished Doctoral Dissertation, Dept. of Educational Leadership: Appalachian State University, 2011.

Taber, N. "Critiquing War in the Classroom: Problematizing the Normalization of Gendered Militarism." In S. Carpenter, S. Dossa, and B. J. Osborne (Eds.), *Proceedings of the 52nd Annual Adult Education Research Conference.* Toronto: Department of Adult Education, University of Toronto, 2011, pp. 676–682.

Taylor, A. "The Impostor Phenomenon: A Look at the Outside, the Inside, and the Other Side through Scholarly Personal Narrative." Unpublished Doctoral Dissertation, School of Education, Colorado State University, 2009.

Taylor, E. W., and Cranton, P. (Eds.). *The Handbook of Transformative Learning: Theory, Research, and Practice.* San Francisco: Jossey-Bass, 2012.

The Yes Men. "Dow Chemical Just Says 'Yes' to Bhopal." In T. Corby (Ed.), *Network Art: Practices and Positions.* New York: Routledge, 2006, pp. 197–213.

Thompson, T., and Wulff, S. "Implementing Guided Self-Directed Learning Strategies (GSDL) in Intermediate and Advanced Chemistry Courses." *International Journal of Self-Directed Learning* 2004, *1*(2), pp. 38–52.

Tyler, J. A. "Charting the Course: How Storytelling Can Foster Communicative Learning in the Workplace." In J. Mezirow and E. Taylor (Eds.), *Transformative Learning in Practice: Insights from Community, Workplace, and Higher Education.* San Francisco: Jossey-Bass, 2009, pp. 136–147.

Vygotsky, L. S. *Mind in Society: The Development of Higher Psychological Processes.* Cambridge, MA: Harvard University Press, 1978.

Wang, V., and Farmer, L. "Adult Teaching Methods in China and Bloom's Taxonomy." *International Journal for the Scholarship of Teaching and Learning,* 2008, 2(2), pp. 1–16.

Williams, H.S. "Black Mama Sauce: Embodied Transformative Education." In B. Fisher-Yoshida, K. D. Geller, and S. A. Schapiro (Eds.), *Innovations in Transformative Learning Theory.* New York: Peter Lang, 2009, pp. 269–286.

Wilson, A. L., and Nesbit, T. "The Problem of Power." In R. J. Hill and R. Kiely (Eds.), *Proceedings of the 46th Annual Adult Education Research Conference.* Athens, GA: Department of Adult Education, University of Georgia, 2005, pp. 449–454.

Zhang, W. "Conceptions of Lifelong Learning in Confucian Culture: Their Impact on Adult Learners." *International Journal of Lifelong Education.* 2008, 2(5), pp. 551–557.

Ziga, P. L. "Self-Directed Learning in Directors of a U.S. Nonprofit Organization." *International Journal of Self-Directed Learning.* 2008, 5(2), pp. 35–49.

Index